John Henry Walsh

The dog, its varieties and management in health

John Henry Walsh

The dog, its varieties and management in health

ISBN/EAN: 9783337814786

Printed in Europe, USA, Canada, Australia, Japan

Cover: Foto ©ninafisch / pixelio.de

More available books at **www.hansebooks.com**

THE DOG

ITS VARIETIES AND MANAGEMENT IN HEALTH

BY

"STONEHENGE"

WITH ITS DISEASES AND THEIR TREATMENT

BY

GEORGE ARMATAGE, M.R.C.V.S.

Formerly Lecturer in the Albert and Glasgow Veterinary Colleges
AUTHOR OF "THE HORSE DOCTOR," "THE CATTLE DOCTOR"
"THE SHEEP DOCTOR," ETC. ETC.

WITH NUMEROUS ILLUSTRATIONS

LONDON
FREDERICK WARNE AND CO.
AND NEW YORK

[All rights reserved]

PREFACE.

OUR dumb friend and companion has advanced to signal prominence in various directions. His mental aptitude, as well as natural capabilities, are better understood, and recent years have witnessed a marvellous increase in his varied spheres of usefulness, with corresponding appreciation of his intelligence and intrinsic worth. His management in health and disease is, therefore, a subject of the first importance. To promote the first and remove the latter is the supreme desire of him who rightly appreciates the virtues of his canine friend. How to effect this forms the prominent theme of the following pages.

The valuable experience of Stonehenge which graced the pages of the first part of former editions has been largely retained, new matter being added where it was expressly needed.

The second part, relating to Disease, has been entirely re-written, and presents the standard of current experience as to its nature and appropriate treatment.

In the endeavour to present reliable views regarding the nature of the maladies of the dog, they are arranged as far as practicable in accordance with the supposed causes; thus, many are conveniently included under the head of Blood Diseases; others are due to specific or contagious elements; while the majority, perhaps, arising from interference with organic function, injury, &c., are conveniently dealt with in connection with the several systems, or groups of organs.

The chapter on Materia Medica deals with the numerous remedies employed in the treatment of disease, their combination and forms of administration, details of which are given in everyday language. The reader will find ample choice, and experience little difficulty in procuring from the nearest chemist, the preparations he may need.

By way of embellishment, faithful portraits of celebrities have been secured, through the kindness of several exhibitors, and especially Mr. Charles Reid, of Wishaw, whose similar efforts have satisfactorily enriched previous companion volumes.

LONDON, 1896.

CONTENTS.

CHAPTER I.

THE DOG AND ITS HABITS.

Origin—Characteristics—Age, &c. &c. . . . . . . PAGE 1

CHAPTER II.

VARIETIES OF THE DOG.

Pointer—Setters—Field Spaniels—Sussex Spaniel—Clumber Spaniel—Norfolk Spaniel—Cocker—Water Spaniels—Old English Water Spaniel—North of Ireland Water Spaniel—South Irish Water Spaniel—English Greyhound . . 4

CHAPTER III.

VARIETIES OF THE DOG (*continued*).

Hounds—The Bloodhound—Staghound—Foxhound—Harrier—Beagle—Dachshund—Otterhound—Fox Terrier—Truffle Dog—Retrievers—Deerhound—The Borzoi . . 28

CHAPTER IV.

USEFUL COMPANIONS OF MAN.

Old English Mastiff—The Great Dane—Newfoundland—St. Bernard—Bulldog—Bull Terriers—Pure Terriers—Smooth English Terrier—Black and Tan English Terrier—Rough or Broken-haired Terrier—Skye Terrier—Dandie Dinmont—Bedlington Terrier—Irish Terrier—Welsh Terrier—Whippet—Bob-tailed Sheep-Dog—Collie—Pomeranian or Spitz 51

Contents.

CHAPTER V.

LADIES' TOY DOGS.

King Charles Spaniel—Blenheim Spaniel—Italian Greyhound—Pug—Maltese Dog—Toy Terrier—Poodle . . . 86

CHAPTER VI.

GENERAL MANAGEMENT OF THE DOG.

General Management of Dogs—Of Whelps—Dressing—Kennels—Management of Pet Dogs 100

CHAPTER VII.

DISEASES OF THE DOG.

General Observations—Health and Disease—Pathology—Fever: Simple, Sympathetic, and Specific—Inflammation—Abscess—Serous Cyst—Prevention of Disease—Classification of Disease 108

CHAPTER VIII.

MATERIA MEDICA.

The Dispensing of Medicines—Nursing—Doses of Medicines—Alteratives—Anodynes—Antiseptics—Antispasmodics—Aperients—Astringents—Blisters—Caustics—Clysters, Enemas, or Injections—Cordials—Demulcents—Diaphoretics—Digestives—Diuretics—Electuaries—Embrocations or Liniments—Emetics—Expectorants—Febrifuges—Fomentations—Hypodermic Injections—Inhalations—Lotions—Ointments—External Parasiticides—Poultices—Stimulants—Stomachics—Styptics—Tonics—Worm Medicines, Internal Parasiticides 116

CHAPTER IX.

BLOOD DISEASES.

Plethora—Obesity—Anæmia—Rheumatism—Rickets, or Rachitis—Inter-breeding—Crooked or Bandy legs—Leuchæmia—Jaundice—Uræmia—Apnœa 138

Contents. xi

CHAPTER X.

SPECIFIC AND CONTAGIOUS DISEASES.

                                                                               PAGE

Anthrax—Cholera—Diphtheria—Distemper—Eczema Epizoötica—Glanders—Measles—Rabies—Relapsing Fever—Septicæmia—Tuberculosis—Variola, or Small Pox . . 146

CHAPTER XI.

DISEASES OF THE RESPIRATORY SYSTEM.

Catarrh, or Coryza—Ozæna—Parasitic Ozæna—Epistaxis—Polypus—Laryngitis—Aphonia—Snoring—Bronchitis—Pneumonia—Pleurisy—Parasitic or Verminous Bronchitis—Chronic Cough—Asthma 170

CHAPTER XII.

DISEASES OF THE CIRCULATORY SYSTEM..

Fatty Degeneration of the Heart—Rupture of the Heart—Valvular Disease—Pericarditis—Invasion by Parasites . 180

CHAPTER XIII.

DISEASES OF THE DIGESTIVE SYSTEM.

The Teeth: Caries—Abscess of the Jaw—Diseases of the Tongue: Glossitis, Wounds, Paralysis—Ptyalism—The Lips: Pharyngitis—Choking—Stricture of the Gullet—Indigestion—Vomition—Gastric Catarrh—Gastritis—Foreign Bodies in the Stomach—Ulceration—Worms in the Stomach—Colic—Diarrhœa—Dysentery—Constipation—Impaction—Enteritis—Prolapsus—Piles—Atony—Thickening—Hernia—Worms in the Bowels—Peritonitis—Ascites, or Dropsy—Hepatitis, Acute and Chronic—Fatty Degeneration—Parasites in the Liver—Diseases of the Spleen and Pancreas—Goitre 184

CHAPTER XIV.

DISEASES OF THE URINARY SYSTEM.

Nephritis, or Inflammation of the Kidneys — Albuminous Nephritis—Calculi, or Stones in the Kidney—Hæmaturia, or Red Water—Atrophy and Hypertrophy—Worm in the Kidney—Impaction of the Ureters—Cystitis, or Inflammation of the Bladder—Stone in the Bladder—Rupture of the Bladder—Diabetes—Paralysis of the Bladder—Disease of the Prostate—Stone in the Urethra—Urethritis—Balanitis—Posthitis—Worm in the Urethra . . . 204

CHAPTER XV.

DISEASES OF THE GENERATIVE SYSTEM.

MALE ORGANS: Gonorrhœa—Imperforate Prepuce—The Penis—Amputation—Scrotal Inflammation—Orchitis—Abscess of the Testicles—Scirrhus. FEMALE ORGANS: Metritis, or Inflammation of the Womb—Dropsy—Inversion, or Prolapsus—Hæmorrhage, or Flooding—Amputation—Tumours in the Vagina—Inversion, or Prolapsus—Amputation—Use of the Catheter. DISEASES OF THE ORGANS OF LACTATION: Retention of Milk—Mammitis, or Inflammation of the Milk Gland—Malignant Tumours—Warts—Œstrum—Parturition 210

CHAPTER XVI.

DISEASES OF THE EYES AND EARS.

ORGANS OF VISION: Simple Ophthalmia, or Conjunctivitis—Cataract—Iritis—Amaurosis, or Gutta Serena—Staphyloma—Hydrophthalmia—Distension, and Dislocation of the Eyeball—Tumour of the Haw—Dermatoid Conjunctiva—Ulceration of the Eyelids—Ectropion—Entropion—Watery Eyes. ORGANS OF HEARING: Otitis—Internal Canker—External Canker—Abscess of the Ear-flap, or Blood Abscess—Polypi, or Tumours within the Ear—Squamula, or Scurfiness of the Ear-flap—Ticks—Mange of the Ear . . 220

CHAPTER XVII.

DISEASES OF THE NERVOUS SYSTEM.

Epilepsy—Vertigo—Neuralgia—Apoplexy—Tetanus, or Lockedjaw—Chorea—Cramp—Injuries to the Head: Concussion—Compression—Apoplexy—Encephalitis—Hydrocephalus—Paralysis—Parasitism 229

CHAPTER XVIII.

DISEASES OF THE SKIN.

Alopecia, or Baldness—Anasarca, or Dropsy of the Cellular Tissue—Eczema, Surfeit, or "Red Mange"—Erythema—Warts—PARASITIC DISEASES OF THE SKIN, ANIMAL PARASITES: Scabies, or Sarcoptic Mange—Follicular Mange.— The Harvest Bug — Fleas — Lice — Ticks —VEGETABLE PARASITES: Tinea Tonsurans, or Ringworm—Tinea Favosa, or Honeycomb Ringworm . . 236

CHAPTER XIX.

LOCAL INJURIES.

Anchylosis, or Stiff-joint—Sprain of Muscle and Sinew—Congenital Deformity—Dislocations—Fracture of Bone—False Joint—Lameness—Sprain of Muscle—Sprain of Tendon—Lameness of the Feet—Carpet Fever—Injuries by Thorns, Nails, &c.—Raw, Bruised and Bleeding Feet—Mange of the Foot — Overgrown Claws — Wounds — Hæmorrhage, or Bleeding 248

CHAPTER XX.

POISONS.

Empirical Poisoning—Accidental Poisoning—Wilful and Malicious Poisoning—Symptoms of Poisoning—Treatment—Mineral Poisons—Vegetable Poisons—Animal Poisons—Snake or Viper-bite—Wasps, Hornets, and Bees—Destruction of Dogs 254

INDEX 261

LIST OF PLATES

I. POINTERS "CHAMPION SANDFORD BANG" AND "CHAMPION HEATHER BEE"	*Frontispiece*	
II. GORDON SETTERS	to face p.	10
III. IRISH SETTER "CHAMPION HEATHER ROY"	,,	12
IV. GREYHOUNDS	,,	20
V. WIREHAIRED FOX TERRIER "JACK ST. LEGER"	,,	40
VI. FLAT COATED RETRIEVER "HELPFUL"	,,	48
VII. DEERHOUND	,,	50
VIII. BORZOI	,,	52
IX. ENGLISH MASTIFF "PRINCE OF WALES"	,,	54
X. NEWFOUNDLAND	,,	56
XI. ROUGH COATED ST. BERNARD	,,	60
XII. BULLDOG	,,	64
XIII. WHITE ENGLISH TERRIER "CHAMPION MORNING STAR"	,,	69
XIV. IRISH TERRIER "BREDA MIXER"	,,	78
XV. ROUGH COATED COLLIE	,,	84
XVI. PUG "PRIMROSE KNIGHT"	,,	96

THE DOG.

CHAPTER I.

THE DOG AND ITS HABITS.

Origin—Characteristics—Age, &c., &c.

THE DOG belongs to the division *Vertebrata*, and the class *Mammalia*. It is also in the order *Feræ*, the family *Felidæ*, and the sub-family *Canina*, which includes the dog, wolf, jackal, and fox. This sub-family is distinguished by having two tubercular teeth behind its canine teeth in the upper jaw; and the *Canis familiaris* has the pupils of the eye round, while in the fox they are like those of the cat, perpendicular slits, and in the wolf oblique ones. Volumes have been written on the origin of the dog, but our knowledge on this subject may easily be summed up in one little word, *nil;* I shall therefore not inflict upon the readers of this book all the various arguments *pro* and *con;* suffice it to say, that the dog is now an inhabitant chiefly of cold and temperate climates; that it rapidly degenerates if transported to a very warm one, as is seen in India and China, but that it will bear every climate from the Arctic circle to the Equator without loss of life. The dog is a carnivorous animal by nature, though he will feed upon and devour any vegetable substance that comes in his way if pressed by hunger. In his domesticated state he thrives best upon a mixed diet, and is usually considered, and with truth, as omnivorous. His teeth are fitted for tearing flesh, and he has no true grinders suited to bruise grain; his stomach is a simple one, and his intestines are of a medium length between the short ones of the true Carnivora, and the long ones of the graminivorous quadrupeds.

It is impossible to fix the epoch, as we have said, when the dog became the servant of man. The oldest traditions, the most ancient historical documents, show us the dog reduced to a state of domesticity. Thus it may be said that the dog forms an integral part of mankind. This is what Toussenel has well said: "Ce qu'il y a de meilleur dans l'homme, c'est le chien." The dog possesses all the qualities of intelligence and spirit. Where can we find a more certain, more constant, or more devoted friendship, a more faithful memory, a stronger attachment, more sincere abnegation, a mind more loyal and frank? The dog does not know what ingratitude is. He does not abandon his benefactor in danger or adversity. With joy he offers to sacrifice his life for those who feed him. He pushes his devotion so far as to forget himself. He does not recall the corrections, the unkind treatment, to which he has been subjected; he thirsts for caresses, while the indifference of those who are dear to him plunges him into deep distress. Noble creature! the favourite of the rich, consolation of the poor, inseparable companion of the unfortunate; thanks to thee, the miserable individual who dies alone in the midst of society, counts at least one friend at his melancholy funeral; he does not descend alone into the cold grave, for thou comest to shed on his tomb the sincere tears of affection and regret, and such is the excess of thy grief, that no one can tear thee from that spot where sleeps the corpse of him thou lovest!

And what intelligence! what penetration! what *finesse* is there in this admirable companion of our gladness and sorrow! How well he can read countenances; how skilfully he knows how to interpret the sentiments conveyed in gestures and words! In vain you may threaten, in vain try to frighten him. Your eye betrays you; that smile, which scarcely appears upon your lips, has unmasked your feelings; and so far from fearing and avoiding you, he comes to solicit your attention.

Volumes might be written, if desirable, relating all the extraordinary stories of which dogs are the heroes. Every day, in ordinary life, we see something of this kind, and which, although of so frequent occurrence, is none the less curious. Is it necessary to recall to memory the dog of Ulysses, the model of fidelity; the dog of Montargis, the vanquisher of crime; of Munito, the brilliant player at dominoes? Must we mention the Newfoundland dog and the dog of Mount St. Bernard, both of them preservers of human life? Is it necessary to speak of intelligent dogs going for provisions for their master, and assisting him in his duties with ability; of the shoeblack's dog, trained to plant his muddy paws on the best polished boots, so as to bring more business to his master, the man of the brush? We should never come to an end if we attempted to register all the exploits of this valuable companion of man.

Dogs are *digitigrade*, or walk on their toes; their claws are not retractile—they have five toes on the fore-feet and generally four on the hind ones. Their teeth are—

$$\text{Incisors } \frac{6}{6} \quad \text{Canine } \frac{1-1}{1-1} \quad \text{Molars } \frac{6\ \ 6}{8\ \ 8}$$

The tongue of the dog is smooth, not lacerating like that of the cat; its application to wounds has a healing tendency when the animal is in health. Dogs live on an average about fourteen or fifteen years.

CHAPTER II.

VARIETIES OF THE DOG.

Pointer—Setters—Field Spaniels—Sussex Spaniel—Clumber Spaniel—Norfolk Spaniel—Cocker—Water Spaniels—Old English Water Spaniel—North of Ireland Water Spaniel—South Irish Water Spaniel—English Greyhound.

THE **Pointer** of the present day is no doubt descended from the old Spanish dog, crossed with the foxhound or greyhound, by which he has obtained greater lightness and activity, united with more lasting powers, but at the expense of his nose, which is not so delicate as that of the source from which he sprang.

The well-bred pointer, in the eyes of the true sportsman, is a grand and graceful dog. His ancestry probably cannot be traced so far back as that of the setter, but as a true sporting dog he is often preferred, to the exclusion of the latter.. The habit of pointing at their game is an innate qualification of the breed, and may be observed in young puppies standing to their game when they are first taken to the field.

At the various shows of the United Kingdom three sizes of this dog may be seen, which are denominated as large, medium, and small weight. Of the first, the dog is estimated to be upwards of 70 lbs., and the bitch over 60 lbs.; medium, dogs, 50 to 70 lbs., and bitches, 45 to 60 lbs.; dogs of small weight are under 50 lbs., the bitches not exceeding 45 lbs. The best colours for show purposes are the lemon and white, quality being more prominent in pointers of this colour. Some sportsmen prefer the liver and white, under the conviction that they are possessed of greater endurance; others regard colour as a secondary matter, resting on the conviction that a good dog cannot possess a bad colour, always looking forward in their selection to obtaining symmetrical proportions, good build, and muscular development, all of which combine towards the essential qualities of the breed, viz., strength, speed, and endurance. A black nose is common to the liver and white pointer, but it is disastrous to the lemon and white in the show ring.

The head of the pointer should be large but not heavy, wide across the ears, and showing a raised forehead. The nose should be long and broad, with its front outline square, the teeth being even. This marks the pointer from the hound, whose nose has a tendency to slope towards the throat, the extreme of which is called the "pig's snout." The lips should be well marked, without running into the flews of the bloodhound. Ears long, soft, and thin, set on low down, and carried quite close to the cheeks. Eyes moderately large, soft, and intelligent, the colour varying from buff to dark brown according to that of the coat. A peculiarly rounded outline on the upper side of the neck marks the well-bred pointer, which can scarcely be described in words. No throatiness is allowable, as it indicates too much of the Spanish strain. This *point* should be divided as follows:—Skull, 10; nose, 10; ears, 5; neck, 5—total, 30

The frame may be divided into loin, hind quarter, shoulders, and chest. The loin, which with the hind quarter constitutes the propelling powers, must be well arched, broad, and deep, and strongly united to the ribs in front, and to the couples behind, which latter should be wide and somewhat ragged. Next in importance are the shoulders, upon the obliquity of which depends the elasticity of the action, while they must be well clothed with muscle, to enable the dog to keep up for many hours in succession. The chest must be full, but not so much so as that of the old barrel-shaped Spanish pointer, the back ribs being required to be very deep. Hind quarters well bent at the stifles, provided with strong hocks, and clothed with powerful muscles. In estimating these *point*s, I should give to the shoulders and chest, 15 points; back and hind quarters, 15 points—total, 30 points.

Without the feet and legs the continued action of each dog must altogether be forbidden, as weakly-formed ones soon give way, and the dog becomes lame. The feet should be round and cat-like, with hard horny soles, pasterns short, large in the bone and tendons, and not sloping backwards towards the knees to any great extent. A long and muscular arm is specially necessary, and the elbow must be neither in nor out. These *points* may be valued as follows, viz. :—feet, 6 ; legs, 6 ; elbows, 4 ; hocks, 2 ; stifles, 2—total, 20.

The general quality and stern indicate by their appearance the amount of breeding, and are therefore necessarily attended to, but the former cannot he described. The stern should be shaped like a bee's sting, having a strong root, a straight, *fine*, and stiff body, and a pointed tip—total value, 10.

Of the colour, symmetry, and coat, the first may be selected according to fancy, but most people prefer a dog with a good deal of white, so that he may readily be seen in turnips. Liver and white, or lemon and white, are the most common, next to which come black and white, which, when mixed with tan on the cheeks, indicates the hound cross. Whole colours are liver, red, black, and white. The texture of the coat should be short and soft, but not too fine, the last-named quality being often accompanied by a delicate constitution. These *points* are put at 10.

Setters of the present day are classed as either English, Scotch (Gordon), Irish, or Russian. It is needless to describe the last-named, as the breed, which was common enough thirty years ago, is now seldom met with, and has no advantage to recommend it. It is a very long-haired animal, almost resembling a poodle in coat, except that there is not so much curl. Hence, in the hot weather so often experienced in August and September, it is soon knocked up, and though possessing a very fine nose, this is of little use at its master's heels.

All the various breeds of the setter are doubtless descended from the spaniel, which dog has a natural propensity to pause before springing on his game. This peculiarity has been encouraged and developed until the innate point has become established, and the setter puppy, if well bred, may be expected to point game on the first or second time of showing it to him, or, if very high-couraged, as soon as he finds he cannot run it down by speed. In the early days, after the breed was first established, it was used solely by the falconer and netter, who were contented with any animal which would find birds, and, setting down on the ground, would allow the net to be drawn over him, or the hawk to be cast off, without moving. Since the introduction of the plan of shooting flying, a faster and stouter dog has become necessary, and one also which will bear the heats of August and September. Hence the object of the breeder has been to get rid of the thick curly coat of the spaniel on the body of the setter, and at the same time to retain and even improve upon the elegant feather beneath the tail, or flag, as it is called, and behind the legs. The three breeds we have mentioned, into which setters are divided, all agree in this point, however much they may differ in others, as we shall presently see.

Youatt's remarks on the setter are interesting. He says:—"The setter is more active than the pointer. He has greater spirit and strength. He loves his master for himself, and not, like the pointer, merely for the pleasure he shares with him. His somewhat inferior scent, however, makes him a little too apt to run into his game, and he occasionally has a will of his own. He requires good breaking and plenty of work, but that breaking must be of a peculiar character; it must not partake of the severity which too often accompanies, and unnecessarily so, the tuition of the pointer." Several distinct breeds of the setter are met with: the Laverack setter, which is probably the purest of the English breeds, the colours being liver and white, flints, or blue, or lemon and white Beltons, or mottles. The Featherston Castle, and also the Newark Castle setters are liver and white, the latter being distinguished by top-knots. The Lort setter is black and white or orange and white. The Earl of Seafield's breed is lemon and white, and that of Lord Lovat is black, white, and tan. The Llewellyn setter is described as a very neat and handsome dog, coming pretty close to the Laverack in many of his points.

As his name implies, the setter *crouches, sits,* or sets his game, a qualification which is carefully estimated by experienced judges. If he stands at his game, the fault is supposed to be derived from the pointer.

The English setter is longer and more open in his frame than the pointer, and has a proportionally longer stride in all his paces. He is capable of harder work than that dog, and as his toes are clothed with hair in the intervals between them, he is not so liable to become "foot-sore," either from very dry or very wet ground. In regard to nose, there is much difference of opinion, but I am inclined to believe that the setter has a slight advantage in this respect. When well bred, the setter is as easily broken as the pointer, to the point and back, but he is seldom quite as tractable in regard to the other elements of his education, and is, moreover, more apt to forget his lessons than his smooth competitor in the shooting-field. These remarks, however, apply more to the setter of the early part of this century than to the dog of the present day, which is a great improvement upon his ancestors.

The head is lighter than the pointer's, and narrower across the ears, but equally high at the forehead. The nose is long, and shows a slight tendency to fall inwards towards the eyes, the corners of which should be not less than four inches from its tip. This should be broad, with large open nostrils, well bedewed with moisture, and of a dark colour. Teeth level, and without the slightest tendency to the "snipe" form. Lips full at the angles, but not pendulous even to the extent allowable in the pointer. Ears must be about 6 inches long, set on low and well forward, carried without any approach to the prick shape, and rounded at the lower edges. Eyes large, but not protruding, and beaming with love of approbation and intelligence. Neck long, thin, and slightly arched above, but showing a clean-cut line where it joins the head. Value of these *points:* head, 10; nose, 10; neck, 5; ears, 5—total, 30.

The frame and outline, though different to the eye of the judge from that of the pointer, cannot be separated from the latter by any verbal description, except that the chest is rarely so wide or barrelled as is allowable in that dog. The hips are also more ragged and the loin slightly more arched. These *points* are : shoulders and chest, 15 ; back and hind quarters, 15—total, 30 points.

In the feet and legs also the remarks on the pointer are equally applicable, but there is some difference of opinion as to the hare-foot, which by many is considered to be necessary to the thorough-bred setter. In this shape the toes are longer than in the cat-foot, more split up, and thickly clothed with strong hair between the toes. No doubt this last feature is of great service in keeping the skin free from inflammation when at work over marshy ground, but the long toes which usually attend this development do not stand so well as the stout cat-like formation of the other foot. It is somewhat difficult to strike the balance between these feet, as one form is best suited to wet ground and the other to hard. If it is possible to get the cat-like foot with sufficient hair upon it, I should no doubt prefer that form, and though I have never seen the two fully united, I do not despair of getting them by careful breeding. Legs and feet, 12; elbows, hocks, and stifles, 8.

In the general quality or character there is not much to alter from the remarks given under the pointer, but the *stern* or *flag* varies a good deal. It should be set on well up the back, but not carried with the slightest curl over it, though there may be a gentle and regular sweep in its upper outline. The feather should be flat, long, and silky, deep in the centre, and tapering to each end. This should be as pointed as in the pointer, and should be carried in the same perpendicular plane as the rest of the flag, without the slightest approach to the corkscrew form. Total value, 10.

The coat must be fine and silky, but still somewhat hard to the touch, a combination that can only be felt, and not imagined. There must be little or no curl, while the shorter it is on the body, and the longer in the feather, the better for the value of the dog. Value in conjunction with symmetry, 10. The order of merit of the various colours met with is as follows, viz. :—1. Orange and white, with freckled nose and legs. 2. Orange and white, plain. 3. Lemon and white. 4. Black and white, especially if ticked slightly with tanned spots on feet and legs, known as "Belton greys." 5. Pure white. 6. Black. 7. Fallow or yellow. 8. Liver or liver and white. 9. Liver and tan.

The Scotch or Gordon Setter has become very fashionable of late years, and especially since dog shows were established. The Gordon differs from the English setter in the following properties:—In stern he is generally shorter, or if long, it has a decided tendency to show the "teapot" form, than which nothing is more ugly. This is probably derived from the collie cross, which, I have no doubt, has been used in some strains with the disadvantage of introducing this defect and a more woolly coat. In my own dog Rex (son of Kent and Regent) whose portrait is here given, the flag is faultless, and is somewhat longer both in bone and feather than is given by the artist, who sketched him while yet in his puppyhood. The Gordon head is perhaps slightly heavier than the English, and his nose and intelligence are proportionably good. In colour he is a rich black and tan, but it is asserted by many experienced breeders, that the original colour was more or less mixed with white, and I believe that black, white, and tan colour is quite as correct as the whole black and tan. His carriage is very lively, and he is full of hunt, but he is apt to be shy and headstrong. My experience of the breed in the field is chiefly confined to Rex, who is certainly one of the most perfect dogs I ever saw out; but though he was selected from a lot as a sample, to test their value, it does not follow that he is not an exceptional animal of his strain. He, like all the dogs of the breed I have seen, does not last more than half a day, but some of the bitches of the same strain are everlasting. The *points* are nearly the same as in the English dog, the only difference being that 5 points are taken off the ears and neck, and added to the colour and coat.

The exact origin of the Gordon setter is somewhat enveloped in doubt. As described by judicious authorities

GORDON SETTERS "GROUSE" AND "ROCK."
The property of the Duchess of Bedford

the original colour was black, white, and tan, these being derived from the collie, bloodhound, and the English or Irish setter, each of which contributed to the genesis of the breed. On the other hand, it is averred that the breed was determined in the Gordon kennels, by crossing the collie with an English setter or spaniel, while the evidence of the bloodhound is not forthcoming. Again, it is urged that the breed was not the outcome of special design or selection in the first instance, but the result of numerous as well as various crosses conducted on the principles above named. Careful in-breeding has since secured the distinctive characteristics of this, as in all other breeds. A true Gordon setter is said to possess in almost equal proportions, the main qualifications of the collie, bloodhound, and the setter. This breed is eminently distinguished by a remarkably acute intelligence and scenting power, combined with great endurance, as a glance at the construction of the head will clearly indicate. A beautiful feature in this dog is his straight and slightly wavy coat of jet black, and the well defined mahogany tan of the muzzle and inside of the thighs, and downwards from the front of the stifle and knees to the ground.

As observed in the field, the essential characteristics of the English and Irish setters are great speed, activity, and endurance, especially in the cold and wet during rough work on the moors. In this respect the Irish setter is more suitable than the English; but both are extremely sensible of the heat of the sun without water. Some dogs of both breeds are quite incapable of work under a hot sun unless they can plunge into a pool; on this account, in the south the pointer, well up to partridge shooting, is generally preferred to the setter, while in the northern moors the setter will range wider and faster, do more work, and endure the vicissitudes of weather, as well as the strong heather, which proves so irritating to the feet and legs of the high-bred pointer. It is supposed that the pointer is also superior with respect to nose, but it is probable that when both are in condition, neither being distressed by heat, but little if any difference will be found. A moderately slow dog will always appear to have a better nose than a very fast one, and will put up less game; but, if too slow, he will lose a great many points which are taken from him by his faster competitor. Hence it follows that there is a medium in point of speed which may be possessed by either breed, and a selection need not be made on that account. The setter is, however, acknowledged to be more difficult to break than the pointer, and is apt to forget his lessons; the pointer, on the other hand, rarely forgets under an intelligent master.

Respecting the **Irish Setter** there is still more difference of opinion as to the shade of colour than in regard to the Gordon. By one party it is asserted that the well-bred Irish setter must be of a deep pure blood-red, without the slightest approach to black or mahogany-colour on the back, ear, or stern. After the publication in the *Field* of the article on this dog, in which this was laid down as the attribute of the breed, Mr. Hungerford opened the controversy by asserting that, according to his experience, they might be either red or red and white, followed by the late Mr. John Walker (the well-known judge at most of the recent dog shows), who raised the question as to the objection to the black tinge, which was answered by Colonel Whyte in the negative, and by Mr. Henry Blake Knox as follows: "The coat should be rather coarse, for you want him for hard work and hardships; smooth or wavy, not curly; hair of moderate length on the upper parts of the body; the foot-half tawny, the tip-half deep senna, appearing as if stained with port wine (blood-red), but never showing black on the ears, back, head, or tail; the legs and under parts, deep or pale tawny; white should not appear anywhere except in the centre of the forehead and the centre of the breast. I breed without any white at all." Captain Hutchinson objects to the black stain, and supports his opinion by adding some high authorities in its favour. On the whole, therefore, it may be assumed that the weight of evidence is against the dark stain. In other respects Mr. Knox's description is so admirable that I quote it *in extenso*:—"The ears should be long, reaching at the end of the hair to nose, pendulous, and

Irish Setter "Champion Heather Roy."
Winner of over fifty First Prizes. The property of Mr. Robert Chapman, Glenboig.

as if lying in a fold, set well back and low on the head; they should never be set high, short in length, or half diamond-shaped; their feather should be moderate. The eye is of a rich hazel or bright brown, well set, full, kind, sensible, and loving, the iris mahogany-colour; it should be gooseberry, black, or prominent and staring, like the King Charles. The nose is mahogany, dark flesh, or blackish mahogany, never black or pink. Even dark flesh is not so much admired, though, with a good clear eye, I like it; but with the gooseberry eye you indeed have a rare brute. My old dog has a dark flesh-colour nose, unlike any of his kind, yet none of his pups got it, all having dark mahogany; the whiskers red; the head itself long and narrow, yet wide in the forehead, arched in the peaked cranium behind. A short bullet head, a wide flat one, or one running to a point at the snout, is very common and very bad; the lips deep or moderately so. The chest should be wide when the dog is sitting on his haunches and the head held back. Too wide a chest is apt to give a dog a waddle and slow gait. The chest ribs cannot be too deep. The loins for speed should be long, moderately wide, and the belly well tucked up. The fore-legs straight, moderately feathered, and the feet close and small, not round like a hound's, or splayed. The ham straight, flat, and muscular, and feathered well with buff-coloured hair, and the hind quarters altogether square and active made. The tail should be well covered with coarse hair curling along the tip, and hanging moderately, though bushy from beneath, but not in silken streamers, or in a great bushy flag like a Newfoundland. It should be carried in a horizontal line with the back, or slightly above it, not cocked or curled. In the field or in excitement, I like it carried low, stiff, and beating the hind legs." As in the case of the Gordon setter, there is no difference in the *points* from those of the English variety.

Field Spaniels are divided into two principal groups, the Springers, or larger variety, used for all sorts of covert game, and the Cockers, kept more especially for woodcocks, to follow which they must be of smaller size. The springer is again subdivided into the Clumber, Sussex,

Norfolk, and other strains; while the cocker includes the Devonshire and Welsh varieties, as well as many other strains without special name.

The **Sussex Spaniel** is now very rare, being replaced by the Clumber, which works mute, and is more easily

Sussex Spaniel.

kept under control, and therefore better for assisting the beaters in our modern *battues*. It is a very old breed, and is probably the earliest of all those used with the gun or net, though by some people the Clumber is considered to have the claim to seniority.

The head of this spaniel should be long and heavy; eye large and languishing, with the forehead prominently over it; muzzle square; lips somewhat pendulous; mouth large, with the under jaw receding slightly, though not to the extent which could constitute a pig-jaw or snipe nose. Ears large and lobe-shaped, well furnished with silky hair, and set on low down. Nostrils large, and the external nose large and liver-coloured. Neck strong and muscular, with the crest slightly arched. Value of these *points:* head, 20; nose, 10; ears, 5; neck, 5—total, 40.

The chest should be very wide, with round or barrel-like ribs, deep behind; shoulders well thrown back; body long and round. Value: chest, 5; shoulders, 5—total, 10.

The legs should be short and strong, well feathered to the feet before and behind. The feet round, with the toes well arched and abundantly furnished with tan between the toes. *Points:* legs, 5; feet, 5.

The loin must be very strong; back ribs very deep and round; tail (docked to about 9 inches in length) set low and carried considerably below the level of the back, never above it. *Points:* loin, 5; back ribs, 5; low set and carriage of tail, 10.

The colour is a golden liver without white. Coat waved (not curly), thick, shiny, and abundant. *Points:* colour, 5; coat, 5; symmetry, 5.

The temperament must be cheerful, courageous, and docile. Weight from 35 lbs. to 40 lbs.

This dog is not mute like the Clumber, but he is not noisy or babbling, seldom throwing his tongue after he is thoroughly broken. He is faster and more enduring than the Clumber, and also bears water better.

The **Clumber Spaniel** has obtained his name from the seat of the Duke of Newcastle, where it is supposed the breed originated. At all events, it was confined to that family until the middle of the nineteenth century. This dog is invariably of great length, low on the leg, and heavy in frame; his weight varying from 40 lbs. to 45 lbs., and his height not exceeding 20 inches. He is devoted to the gun, but cares little for his master without that accompaniment. Dogs of this breed never throw their tongue when at work, being perfectly mute if pure in blood. They are capable of very high training, and a team of them, consisting of three or four couples, may be broken to do anything but talk. Hence, where dogs are used in covert, the clumber has become the general favourite, and it is a treat to shoot over a perfect team.

The head is large and long, and should be marked with lemon to a line just in front of the eyes, with a blaze up

Clumber Spaniel.

the face. Eyes large and thoughtful; nose and lips flesh or liver-colour, sometimes cherry. Ears large, but not lobe-shaped or so heavy as those of the Sussex, and with less feather. Neck strong and long. Total value, 40.

Back long and straight; chest wide and deep, showing scarcely any daylight under it. Shoulders thick and wide through them; loin straight but strong, with wide couples; back ribs very deep. Total value, 50.

The legs must be straight, very stout, and very strong.

Fore-arm immense; shanks and hind legs well developed in bone, and clothed with strong muscles. Value, 10.

The stern should be set low (it is generally docked, but not always; if docked, it is left fully 11 in. long). It is carried low and is tufted at its extremity, but not to the same extent. Value, 10.

The colour must be a true lemon, the paler the better. Orange is often thrown, but is objectionable. Any other colour is a mark of impurity. The texture of coat is soft, shiny, silky, and nearly straight. Value, 10.

These dogs last many years, and seldom give up work till incapacitated by old age or disease.

The **Norfolk Spaniel** differs chiefly in length and colour from the Clumber, being shorter and of various shades of black, liver, and yellow, more or less mixed with white. There are no positive signs by which he may be distinguished from the various mixed breeds of springers found throughout the country.

The **Cocker** is a much smaller dog than the springer, seldom exceeding 18 lbs. in weight for bitches, and 25 lbs. for dogs. He is much more active than the springer, and of any colour more or less marked with white. The Devonshire and Welsh cocker are, however, of a deep liver-colour, without white, and closely resemble each other in other respects. They are nearly mute, but whimper slightly on a scent, and when well broken they distinguish each kind of game by the note they give out, especially the woodcock, of which they are particularly fond. The head of the cocker should be round and of a medium length. It should not be square, like that of a Clumber spaniel or Sussex spaniel. The muzzle should neither be snipy nor pointed. It should be wide and well developed, and should taper slightly close to the end. The forehead should take a sudden rise from the top end of the muzzle, near the eye, into a finely-arched skull, with a somewhat knotty or jutting occiput, resembling the occiput of a bloodhound. The eye should be of a medium size, not too full (which would indicate a cross with the King Charles spaniel), but should have a gentle, and at the same time a "knowing" expression. The ears should measure 22 in. to 24 in. across the head from tip to tip, including the hair, which should be soft and silky. They should lie close to the head, and be set well back. They should not be fixed on the top of the head, but be set rather low. The neck strong and muscular. The shoulders broad and prominent. The chest of medium depth, broad, well developed, and muscular. The body and loins strong and powerful; loins slightly drooping towards root of tail. The legs: fore-legs strong, muscular, straight, and not inclined to be bandied; hind legs strong and should be like those of a greyhound, well bent, and very short from hock to foot. The feet strong and round, of a good medium size (not too small), and they should be well feathered between the toes. The tail, thin and straight, should be set low, and always carried below the level of the back, with a downward tendency. The coat waved and silky, but never wiry or woolly; it should be 3 in. to 4 in. in length. The feathering on the legs, hams, and tail, and the frill on the breast, should be 4 in. to 5 in. in length. The colours, black, brown, liver, black and white, liver and white, and lemon and white. The *points* are: head, neck, and ears, 30; chest and shoulders, 10; back and ribs, 10; legs and feet, 10; low carriage of tail, 10; symmetry, 10; colour and coat, 5.

Water Spaniels may be classed as English or Irish, besides which there is the Tweedside breed, which resembles a good deal in appearance a small ordinary English retriever of a liver-colour.

The **Old English Water Spaniel** is now seldom or never seen in any degree of purity, and it is scarcely necessary, or even possible, to describe it with any degree of certainty as to the truth of the particulars. I shall therefore pass on to the Irish breeds.

The **North of Ireland Water Spaniel** resembles greatly the old English dog, except in having shorter ears without feather, and in being longer on the legs, which also are without feather. It is seldom met with in this country.

The **Southern Irish Water Spaniel** is, on the contrary, more frequently found in England and Ireland,

and is highly prized since it was brought to perfection by Mr. McCarthy. He is a very intelligent companion, capable of being broke to retrieve with facility, and a most useful general attendant on the gunner, though specially good at his own vocation in the water. His height is about 21 in. or 22 in., and his weight a little above 40 lbs.

The head is capacious—forehead high, and eyes intelligent, though rather small. The face is clothed with short hair, over which hangs a top-knot of considerable length, coming forward to a peak; these two points being indicative of true breeding. Ears very long, measuring fully 26 in. across when extended.

Body moderately long and very strong, covered with short crisp curls, which often become daggled towards the moulting season. Tail round, without feather, terminating in a sharp point, and rather short.

Colour, a pure deep puce, without white. In other particulars these dogs should resemble the ordinary spaniel, so that it is needless to recapitulate them.

Points: head and nose, 20; top-knot and bareness of face, 10; ears, 10; feet and legs, 10; back and quarters, 10; symmetry, 10; coat and colour, 20; tail 10.

The spaniel, as the name implies, was originally a native of Spain, his class forming the oldest, and possibly the most useful, among the various breeds of sporting dogs. In the field they prove most intelligent, persevering and persistent; and at home are remarkable for their gentleness and loving companionship, besides being exceedingly graceful, docile, and easily trained to almost every degree of house refinement within the compass of canine intelligence. We have similar experience. A dog of this breed was offered to us as a gift, on account of his somewhat "warm temper," which proved to be the result of ill-usage. We took him into our care and he became exceedingly clever, a most faithful guard and amusing companion. One day, a fiend in human form struck him and fractured his fore-leg, when he returned home, limping, and crying piteously, holding the injured member for inspection. It was speedily set and bound in the usual manner, and he was put to rest. Some hours afterwards we heard a banging at the door, and on opening it there stood our maimed friend using his tail to attract attention. We found the member unduly swollen and painful, and at once removed the appliances, afterwards replacing them with greater com-

Irish Water Spaniel.

fort and less pressure. He then barked his thanks, licked our hands, and returned to his bed rejoicingly. He lived some years and endeared himself to us by many acts of true devotion.

The **Scotch Greyhound** is now seldom met with in any degree of purity except in the highland districts of Scotland and Wales, where his rough coat is supposed to render him less obnoxious to cold than the smooth dog. In public coursing he has for some years been invariably

GREYHOUNDS.

beaten by the smooth greyhound, and therefore his use is confined to the districts I have mentioned, where the nature of the country forbids anything in the shape of coursing for sport, and "fox-hunting" is the order of the day. For this purpose he is well qualified, as he soon learns to stoop to a scent. In appearance he exactly resembles the deerhound, but in action he may be known from that dog by the different carriage of the head. With the exception of his rough coat, he closely resembles the English or smooth dog.

The **Greyhound** is the thorough-bred racer among dogs, and the points which give the faculty are easily recognized by the eye, though all dogs which have them are not necessarily fast. These points are—first, length from the hip-joint to the hock, *when extended;* and secondly, powerful and flexible shoulders.

The head should be wide behind, and should be considerably larger in circumference, if measured over the ears, than over the eyebrows. For dogs of good size, I believe the measure over the ears should be about 15 in., and for bitches from 14 to $14\frac{1}{2}$ in., according to the general size of the head, which is sometimes very small and neat in them without injury. The jaw should be very lean, with a good muscular development on the cheek, which gives a strong hold, and enables the dog to bear his hare in striking at her. The head of the greyhound is compared to that of the snake, but it is a far-fetched comparison, save in the flatness of the top, and the width, which certainly are points of resemblance; the nose, however, is so different that the likeness is a very poor one. The teeth should be good, and in young dogs white and free from tartar; indeed, in a well-reared dog, the whiteness is of such a kind as to excel the finest ivory. This is a strong mark of good rearing, and indicates the habitual use of bones, the gnawing of which not only cleans the teeth, but aids in their formation, and also increases the general health of the whole system. The eye should be bright and tolerably full. I have never been able to satisfy myself as to the general possession of any one kind of eye by good public greyhounds. I have seen, I think, as many of any one colour which can be mentioned, as of others common in the greyhound. So with the ears; different breeds are so very variously furnished with this appendage, that nothing can be made of

Greyhound.

it as a sign of good or bad qualities. Some good ones are possessed of falling, soft, and broad ears; others of sharp and screwed-up ears; and others again of foxy, pricked ears; and these are very remarkable in the descendants of Heather-jock, belonging to Dr. Brown, in Scotland, who often inherit this peculiarity to the third and fourth generation.

The neck is a very beautiful part of the high-bred greyhound, and is properly compared with that of the drake, though not quite coming up to the elegance of that bird,

In many breeds, however, the neck is extremely long and swan-like; and this point gives great power of reaching the hare without losing the stride, which would be a fatal drawback in the fast dog.

The chest and neck together constitute the body or trunk. The chest is a conical cavity adapted to contain the lungs, heart, and great vessels, to protect them from injury, and to inflate the lungs by enlarging the capacity of the chamber which contains them. Such a cavity must therefore be of sufficient volume for the first purpose, of sufficient strength for the second, and of sufficiently varying capacity for the third; and all these offices the chest of the greyhound efficiently performs. But not only must it be thus formed, but it must also be so flattened on the sides that the shoulder-blades shall lie smoothly upon them, and have free play to extend themselves. In order to meet all these requirements, the chest of the greyhound is deeper than in most animals, so as to give increase of volume without separating the shoulders too much, or placing their blades on too convex a surface. But if the chest is prolonged too far downwards, it strikes the ground in the efforts made to stop the speed at the turns, and in that way is prejudicial to the going of the dog. Thus a happy medium is required in this department, and the chest must be wide, but not too round, and deep, without being so much so as to interfere with the working powers. Besides these two points, it is important that the ribs shall be well separated from each other, so that they may expand the cavity properly, otherwise respiration is not performed with sufficient power and velocity. This width of the spaces is known to exist by the comparative length between the breast and the last rib at the loin; but, again, this must not be too great, or the back is rendered weak, and incapable of those vigorous and quick efforts which the gallop requires.

The back ought to be well let into the shoulders—that is to say, the muscles which compose it ought to run well forward towards the shoulder-blades, and should leave a strong ridge of muscle standing up above the ribs on each side of the spine. This is a very important point, and one which almost every good greyhound exhibits. Its absence betokens great weakness and a want of endurance; for though the dog may be fast without it, he is seldom capable of continuing his speed.

The hind quarter is the main element of progression, and upon it in a great measure depend the speed and power of the greyhound. As in all other cases, size is power; and the greater the length and size of the hind quarter, so will be the power of propulsion. This length is variously displayed: sometimes the hind leg being long, but straight; whilst in others it is more or less bent in two places—the stifle and hock. It will generally be observed that when the part of the leg below the hock is comparatively short, the bones above that part are bent at the stifle, and the whole hind quarter is long, without raising the back from the ground, as would be the case with the same length of limb in a more straight form. As far as my observation goes, the bent hind quarter is the more favourable form; but I have seen many good dogs with very straight stifles, and there can be no reason why these should not serve the purpose of propulsion as well as the bent ones. But though they can propel as well, and perhaps even better under some circumstances, they are quite useless unless they are accompanied by a low fore-quarter; for if otherwise, the fore-leg is too long in proportion, and the power of working and killing is at a very low ebb.

Two essentials are required,—speed and working power. Now, speed may be given from length of hind quarter, whether that length is usually in an extended or in a bent form, because, when in action, they both assume the same condition, and are then precisely similar the one to the other; but the working power is deficient if there is the *usual* accompaniment of the straight hind quarter—viz., a long fore-leg. It will be evident that if the hind quarter is straight, and the fore-leg is properly proportioned—that is to say, short enough for the working powers—the fore-quarter will appear very low, and the hips will stand up far above the shoulder.

Now, if this formation co-exists with the straight hind

leg, all may be in good proportion; but if not, it seldom happens that the dog can stoop to reach his hare without spoiling his stride. Nevertheless, a remarkable exception is sometimes seen, in which there is great working and killing power displayed, with a high shoulder and long fore-legs. This, however, is contrary to rule; and in selecting a good shape, no experienced courser would take such a formation without a practical proof of its efficiency in that particular instance. Next to the length of limb, the due development of the joints is of great importance; the stifle-joints ought to be strong and broad, and the bony processes powerful and large. The hocks, also, should be long and powerful, and well separated from the leg-bone by that thin double layer of skin which may be felt, and almost seen through. The muscles are divided into two large masses—the upper thigh, which is scarcely to be made out without the touch, being, as it were, buried in the body and flank; and the lower thigh, which is much more distinct, and of very great importance to the powers of galloping. This lower thigh is a very desirable point, if well developed; and in making a selection for breeding, its large size should be especially insisted upon. Good hind feet, again, are necessary, but I do not like them too round and cat-like; at the same time, a long flat foot is opposed to high speed, and also prevents a due hold being taken of the ground. Wherever there is this long, flat, and broken-down foot, I should not look either for high speed or for the power of continuing the efforts of the greyhound; there is a want of that elasticity and springiness which characterize the movements of this graceful animal, and he goes dull and dead instead of being animated and ready for any exertion.

The fore-quarter is the complement to the hind quarter, and can do nothing until set in motion by that part of the animal economy: but, in spite of this secondary part in the locomotive department, it is not less important than the primary cause of motion, because, though not originating it, it can and does neutralize the efforts of the hind quarter, if not calculated to carry them out. The great purpose of the fore-quarter is to enable the animal to take advantage of the propulsion given by the vigorous contraction of the hind one, and thus to carry the animal on in the intervals of the strokes. If, therefore, the forequarter is dull, heavy, and incapable of extension, the stroke is broken and suspended, and the pace is reduced accordingly. But besides this purpose, in which the forequarter of the race horse bears a similar part, that of the greyhound is also used in stopping the speed, and turning the body to the right or left, when the hare makes one of those turns which she delights in. Here the shoulder requires to be pliable yet strong, and there must be considerable play in all its parts, or it will give way in the violent effort made to change the direction of the speed. The outward formation for these purposes is well known and recognized by all in its general principles, though there may be a difference of opinion as to its details. Every one is agreed that the line through the shoulder-blade should be oblique, because that gives, in the first place, greater absolute length of blade ; and, in the second, it gives greater power over the arm, so that it may be protruded further and with greater force than is the case with a short and upright blade. It is acknowledged as a fact, that such oblique shoulders conduce to that conjunction of speed and working power which is desired. At the same time, I think I have seen so many cases of upright shoulders united with great pace and cleverness, that the rule is by no means an absolute one. But one rule is, I think, of that nature—viz., that where there are confined shoulders not acting with any liberty, but glued in their places, then the speed is not good, and the working power is absolutely null. With good sloping shoulder-blades there is almost always combined a formation which is of the greatest consequence, and that is a long upper arm—that is to say, a long bone intervening between the shoulder-blade and the elbow. This length of arm generally coincides with good length from the hip to the hock ; and when that quarter is bent as I have already described, the oblique shoulder-blade, long upper arm, and low elbow, usually accompany it ;

in most cases, also, there is a knee close to the ground, and thus the fore and hind quarters agree in formation, and will assuredly act together. When these points are combined, they make a perfect fore-quarter, and only want a strong useful foot, with a thick horny sole, to complete the requisites. As with the hind foot, so with this: I am not fond of the very upright, small, and round foot: such feet are always drawing their nails, though they are certainly well suited for fine turf; but on fallows, or rough ground of any kind, the strong and moderately flat foot is the more useful kind. The knuckles ought to be strong and well up, but the dog should not be too much on his toes; a spreading foot, however, with a thin sole devoid of horn, will never stand work, and should on that account be avoided.

The colour is one of those points in the greyhound which has been most disputed by different judges of his merits; one party considering it of the greatest importance, while the other decides that " a good dog, like a good horse, cannot be of a bad colour." With most people there is more or less of prejudice in this matter, and I am not perhaps exempt from this failing, when I own my leaning is to blacks and reds. This leaning, however, is not entirely guided by the eye, because it will be found that a large proportion of the winners in *The Coursing Calendar* are of one or other of those colours. Indeed, my belief is, that all the colours exhibited by the greyhound are to be traced to them, and that when united with white (the result of domestication) they will produce any of the many other shades which appear in the lists. Thus, by ringing the changes of black, red, and white, every shade will be produced, as shown in the following table:—

The Mixture of	Result.
Black and red, No. 1	Red, with black muzzle.
Do. No. 2	Red-brindle.
Do. No. 3	Black and tan.
Black and white	Blue.
Red and white	Fawn or cream.
Black, red, and white, No. 1	Blue-fawn.
Do. do. No. 2	Fawn-brindle.
Do. do. No. 3	Blue-brindle.

These colours only result when they are mixed together in the coat generally; for when that is not the case, the dog is patched with these colours in blotches, either of colour on a white ground, or of white on a coloured ground.

The *points* of the greyhound are as follows :—Head, 10; neck, 5; legs, 10; feet, 10; shoulders, 15; hind quarters, 20; back, 10; general symmetry, 10; tail, 5; colour and coat, 5.

CHAPTER III.

VARIETIES OF THE DOG (CONTINUED.)

Hounds—The Bloodhound—Staghound—Foxhound—Harrier—Beagle—Otterhound—Fox Terrier—Truffle Dog—Retrievers—Deerhound—The Borzoi.

THE various hounds used in the present day for the pursuit of the stag, fox, hare, rabbit, and otter are no doubt descended from one common ancestor, the nearest type of which now existing is the bloodhound; and, indeed, it is supposed by many high authorities that this dog is identical with the old Southern hound in all respects but colour. The latter was usually white, mottled with blue or badger-colour, whilst the bloodhound has always been known to possess the deep black and tan by which he is now recognized.

The **Bloodhound**. Gervase Markham, in his " Maison Rustique," speaking of hounds, says: "The baiecoloured ones have the second place for goodnesse, and are of great courage, ventring far, and of a quicke scent, finding out very well the turnes and windings . . . .
They runne surely, and with great boldnesse, loving the stagge more than any other beast; but they make no account of hares. It is true that they be more headstrong and harde to reclaime than the white, and put men to more paine and travaill about the same."

The exact origin of the bloodhound has not been satisfactorily defined. As we see him to-day, he is the evidence of careful selection, and the production of development of the highest order. He is the perfect combination of dignity, with a consciousness of inherent power, yet his movements as a massive animal are really graceful. In temperament he is docile, obedient, affec-

Bloodhound.

tionate, faithful, and reliable, and on this account proves the perfect companion and protector to child or adult, qualities derived only under careful training, as the lessons are begun in puppyhood. Even in this he is apt to become self-willed and turbulent, but under prompt repression, good lessons are carried home, and at length he assumes his position as companion and protector, his faithfulness being equal if not superior to that of any other breed. His proportions are large, even massive, and in detail, important and interesting. The head is long, expansive, highly arched, and crested behind, the width not being in proportion to the length. The facial and maxillary bones are unusually developed, and, extending forwards, secure the formation of spacious nasal chambers and voluminous turbinated bones, whereby the sense of scent or smell is surprisingly acute. The lower jaws accommodate large and powerful muscles, which are covered with loose and pliant skin, forming folds or wrinkles at the forehead, and descending down the cheeks are lost in the flows or lips, the upper covering the lower, and in the dewlap, which confers the characteristic "throaty" appearance. These provisions not only confer the needful power to seize, but also to retain the hold of large objects. The ears are set on low, and descend gracefully to the shoulder. The eye is deeply set in the orbit, is calm and impressive, and protected by the largely developed "haw"; the neck is long, but stoutly muscular; shoulders massive and sloping; forelegs straight, strong, and muscular, firmly standing on round and well-padded feet, and the claws are very large, strong, and black. The ribs are well arched, and, carried backwards, give the appearance of needful width and strength to the back loins and hind quarters; the tail well set on, thick at the base and tapering, carried moderately high and waving. With regard to colour, various opinions are entertained. "Black-tan, or a reddish fawn" was the favourite with "Stonehenge," who admitted no white, "but on just the tip of the stern." The old adage, that "good dogs cannot be of a bad colour," holds good in this instance, and among the varieties white spots, and the flake or dapple are not uncommon. The coat is largely influenced by method of treatment and work, as well as by breeding and rearing, but, as a rule, the tendency is to be thickly set, but fine and short. The voice is deep-toned, full, and loud, and as echoed by the hills in the stillness of night, is peculiarly impressive.

The critical judges of this breed are now watching with some interest the result of the introduction of a cross of the old southern hound, the object being to remedy the present defective constitution. This has resulted in all probability from what is understood to be "close breeding," which, being freely translated, signifies breeding from defective animals. Close consanguinity with the best and healthiest animals gave us our unparalleled flocks and herds, and the same will hold good with dogs of all breeds. "Like produces like," was the watchword of Bakewell, and as he followed with unerring precision the principles embodied in the phrase, he produced the best animals, and, conversely, he realised that unless he did so, the produce would be anything but good. It is not generally understood how unerringly the defects of an animal are handed down from parent to offspring, and it is chiefly to this that the incongruous mating of animals is due. The general idea is that if a sire possesses a quality which is absent in the dam, the offspring, in accordance with laws hitherto unexplained, will certainly derive that quality. We shall not attempt to argue that this is impossible, but feel at liberty to quote from experience, and state unhesitatingly whether the desirable qualification is, or is not handed down, it is quite certain, if there are serious defects they will be assuredly transmitted to the offspring. All men of shrewd character and experience in these matters are thoroughly well agreed on the point that half a dozen excellent qualities in the sire will not dissipate or neutralise one bad one in the dam. Whatsoever, therefore, we desire in the offspring, we must assure ourselves are to be found in the parents, whether it be soundness of constitution, perfection in form, action, etc., and when these are present, closeness of consanguinity will unerringly perpetuate them. On the other hand, all the desirable qualifications may be found in two strange animals; if so, there is no reason why they should not be mated. This is the simple law of the question.

The most celebrated breeders in past years were Lords Yarborough, Fitzwilliam, and Faversham; the Honourable Grantley Berkeley; Mr. Jennings, of Pickering, Yorkshire; Mr. Cowen, of Blaydon-on-Tyne; Mr. Harrison, of Dudley; and Mr. Halford, of Ware, Herts. Of the various dogs exhibited from the above kennels, Mr. Jennings's Druid, to Prince Napoleon, was said to be the best specimen of the breed. Mr. Cowen's Druid was also a grand dog in his prime; but his head was not equal to that of Mr. Jennings's old favourite. Mr. Hallford's Regent, a son of Cowen's Druid, was also a magnificent animal, and almost, if not quite, equal to Jennings's Druid. From these have descended the best blood of the present day.

The **Staghound** as a distinct breed is completely unknown in this country; all those packs which hunt stag being pure foxhounds, with the exception of Mr. Nevill's, in Hampshire, which he calls "Black St. Huberts," but which seem to be relics of the old Southern hound.

The modern **Foxhound** has had more attention paid to his shape, and has been kept more pure than any other breed of dogs in existence. Most kennels of any standing possess stud-books going back from 80 to 100 years, and can trace the pedigree of every hound in their packs for that time. This is almost equal to that of the English thorough-bred horse, and far greater than that of the greyhound, few pedigrees of which go back in all their lines more than ten generations. "Cecil" has lately published the "Hound Stud-book," which proves this statement without a doubt, and makes the study of the various strains of the foxhound doubly interesting. His points are as follows:—The head varies a good deal, from the comparatively heavy form characterizing the Beaufort Grasper, to the snipe-nosed light shape of the Puckeridge. It should, however, in any case be light, airy, and sensible, yet full of dignity. There should be a slight tendency to chop without actual flew, and the forehead should be a little wrinkled. Circumference of skull in front of the ears, 16 to 17 in., and at least $4\frac{1}{2}$ in. from the eye to the point of the nose. Neck long and clean; the least looseness or approach to throatiness is tabooed. Where it joins the head it must be fine, and gradually deepen towards the shoulders. Length of neck is necessary to allow the hound to stoop to a scent without losing pace. Ears set on low down, and carried close to the head—of course rounded. Total value, 20.

The back must be straight, wide, and muscular, with an equally strong and square loin, very slightly arched. Back ribs especially deep and wide, not flat. Chest deep, and at the same time, if possible, wide, increasing behind

Foxhound.

the elbows to at least 30 in., sometimes 31 in. Shoulders long, sloping, and powerful, elbows perfectly straight and well let down. Value—back and loins, 20 ; shoulders, 20.

The fore-legs, it is insisted by huntsmen, must be as straight as possible, without the slightest tendency backwards. This, however, I believe to be an exaggerated conception of the form which is best for standing work, as I have no doubt a very slight angle at the pastern is advantageous. The bone of the leg must be as large as possible, and the muscle of the fore-arm, as well as the tendons of the pasterns and toes, proportionably strong. If the foot is not perfectly straight, it must turn in, not out. In shape it should be round and cat-like, but very highly arched toes are apt to give way. Sole hard and thick. Value of legs and feet, 20 points.

The hind quarters must be as strong as possible, wide as well as deep. Bone of pastern strong and large; hocks strong and straight. Value, 10.

The stern should be carried gaily upwards without hooping; it should be slightly rough beneath its lower edge, but not feathered; point straight. The coat should be dense, smooth, and glossy. Colour, black, white, and tan, black and white, or pied with hare, badger, red, tan, or yellow, which colours are preferred in the order I have given. Value, 10, in conjunction with the general symmetry. Height from 22 to 25 in.; the best average is $22\frac{1}{2}$ in. for bitches, and 24 in. for dogs; or for a mixed pack, 23 in.

The **Harrier** comes next in order. His head is heavier in proportion than that of the foxhound, and the ears of thinner texture; they are sometimes slightly rounded, but the general practice is to leave them in their natural state.

In other respects there is little difference between the two breeds, though the eye of the master will readily pick out a true harrier from a foxhound without seeing the head. The *points* are the same as in the foxhound.

The **Beagle.**—The exact origin of this dog is not quite clear. He has been described as a dwarf southern hound, as it was thought the resemblance to him was closer than is observed in the foxhound or harrier. Like the southern hound, he also possesses an extraordinary power of scenting; his intelligence is acute, and when carefully selected with respect to these requirements, as well as uniformity in size, the pack works evenly and efficiently, giving forth enspiriting music. The Master of the Cockermouth Beagles gives the following description and points of the breed: "*Head* like that of a foxhound, with sweet, intelligent countenance; the head long, and the nose should not come to a sharp point.

Ears long, set on low down, and carried close to head; not too broad, and the thinner in the leather the better. *Neck* and throat long and lean; but some of the heavier hounds are very loose in throat, and have a deep voice. *Shoulders*, long and strong, well clothed with muscle. *Chest*, deep and wide; ribs also deep. *Back*,

Harrier.

strong and wide, and especially wide across loins. Bitches are generally better across loins than dogs, for their size. *Hind-quarters*, the stronger the better, wide and deep; stern strong at set on, and tapering, carried high, but not curled. *Legs* straight, although for work they are no worse standing a little over on the forelegs; strong of bone; feet round, like those of the cat. *Colour*, black, white, and tan: black and white. I had a heavy dog the latter colour, that was always first to find game, and always led. He was well known among the Cumbrians, and they knew his voice, and said: "'Dar, that's auld Duster; we'll have a run noo.' Occasionally beagles are the colour of bloodhounds. The beagle should be hard in condition, with plenty of muscle." These beagles hunt the hare on Skiddaw, and in the Lake District, capital runs being "enjoyed about Buttermere, where it is a grand sight to see the little hounds on the breast of a mountain, when a sheet could cover them sometimes, and their cry is melodious. We do not mount our huntsmen." The height of the dogs at the shoulder varies from 14 in. to 15 in., and the weight from 25 lbs. to $27\frac{1}{2}$ lbs. Some having the harrier cross are higher. The Royal Rock Pack, said to be pure beagles, stand 16 inches high. The rabbit beagle, so called, is probably a cross with beagle and the terrier.

The Dachshund, or German Badger Terrier is not a hound as some conclude. The terminal "hund," signifies a dog, notwithstanding many of his characteristics are those of a hound; indeed, it is said he comes of a cross with the old English hound and the beagle, and, according to Bewick, known as the Kibblehound. The dog of the present day has a singularly long back, and apparently ill-formed legs. Our friend *Punch* says he is "sold by the yard." Many years ago, an engineer seeing one of the early specimens, and viewing him only in the light of mechanics, said thoughtfully, "his bearings are too wide apart," and suggested taking "a piece out of his middle and welding him together again." The breed is self-coloured, excepting a stray "beauty spot" on the breast or toes. Black and tan, or fallow red are preferred, though good dogs have shades of red, and smutty, or tawny markings. The *Head* is of the bloodhound type, and the ears, long and pendulous, measure 13 or 14 inches across the head from tip to tip. The *Nose* is square, and the muzzle about $8\frac{1}{2}$ inches in girth. The *Eye*, which is lustrous and mild in expression, has the colour of the coat. The *Teeth* should be white, sound, strong, and recurvate for grip; a diseased and offensive mouth being fatal for any purpose. The *Neck* is long and muscular, the *Chest* wide, and the brisket well up to the throat. The *Shoulders* are muscular, covered with loose skin, and the chest apparently swings between them. The limbs are very large and bony, and the elbows turn widely outwards, while the knees are twisted inwards. "Knuckling" of the latter is a serious deformity. The feet are large, armed with powerful claws, and are turned outwards for making way in the burrow. To these qualifications must be added a good nose for tracking, length of body to conform to the windings of the badger earth, and lion courage to grapple and seize the quarry, in the earth or in the open. In Germany the dog is used to drive out deer from the thick and short underwood, and to track wounded deer, but are little used for badgering. In Hanover he is employed to kill foxes, for which purpose he will lie at the hole for days, being fed meanwhile, until the prisoner ventures forth to avoid starvation, but to be summarily destroyed. Dachshunds are remarkable travellers, and good water dogs, extremely affectionate with themselves, and their masters especially, but remarkably jealous of his favours being transferred to another dog.

The **Otterhound** is still more like the old Southern hound than the beagle, being of the same size as the former, and only differing from him in having a long and rough coat.

His head is heavier in mould and in its flews than that of the foxhound, eyes deeply set like those of the bloodhound, and with the same deep expression, often amounting to engaging; forehead long and narrow, but less so than that of the bloodhound; nose large and black, with a decidedly wiry-haired muzzle; lips ample and pendent; ears large, thin, and coated with strong wiry hair, but not feathered at the edges like those of the spaniel or setter; forehead wrinkled deeply; neck long and muscular, with a loose skin and some throatiness. Value: head, 15 · ears, 10; neck, 5.

Chest deep but not wide; elbow let down very low; back ribs very deep; loins strong and straight, but looser than those of the foxhound; shoulders powerful and sloping.

Arms very large and powerful; ankles short, and the feet round, but more open than those of the foxhound; thighs large and strong; with powerful hocks.

The stern should be coated moderately but not in-

Otterhound.

creasing, to the tip, which should be well pointed, whilst the root should be large; carriage like that of all hounds. Coat hard, wiry, and abundant; the colours may be black, white, and *pale* tan; mixed, or black pied, with the colours strongly linked with white.

The origin of this hound is uncertain, but he is most probably descended from the old Southern hound or Talbot.

This dog is sometimes confounded with the otter terrier. The otterhound is in all respects what the name implies, a dog comprising all the attributes of the hound, combined with acute scent, great endurance, strength, and remarkable intelligence. He is not so large as the bloodhound, but greatly resembles him in symmetry, strength of limb, formation of the head, with long drooping ears, well-developed nostrils, and eyes deeply set, over which the haw fully protrudes. Whatever may be his true origin, one thing is quite certain, the pure bred dog is always ready when wanted. Few can compare with his indomitable pluck, strength, solid wisdom and cunning, wonderful sight and scent. Unfortunately, however, many miserable attempts have been made to improve his breed. He has been crossed with the otter terrier, and the issue is a breed far too small for the common requirements, besides being impudent and tricky, lacking the nobility and grace of the true hound. In order to overcome such an expert, strong, and cunning animal as the otter, he needs the highest endowment of sight, scent, and sound. The first enables him to mark the significant sign of the otter's movement by the smallest ascending bubble; his nose will scent out the coldest trail, and he follows it with astonishing pertinacity, and his sense of hearing is so acute, that amid a very babel of voices, he is obedient to that of the huntsman alone.

The **Fox Terrier.**—To class the fox terrier with the hounds may seem a misnomer, but as he is kept specially for the purpose of being used in their aid when a fox is to be bolted, he is certainly not out of place in this subsection.

In the early part of the present century, when hunting the fox was considered of more interest than galloping after him, one or two terriers were added to the pack, and were not merely kept in readiness to bolt him from his earth when driven to ground by the hounds, but regularly drew each covert with them, and throughout the run followed the line as well as they could, being generally in at the death before the breaking up was over.

When, however, the fields of horsemen increased in numbers from two or three score to two or three hundred—when their riding became either a steeplechase between those who went straight, or a flat race among the "macadamisers;"—and when hounds were bred fast enough to get away from all, the little terrier stood a poor chance of escaping with life and limb, and his services were confined to underground work, for which he is now kept handy to the part of the country which is to be hunted, his absence being supplied by the nearest rat or rabbit terrier that can be obtained. In the cub-hunting he is specially serviceable, and, indeed, it is for this purpose that he is chiefly kept by the huntsmen of our various packs; for it is but seldom that a regularly entered fox terrier attached to the pack is at hand when a fox is run to ground during the season.

The fox terrier is a clever, strong little dog, possessing great endurance and remarkable courage, and a nose almost as sensitive as the harrier or beagle. He derives his pluck from the bull-dog, like other useful vermin killers, and is generally kept for the purpose of destroying those vermin which prove more than a match for the harrier or beagle. In his encounters with such, the fox terrier is rendered more determined, and his natural prowess is encouraged, as with superior ability he brings his antagonist to a state of helplessness or destruction. Hence he becomes the attendant and companion of the ratcatcher, gamekeeper, or farmer, who make use of his attainments in clearing the barns, stables, kennels, etc., of rats and mice, and occasionally other vermin. In former days it was the practice of adding a couple of fox terriers to each pack of fox hounds, for the purpose of bolting the fox when he takes refuge from his pursuers in some accessible drain, or otherwise goes to ground. The pluck and endurance of the fox terrier enables him to follow steadily in the track, finally coming up to do the required unearthing when other means are not available. In later years, hounds have been bred to greater speed, and the terrier has been dispensed with, but retained as a companion or guard, and for destroying ground

Wire-haired Fox Terrier "Champion Jack St. Leger."
Winner of one hundred First Prizes and Cups, including the Fox Terrier Club's Fifty Guinea Challenge Cup five times. The property of Mr. Albert E. Clear, Maldon, Essex.

vermin. He is faithful and tractable, and, under proper care and training, is rarely surpassed.

The entering and breaking of the fox terrier as a vermin killer is not a process of great difficulty. His innate intelligence rapidly leads him to look upon rats, mice, etc., as his mortal foes, and himself as their especial exterminator. When he is to be used with ferrets, he must be broken to leave them alone, as they are apt to make their appearance suddenly at one hole, from which they pass to another. In order to accomplish this, the ferret and the terrier should be allowed to be in the company of each other within a yard, stable, etc., when the terrier must be carefully watched and cautioned not to molest his companion. After a few such lessons, both animals grow friendly, or at least the terrier learns not to molest the ferret. Some terriers, owing to their breeding, prove to be great cowards, and will not bear the bites of their foes, which renders them perfectly useless as vermin destroyers, to say nothing of the more formidable operation of unearthing the fox. To complete their necessary courage, some breeders contend they should have the evident cross of the bull-dog. But sometimes young dogs of this cross may prove rather timid at first, when they should be encouraged by first trying their skill on young rats, singly. They will thus gain confidence, and rapidly increase in needful courage. This precaution, however, is scarcely called for with respect to well-bred terriers; as with the opportunity for practice in the exercise of the allotted vocation, they rapidly acquire the proficiency for which the breed is remarkable.

There has been a good deal of controversy among those interested in this breed on the subject of the bull cross, but the preponderance of evidence is certainly against it. The chief argument is that this cross makes the dog lie too close to his game, and punish him too much if he can reach him, often absolutely preventing his bolting by hanging on to him. In any case it is admitted that the strain should not be made visible in the mouth, and that the teeth should be therefore quite level. What is really wanted is a dog small enough to enter any drain or earth which will admit a fox, and consequently not above 16 lbs.

weight; while, to give him strength enough for the task which he has to perform, he should be at least 14 lbs.

The head should be flat and narrow forward, gradually widening towards the ears, which must be small and fold over, so as to keep out the dirt from their interior in digging, being also set on forward and carried close to the cheeks. Jaw strong and well clothed with muscle; mouth level and well furnished with teeth; eyes small, keen, and full of expression; nose pointed, long, and tipped with black. The back should be strong; chest deep; neck light and airy, coming nicely out of oblique but powerful shoulders; loins straightly arched, without slackness; ribs carried well backwards; quarters and thighs muscular; hocks well let down; the legs and feet strong and straight, and the stifles not turned outwards; the stern set high, carried gaily, but not over the back. Traces of the bull breed are disqualifying, likewise a long head and narrow chest, minus the needful muscular shoulders, which are serious congenital defects, or due to want of development under suitable care and exercise.

The symmetry also must be appreciated on the same principle as that of the foxhound, but it is important as showing breeding and general fitness for work. Value, 10 points.

Colour, for which 5 points are allowed, is only to be regarded as leading to the dog becoming easily seen either underground or above; hence there must be a preponderance of white. With this external configuration the fox terrier must be hardy in constitution, so as to withstand cold, wet, and fatigue, and he must have that degree of courage which will induce him to face any amount of punishment. Possessed of all these qualifications, this dog becomes an excellent companion independently of his use to the M.F.H., and the breed has been in high favour for this purpose since the introduction of dog shows; from £200 to £300 having sometimes been given for a prize winner.

The **Truffle Dog** is little known out of the districts which furnish that esculent, in our knowledge of which we are far behind the Germans, French, and Italians. Our Continental neighbours are far more skilled both in its preservation and production. They can dry it, or preserve it in oil, vinegar, or brine; and in neither case does the conserve lose much of its aroma, flavour, or nutritious quality. One Italian species is produced by scattering a shallow layer of soil upon a porous slab of stone, and occasionally moistening it with water; another, by slightly burning, and subsequently watering, blocks of hazel-wood; and a third (a species of *Agaricus*) is cultivated by placing the grounds of coffee in places favourable for its growth. The market returns of Rome show that as much as £4,000 a year are expended on these productions; and that the peasantry of France, Germany, and Italy in many places subsist to a great extent upon them, is an established fact.

The truffle—an edible underground fungus—is classed by Berkeley with *morel*, as one of the *Ascimycetes*, because in these, "spores," or organs of reproduction, are arranged in *asci* (tubular sacs, or vesicles). The best writers on fungi have arrived at this learned conclusion; but in spite of all their discoveries, and their elaborate remarks on "spheroidal cells," and "spores," and "fructification taking place in some particular membrane," we believe attempts to cultivate the truffle have failed.

Science has ascertained that it forms an intermediate link between the animal and vegetable kingdom, for it does not absorb carbonic acid from the air and give out oxygen, but, like animals, it absorbs oxygen and gives out carbonic acid.

The truffle is found in many districts of France, Spain, and Italy; and in other parts of these countries, doubtless (as in England), it exists, though it has not been discovered.

In this country it may be found on almost every chalky down, especially where plantations of beech flourish, and in many gentlemen's parks, and on lawns. Hampshire, Wilts, Dorset, and Kent, all these counties produce truffles of rich quality and in great abundance. Beneath the beech, the cedar, the lime, the oak, the hazel, the Scotch fir, it is frequently to be found in clusters, one, two, or three feet apart. It is known to be in Tedworth (the seat of the late Mr. T. Assheton Smith); at Charbro' Park, Dorset (the seat of Mr. Drax); at Olantigh Towers, in Kent, and at Holnest House, in Dorset (both seats belonging to the same gentleman); whilst Kingston Lacey, in Dorset (the property of the Bankes family), produces both morels and truffles. Truffles are also found at Eastwell Park, Kent; at Sir J. Sebright's, in Beechwood Park; at Lord Barrington's; at Lord Jersey's; at Longleat, Wilts; at the Countess Bridgewater's; at Lord Winchilsea's; and, we believe, at the Earl of Abingdon's seat, near Oxford.

In Italy, this fungus is hunted with a pig (a fact confirmed by Youatt); in France (as with us) the trufflehunter depends upon his dog. The breed is rare, and the men dislike to sell them. It is said that, about two hundred years ago, an old Spaniard brought two dogs into Wiltshire, and made a great deal of money by the sale of truffles which his dogs found for him; that at his death he left his money and his dogs to a farmer from whom he had received some kindness, and that the hunters derive their dogs from those he left that farmer.

The truffle dog is a small poodle (nearly a pure poodle), and weighing about 15 lbs. He is white, or black and white, or black, with the black mouth and under-lip of his race. He is a sharp, intelligent, quaint companion, and has the "homeing" faculty of a pigeon. When sold to a new master, he has been known to find his way home for sixty miles, and to have travelled the greater part of the way by night.

It is mute in its quest, and should be thoroughly broken from all game. These are essential qualities in a dog whose owner frequently hunts truffles at night—in the shrubberies of mansions protected by keepers and watchmen, who regard him with suspicion. In order to distinguish a *black* dog on these occasions, the hunter furnishes his animal with a white shirt, and occasionally hunts him in a line.

These dogs are rather longer on the leg than the true poodle, have exquisite noses, and hunt close to the ground. On the scent of a truffle (especially in the morning or evening, when it gives out most smell), they show all the keenness of the spaniel, working their short-cropped tails, and feathering along the surface of the ground, for from twenty to fifty yards. Arrived at the spot where the fungus lies buried some two or three inches beneath the surface, they dig like a terrier at a rat's hole, and the best of them, if left alone, will disinter the fungus and carry it to his master. It is not usual, however, to allow the dog to exhaust himself in this way, and the owner forks up the truffle, and gives the dog his usual reward, a piece of bread or cheese; for this he looks, from long habit, with the keen glance of a Spanish gipsy.

The truffle-hunter is set up in business when he possesses a good dog; all he requires besides will be a short staff, about 2 ft. 6 in. long, shod with a strong iron point, and at the other end furnished with a two-fanged iron fork. With this implement he can dig the largest truffle, or draw aside the briars or boughs in copsewood, to give his dog free scope to use his nose. He travels frequently thirty or forty miles on his hunting expeditions, and with this (to use a business term) inexpensive "plant," keeps a wife and children easily. I know personally one blue grizzled dog of the old truffle breed which supports a family of ten children.

The truffle dog is a delicate animal to rear, and a choice feeder. Being continually propagated from one stock, he has become peculiarly susceptible of all dog diseases, and when that fatal year comes round which desolates the kennel in his quarter, many truffle-hunters are left destitute of dogs, and consequently short of bread; for they will not believe (as I believe) that any dog with a keen nose and lively temper may be taught to hunt and find truffles.

The education of the dog commences when he is about three months old. At first he is taught to fetch a truffle, and when he does this well and cheerfully, his master places it on the ground, and slightly covers it with earth, selecting one of peculiar fragrance for the purpose. As the dog becomes more expert and keen for the amusement, he buries the truffle deeper, and rewards him in proportion to his progress. He then takes him where he knows truffles to be abundant, or where they have been previously found by a well-broken animal, and marked. Thus he gradually learns his trade, and becomes (as his

Curly-coated Retriever.

forefathers have been for many generations) the breadwinner for his master and all his master's family; unless he is so fortunate as to become *attaché* to some lordly mansion, or possibly to a Royal palace, in which case he is a fortunate dog indeed. With regard to *points*, as he is never shown, none can be laid down.

The dogs which retrieve game previously wounded by man are very useful, and in the present day, when driving and walking up game are practised extensively without pointers or setters, the retriever is an indispensable accompaniment to every shooter who indulges in this kind of sport. There is no distinct breed recognized, though the cross of the spaniel or setter with the small Newfoundland has become now quite as much so as the

Wavy-coated Retriever.

modern Leicester or Southdown sheep. Indeed, the recurrence to this cross is seldom employed in breeding retrievers, males and females of that strain being chosen on each side. I have a great fancy that the modern rough St. Bernard, of which the Rev. J. C. Macdona has some magnificent specimens, will, if crossed with good setter blood, produce an excellent result, and I intended to try the experiment, that gentleman having kindly given me a daughter of his celebrated Tell and Hedwig for the purpose, but unfortunately the puppy died of abscess in the head. Intelligence and docility are the qualities which must be looked for, and these are possessed by the St. Bernard in the highest degree, while the setter must furnish nose and the desire to hunt game.

The modern **Retriever** is now almost always a cross of the setter and Newfoundland (showing the smooth or wavy coat), or of the water spaniel (generally Irish) with the same dog, in which case the coat is curly. Very often the two kinds are intermixed, the result of which is a coat showing more or less of each texture. There has been a good deal of discussion on the relative value of these strains, and the question is by no means settled. My own impression is in favour of the smooth, wavy coat, indicative of the setter origin rather than the spaniel, as I believe this cross is more docile and better fitted to be broken to the extent of implicit obedience which is required. It is a great nuisance to have to work a retriever in a slip, but there are very few curly-coated dogs with which it can be dispensed with, whereas it is comparatively easy to do so with the smooth kind.

The **Norfolk Retriever** is a breed introduced within recent years. The colour of the coat is sandy-brown, though this may run so dark as to be called black, and curls somewhat loosely, being open, short, woolly, coarse and harsh under the fingers. The head is massive, and has the appearance of intelligence; the ears are large, the hair upon them being thick and curly, and the muzzle is broad and square or deep. Along the back the hair lies short and straight. The limbs are strong, stout, well-set, and terminate in feet which are largely developed, and fully webbed. It is stated by "Saxon" to be the usual custom to dock the tail, the utility of which seems questionable in the opinion of sportsmen outside the county. The dogs of this breed run somewhat above the medium size, being also strong and well set. They exhibit a remarkable degree of intelligence and tractability, which under efficient training renders them exceedingly clever under the gun, or as the amusing companion in leisure hours. Uncertainty of temper is somewhat

rare among them, and any appearance of impatience under restraint, or other defects in the field may as a rule be attributed to imperfect training, or such may be the result of impure descent. They are excellent swimmers, not in smooth water alone, but prove themselves invaluable on the sea shore, when against surf and swell they resolutely search for the dead or maimed bird.

The retriever proper should have a long head, wide and flat, and a moderately large eye, full of intelligence and docility; mouth capacious; ears small, lying close to the face, and set low, with short hair only on them; nose large; neck long; and face covered with short hair only. Head, 10; nose, 10; ears, 2; neck, 8—total, 30.

The loins and back must be strong and firmly coupled, without which this big heavy dog soon tires, and as he sometimes has to carry a hare for half a mile, and to jump gates and brooks with her in his mouth, this point is of great importance. Quarters also must be thick, and clothed strongly with muscle. Shoulders strong and oblique; chest broad and also deep. Loins and back, 10; hind quarters, 10; shoulders, 6; chest, 4.

Legs long, straight, and muscular; feet round and compact; toes well arched and not spreading; hocks powerful; stifles strong and wide. Value: feet, 6; legs, 6; hocks, 6; stifles, 2—total, 20.

Coat either flat and wavy, or short, curly, and crisp; the former being in my opinion the best, but in dog shows there is generally now a prize for each kind. Colour either jet black without white, or liver, also without white, or black and tan, or black with brindled legs, or, lastly, whole brindled. Stern well feathered, rather short, but tapering to a point, and carried gaily but not over the back. Colour and coat, 15; stern, 5. The height should be at least 24 in., weight from 70 lbs. to 80 lbs.

The Irish Water Spaniel, and the English dog of the same breed, are often used as retrievers proper, but I have classed them with the other spaniels, since they are generally used for seeking live as well as dead game.

Crosses of the terrier and spaniel, and true terriers, are

also sometimes employed as retrievers; and, indeed, foxhounds, bloodhounds, and pure setters are occasionally broken to this trade.

The **Deerhound** is a distinct breed, having been for many years employed to hunt down wounded deer, and, if necessary, bring them to bay till the deerstalker comes up to give the *coup de grâce* with bullet or knife. In the present day he closely resembles in appearance the rough Scotch greyhound, but having each been kept to its separate work, they show their specific natures distinctly when taken to their respective game.

The points of this dog are the same as those of the rough greyhound, except that he is at least 28 in. high, with a girth of 32 in. In colour he must be fawn, yellow, brindled, or grey, with a rough coat, especially about the face.

The Borzoi.—Under this name are included several breeds of the deerhound type, especially used in their native wilds for hunting the wolf. The most familiar are the Siberian, or Russian, Pyrenean, and Circassian wolfhounds. The Siberian wolfhound is of the type and size of the Scotch deerhound, the grisly hue of the coat being replaced by white, with markings of yellow, or fawn, and in a few dark grey. These dogs are singularly handsome, and in movement majestic, good specimens exhibiting the build of our best deerhounds, having a remarkably deep chest, well-shaped and sloping shoulder, and airy neck even with the back. The head is clean throughout, the skull flat, and somewhat narrow, separated by a slight indentation from the long and tapering snout. The nose is black, eyes dark, expressive and almond shape, ears small, somewhat rounded at the tip, set high and almost meet when thrown over the head. The back is strong, and arched in the dog, but level in the bitch; ribs flat, elongated, and extending to the elbows or lower; groin capacious in the bitch, and short in the dog. The forelegs are lean and straight, and, as seen from the front, are narrow and tapering to the feet. The hind legs are slightly beneath the body when standing, free from dewclaws, and not wide apart, the stifle is slightly flexed;

Deer Hound "Ben-Avon."

Winner of many first and special prizes. The property of Mr. John Anderson, Garnethill, Glasgow.

pasterns short, toes long and close together; nails strong, short, and mainly supporting the weight of the animal: tail long and shaped like a sickle; coat long, wavy and silky, curly only in places. The muscles of the shoulders, chest, and hind quarters are long and flat, roundness or convexity being objectionable. Average height of the dog 28 to 33 inches; of the bitch 24 to 28 inches. The frill on the neck is long and rather curly, and the forelegs are well-feathered. The hair on the hind quarters and tail is long; curling is objectionable.

The Circassian or Orloff Wolfhound is said to be derived from the Siberian, climatic and other influences combining to produce variations in form and colour. He is swifter than the Siberian, and said to be more intelligent.

As ornamental dogs these wolfhounds are graceful and dignified, and as companions, gentle, faithful, watchfull and obedient.

The Pyrenean Wolfhound is a dog of stronger build, and somewhat shorter, suggesting a cross with the collie and deerhound. The breed is well adapted for the tending of mountain sheep, being employed with especial reference to warfare with wolves and foxes, the enemies of the flock.

CHAPTER IV.

USEFUL COMPANIONS OF MAN.

Old English Mastiff—The Great Dane—Newfoundland—St. Bernard—Bulldog—Bull Terrier—Smooth English Terrier—Black and Tan English Terrier—Rough or Broken Haired Terrier—Skye Terrier—Dandie Dinmont—Bedlington Terrier—Irish Terrier—Welsh Terrier—Whippet—Bob-tailed Sheep Dog—Scotch Collie—Pomeranian or Spitz.

UNDER this division are included those dogs which serve some purpose in their companionship, either as guards of man or his herds or flocks; thus, the Newfoundland, the mastiff, the St. Bernard, the bulldog, the bull terrier, and other large terriers, the collie, and the drover's dog, all come under the designation.

The **Old English Mastiff**, as being a native of this country, should stand at the head of this section, though by no means so generally met with as the Newfoundland. Like the bulldog, he is peculiar to this country, though a near approach to him, the Cuban mastiff, is met with in the West Indies and America. Whether any of the modern strains can be shown to be really indigenous in their origin it would be difficult to say, as their pedigrees cannot be traced for many generations.

Mr. Edgar Hanbury, of Eastrop Grange, Wilts, and Mr. Lukey, of Lock's Bottom, Bromley, Kent, have bred the best specimens of the English mastiff of late years, and neither of these gentlemen can trace back their blood far enough to enable us to decide whether they are purely English or not. Mr. Hanbury commenced with a bitch without pedigree, but a beautiful animal. This bitch was put to a dog from Wales, also without pedigree, so that his kennel dates from his own knowledge. Mr. Lukey began with a brindled bitch bred by the Duke of Devonshire, which he crossed with Lord Waldegrave's celebrated dog " Turk," a black-muzzled fawn, of great courage and symmetry. The produce consisted of two brindled bitches, which he put to the Marquis of Hertford's Pluto, since which, for a long time, he bred in-and-in from their descendants. Seven or eight years ago, however, he obtained possession of his magnificent stud dog Governor, by Lieut. Garnier's Lion out of Countess, a daughter of Mr. Bruce's Duchess, and this dog has proved a most valuable sire, having been extensively used by Mr. Hanbury and other breeders. Mr. Hanbury's Prince, descended from Governor and Duchess, is a magnificent specimen, and quite as good as, or better than, his celebrated sire.

The remarkable power and courage of the mastiff render him peculiarly fit to be the dog of the keeper, when associated with the fine temper which ought never to be dispensed with, since a savage mastiff is a dangerous brute, and should never be unloosed from his kennel. A

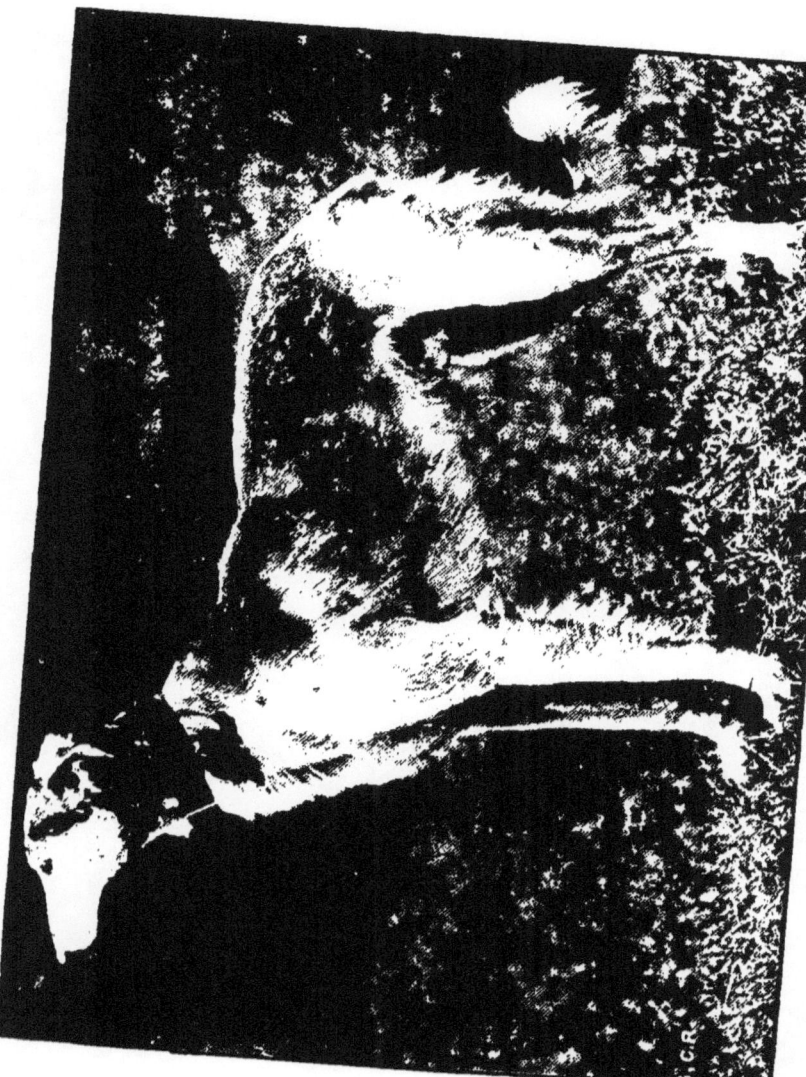

Albanian Wolf Hound (Borzoi).

well-broken one of good temper may be taken anywhere, and is far more trustworthy than the Newfoundland, and quite equal to the St. Bernard. The sense of smell is acute, and the mastiff has been known to draw up to a covey of partridges like a pointer.

The mastiff is remarkable for the combination of his general development. The conformation of the head bespeaks an unusual brain power, which is under admirable control. He is a creature of strong and sincere attachment to man, endowed with a wonderful power of discrimination and true nobility of character, all of which he freely exercises in the interests of those for whom alone he seems to live. He is by nature docile and gentle to a fault. He lays aside his giant strength to unite in the gambols of the child with the same spirit of tenderness and grace. If his conduct be otherwise it bespeaks his origin in the mongrel or nondescript races, and his general conformation does not, as a rule, correspond to the portrait we have so feebly outlined. It is possible for apparently well bred animals to inherit the "bad blood of their forefathers;" but as greater attention is now paid to a careful system of selection and in-breeding, this dangerous element in the character may be kept in abeyance, in common with other serious defects. The well-bred mastiff allies himself to man as his friend, to whom he becomes the closest companion, and serves him with the truest devotion and sincerity. This animal should not be subjected to the restraint of the chain; if he is, whether young or old, he will be inevitably spoiled in outward form as well as temper.

The *points* of this breed are as follows:—The head should be massive, with a broad and flat forehead; ears small and wholly pendent, lying close to the cheek, though set on farther back than in the hound, pointer, and setter; eyes small, but mild and intelligent in expression; face short, with a square muzzle, not tapering towards the point of the noise; teeth level, but sometimes there is a slight projection of the lower; flews deep; neck muscular, with the head well set into it, showing a slight prominence at the upper point of junction; body very large, with deep and wide chest, well ribbed up, and a powerful loin; legs straight, with great bone (this point is not generally well displayed, owing to confinement, as is also the case with all large breeds); feet round and close; coat short, and tail fine, but with a very slight indication of roughness: it should be carried high when the dog is excited; colour most to be desired is fallow (fawn), with black muzzle, and the richer the black the better; next to this comes brindle, then red with black muzzle, or black; sometimes there is a considerable admixture of white, but this is not desirable. Height, from 29 to 31 in. in the dog, and even more if a fine symmetry can be obtained, but his good shape is seldom met with in so large an animal; bitches are 2 or 3 in. lower. A dog standing 29 in. high ought to weigh, in good condition (not fat), from 120 lbs. to 130 lbs.

The Great Dane.—This champion among canine athletes has rapidly advanced to prominent favour. The best specimens stand over 34 inches, and in the scale raise 180 pounds or thereabouts. He is powerful, and elegant in carriage, his enormous size combining to render his general appearance exceptionally grand. In detail he is also remarkable for strict proportion. His faithfulness and intelligence are equally acute, and his courage unfailing. He is minus the repellant ferocity of the bulldog, but when occasion demands, his qualities as a mighty defender are never absent. He is a dog of wonderful mould, especial temperament and capabilities, as the close companion of man. The following are the various points adopted by the Great Dane Club: The *Head* is long, the forehead being slightly elevated and indented between the eyes. *Skull* not too broad. *Muzzle* strong and obtuse; nose large and arched; cheek muscles large and firm; lips blunted perpendicularly in front, not hanging too loose at the sides, but with well defined folds at the angles of the mouth. The lower jaw slightly projects. *Eyes* small, deeply set and expressive, *Ears* very small, and carried erect. Fashion, however, calls in the aid of cropping. The *Neck* is strong, muscular, well-arched. No dewlap or loose skin about the throat.

MASTIFF.

Junction of head and neck sharply defined. *Chest* very deep at the brisket, but not too wide. *Back* of medium length; *Loins* arched and falling in beautiful curve to the insertion of the tail. The latter should reach to the hocks, be strong at the insertion, tapering and ending in a fine curve. During carriage it is elevated, and more curved, but not carried over the back. The belly is well drawn up. *Shoulders* sloping; *Elbows* well under, neither turned inwards nor outwards. *Forearm* muscular, ample bone development throughout, and leg straight. *Thighs* muscular; second thighs long and strong as in the Greyhound; hocks well let down, and turning neither in nor out. *Feet* large, round and parallel to the front. *Toes* well-arched and closed. *Nails* very strong and curved. *Hair* very short, hard, and dense, and not much longer on the under part of the tail. The recognised colours are the various shades of grey (commonly termed "blue"), red, black, or pure white, or white with patches of the before-mentioned colours. These colours are sometimes accompanied with markings of a darker tint about the eyes and muzzle, and with a line of the same tint (called a "trace") along the course of the spine. The above ground colours also appear in the brindles, and are also the ground colours of the mottled specimens. In the whole coloured specimens the china or wall eye rarely appears, and the nose more or less approaches black, according to the prevailing tint of the dog, and the eyes vary in colour also. The mottled specimens have irregular patches or "clouds" upon the above named ground colours, in some instances the clouds or markings being of two or more tints. With the mottled specimens the wall or china eye is not uncommon, and the nose is often parti-coloured or wholly flesh-coloured. The whole coloured reddish-yellow, with black muzzle and ears, is the colour least cared for, as indicative of the mastiff cross.

The **Newfoundland Dog** is of two distinct breeds, the large and the small, the latter being also called the St. John or Lesser Labrador. The former—subdivided into the Newfoundland proper and the Larger Labrador—

is the most common in this country, and is a dog of massive form, possessing great character and intelligence. My own opinion, however, is that these breeds are so intermixed that they cannot be called distinct, and that though without doubt these several varieties are met with, they occur indiscriminately, and often two are met with in the same litter. "Index," who has studied the subject a good deal, lays it down in the *Field* that the three breeds may be known by the coat, as follows:—" The dog with long shaggy hair is the Newfoundland pure and simple, and recognized as such in both countries; the dog with the completely curly coat is the Labrador; and the dog with the close smooth coat is the lesser or smaller Labrador." In Newfoundland he is used as a beast of draught, being harnessed to sledges, which his great form, large feet, and endurance enable him to draw over the snow, while his thick coat and hardy constitution render him little amenable to the effects of cold and wet. As a water dog he has no equal, and he floats or swims for hours without suffering from the immersion. His patronage of children, especially when in danger of drowning, is one of the most remarkable features in the canine race, and the way in which he suffers himself to be pulled about by them makes him, when not exceptionally ill-tempered, the pet of many a family. Still it will not always do to trust him, and I have known many examples which were absolutely dangerous even to their masters when excited by deprivation of food or anger against some offender of their own species.

In dealing with the merits of the Newfoundlander, as he was originally named, we are in company with the aristocracy of the canine race. Faithful and gentle to a degree, sagacious above his fellows of indigenous breeds, grand in appearance, firm in his attachment, and noble in his behaviour, he becomes at once the general favourite with every child, and the intimate companion of man. Since his introduction to this land his breeding has been considerably improved, and a more graceful or noble creature can scarcely be conceived, as a glance at the picture of Landseer, "A Member of the

Newfoundland Dog.

Royal Humane Society," will bear out. Formerly his colours were red, brown, brown and white, bronze, red and white, or black and white, but thanks to the interest developed by periodical shows, and the earnest care of the fanciers, the too common degeneration of breed by indiscriminate crossing has been greatly avoided. The true Newfoundland dog is very large, certainly larger than many now commonly called after him. His coat is jet black, long, and straight, and the tail bushy. His countenance is especially expressive, and the eyes indicate deep intelligence. The Landseer dog is black and white as already referred to, but he is the animal of the same mould, the markings being somewhat prettily dispersed. Like all dogs of his class, he is apt to become leggy, with increase of size, and probably cow-hocked, which militates against beauty and action alike.

In all three varieties the head is remarkable, grand, and full of character, with an expression of mildness and benevolence which is shared with this breed by the St. Bernard. Across the eyes the breadth is great, with a flatness behind them, before which the skin is wrinkled, but without any perceptible forehead. Eyes small, bright, and intelligent, deeply set, but not showing the haws, which gives the appearance of being bloodshot, so remarkable in the bloodhound. Ears small and set low, hanging close to the face, and with little hair on them. Nose large, muzzle long and smooth; mouth capacious, with level teeth. Neck shorter than in most breeds. *Points:* head, 30; temper, 20; neck, 10.

Back often weak and slack in the loin, but this is a fault which, though common, is not universal. There is also very often a want of depth in the back ribs which ought not to be passed over. Back and loin, 10.

Feet and legs large and muscular; the former being too flat for much work over hard ground, and are more adapted for the snow of his native land, or for swimming. Feet and legs, 10.

Colour black, or black and white, the former greatly for choice, with as little white as possible. Sometimes the black has brindled legs, or of a rufous dun-colour, and occasionally fully-bred dogs are met with brindled, or rufous dun mixed with white. There are several varieties in texture of coat. The smooth dog is almost as free from any approach to feather as a mastiff. If this dog has any tendency to feather, it will declare itself in profile just below the set on of the head. His coat, if well examined, will be found more dense than a mastiff's, and of greater volume. The shaggy-coated Newfoundland has a smooth face, but within two inches of the skull the coat suddenly elongates, and except that he is very clean to the angle of his neck, he is thoroughly feathered in his outline. His coat generally parts down the back, and this parting is continued to the end of his tail. His hind legs are close-coated from the hock, and his feet all round are nearly as free of feather as a cat's. Colour and coats, 10 points.

The stern is long and bushy, usually slightly turned on one side, and carried in a trailing fashion. The gait is rather loose and waddling, but this is a defect owing to the slackness of loin. Carriage, 5; stern, 5. In height this dog is sometimes 33 or 34 in., averaging 29 or 30.

The St. Bernard Dog has been so well described by an experienced hand in the *Field* newspaper, that I extract his account *verbatim*:—

"About the year 962, Bernard de Meuthon built two '*hospitia*,' one on Mont Joux, where a temple of Jupiter stood—constructing his hospice from the ruins of the temple; the other on the road that leads over the Grison Alps at Colonne Joux, so named from a column dedicated to the same heathen deity. The benevolent builder presided over both *hospitia* for forty years, and left to his monks the duty of affording refuge to travellers, and searching for those who were lost in the snow. St. Bernard's portrait, and that of his dog on the same panel, is still in existence, and the dog appears to be a bloodhound. The Hospice of St. Bernard Pass stands 7,668 feet above the sea level, and is undoubtedly the highest inhabited spot in Europe. Nine months in the year the snow is thick on the ground, and in the very worst part of winter from 1,500 to 2,000 of the poor inhabitants of the low countries pass over the mountains. During this inclement season all travellers from Martigny are desired to pass the night at the first house of refuge. Every morning a servant, accompanied by a St. Bernard dog, descends from the hospice to take all the travellers under his direction. The dog leads the way, for he can not only discover the buried traveller by his marvellous

St Bernard.

powers of scent, but he can also to a certainty keep the track, in spite of snowstorms and bewildering drifts. The dogs have been used by the monks in these ways, *and in no other*, for years, and they have acquired a well-deserved high reputation for perseverance, sagacity, and power of scent.

"The old breed died out many years ago, and we doubt whether the monks have possessed the present race of dogs more than forty or fifty years.

"About forty years ago, or a little more, all their dogs and several servants were swept away by an avalanche; but two the monks had given away were returned to them, and the breed was thus preserved. One of the St. Bernard dogs, Barry, a brindled and white one, saved the lives of forty-two persons, and was vigorous and active at the age of fifteen years, although they generally succumb to rheumatism in their tenth year. He is preserved in the Berne Museum, wearing an iron collar with large spikes, which had often protected him from the wolves. We are told he had discovered a man lost in a snow-drift, and, being mistaken for a wolf, the poor fellow received a blow on the head, and '*il était obligé de mourir.*'

"At the time we were the guests of the monks, they possessed but three dogs, Barry, Pluto, and Pallas. The finest specimen had goitre or bronchocele, and wore a muzzle, as he was of an uncertain disposition; and a very fine bitch was expected soon to add to the strength of the company. Two dogs were placed out at some neighbouring hospice. We purchased a young dog at the Hôtel des Alpes (on our way home), from the proprietor: the mother had been procured from the hospice; the father was the fine specimen we have seen there. Subsequently we found him very intelligent and good tempered; he was very pleased to carry and fetch, and he appeared to have an excellent nose: but, alas! when nearly twelve months old, like Barry, '*il était obligé de mourir.*' All of these dogs were *orange tawny;* they had white legs, flecked *slightly* with orange, white belly, white collar round the neck; the head remarkably fine, majestic, and full of character; the ears small and set low; the eyes deeply set, a crease between them giving a mastiff character to the whole animal; from the eyes half-way down the face black, then suddenly white to the nose (which is black); the lips, which are pendulous, spotted with orange and black; the white above the nose is continued in a blaze or streak up the forehead, and *extends in a narrow line down the poll, meeting the white collar round the neck.*

"The monks begged us to observe this peculiar mark, and compared it to the badge of their order—a white

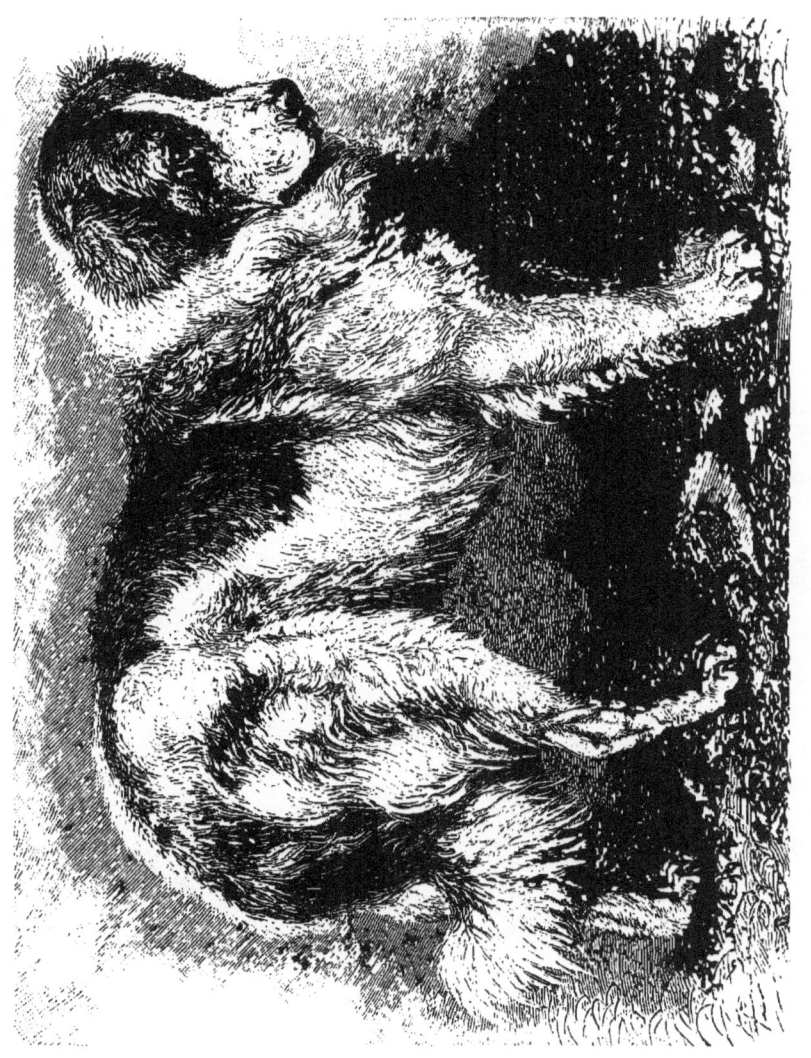

Rough-coated St. Bernard.

band or tape, single behind, slit to pass over the neck, and the two ends tucked into the black dress in front at the waist. Some very fine specimens, however, are brindled instead of orange tawny, and many have no white in the face at all, nor down the poll. The coat, which appears to the casual observer hard and smooth, when closely examined proves to be very thick and fleecy, and it is well suited to repel cold by retaining the animal heat. The tail is bushy, but carried generally down between the hocks, and the gait or carriage of the dog much resembles the march of the lion.

"The character of the dog is majestic and important. He has that true nobility possessed by the highest type of Newfoundland. The same thoughtful, observant eye, the wide brow, the muscular neck, the enormous loin, and sinewy arms and thighs, and the large round arched feet and toes ('*pattes enormes*,' the monks called them), and that general intimation of power, and sense, and benevolence which no other domesticated animal possesses in the same compass.

"Tell, the noble specimen we have engraved, has the true form of the St. Bernard dog, and we believe him to be the best dog of his class in England. His owner, Mr. Macdona, proceeded to Switzerland, in the winter of 1864, to obtain, at any cost, the best specimen to be had for money, and, after rejecting many fine examples, at length bought the only one that came up to his ideal.

"The following are the measurements and weight of Tell :—

	ft.	in.
Height at shoulder	0	30½
Length from nose to tip of tail	7	0
Girth of chest	0	36
,, arm	0	13
,, head	0	22
Length of head	0	13

Weight, 147 lbs.

"He is a red or tawny brindle, the muzzle black, as far as the lower line of the eyes. Chest white. The two fore-paws white; the ankles white; belly white. Tail heavily feathered, and sometimes carried gaily. Hind quarters beautifully furnished with coat. Head massive, eyes quick and intelligent, ears small and well set. He has *the peculiar slinging gait of his tribe.* He has *the retriever instinct,* and is very fond of carrying or retrieving from water. He is of the rough or shaggy-coated breed. There is, we are credibly informed, a smooth variety now existing.

"Captain Tyler's Thün answers this description. He is very large, and of the orange tawny colour, with little white, and is by Leo—Leo by Turk, who came from the monastery.

"The description we have given of the St. Bernard dog is a repetition of the information afforded us personally by the monks, and we have formed an opinion of the class from the specimens the hospice contained."

The double dewclaw is considered to be a mark of the true breed.

I should give the *points* of the St. Bernard as follows:—Head, 20; line down the poll, 10; frame, 10; feet and legs, 10; symmetry, 10; size, 20; dewclaws, 10; coat, 10.

It is a disputed point whether the smooth-coated variety or the rough-coated is the real breed. Mr. Macdona has both in his kennels. Except in coat, there is no difference between them.

Since the preceding paragraph was penned, authorities are pretty well agreed as to the identity of the two. In numerous litters of the rough St. Bernards, there are one or more puppies having smooth coats, which are retained as such throughout their life. Nevertheless the distinction is still observed at the various dog shows, for which separate classes are provided. The modern dog is a fine, commanding fellow, with a beautifully formed head, affording ample space for his largely developed brain; his eyes are large and full, beaming with intelligence, and the movements of his massive body and limbs are pleasing and graceful. In him are blended the power of the British mastiff, with the alertness of the true Newfoundland. In point of size and build the St. Bernard proves himself a perfect Goliath among other breeds. Careful attention to breeding has developed both size and weight. "Sir Redvers," when he was exported to America, stood 34½ inches at the shoulder, and his weight was upwards of 200 pounds; and "Lord Bute," stood 36 inches high, and weighed 220 pounds when he was just turned two years old. The leading animal of recent days is the rough coated bitch "Lady Mignon," the property of Mr. Samuel Jagger, of Honley, near Huddersfield. Her career has been unexceptional, having secured no less than fifty-four first prizes, specials, and championship Birmingham, in one year, the winner being under two years old.

The **Bulldog** is indisputably of British origin, and has never been permanently introduced into any other country. His courage is so great that it has become proverbial, and, with the exception of the game cock, there is no other domestic animal at all coming up to him. Independently of this quality, there is much difference of opinion as to the mental peculiarities of this breed. By some authorities the bulldog is stated to be quarrelsome and wantonly savage, so that he can never be made a safe companion; while others allege that he is mild and gentle in disposition, never showing his teeth until he is induced to do so by some special cause. As usual in such cases, the truth lies between two extremes. The bulldog is no doubt dangerous when his blood is up, and even his master runs some risk in meddling with him then, but he may generally be controlled with perfect facility, and he is mild, fondling, and gentle in his manner as a general rule. Still, he is not capable of strong attachment, and he cannot be taught more than the commonest forms of obedience. He is silent in his attacks, so that he does not make a good watch-dog. Formerly the breed was kept pure with great care, for the purpose of baiting the bull, in which his tendency to pin the most vulnerable point (the nose) made him invaluable, no other dog having either the same desire to go at the head in preference to all other parts, or the same unflinching hold of the grasp when once obtained. Bulldogs have had their legs cut off after pinning a bull, without letting go, and other equally horrible cruelties have been practised to show this peculiarity. In the present day, when bull-baiting is interdicted by act of parliament, the use of the bulldog is confined to the improvement in courage of other breeds, by crossing with them, and in this way the greyhound is supposed to have been brought to perfection by Lord Orford and Mr. Etwall in England, and by Mr. Raimes in Scotland, but a later experiment made by Mr. Hanly has been entirely unsuccessful. The cross with the terrier is an excellent one for general purposes, as I shall presently show.

The *points* of the bulldog are as follows, though there is some difference of opinion upon certain of them. The skull should be large, and high, and broad, the cheeks extending prominently beyond the eyes, and the forehead should be well creased or wrinkled, and flat. The eyes should be black and round, not very large, situated in front of the head, wide apart, and neither prominent nor deeply set, the corners at right angles with a line drawn down the centre of the face. The stop (which is an indentation between the eyes) should extend up the face for a considerable length. The face as short as possible from the front of the cheek-bone to the end of the nose—deeply wrinkled. The muzzle should turn up. The chop—that is, the fleshy part of the muzzle—should be broad and deep, and should perfectly cover the teeth. The nose should be large and black. The lower jaw should project, and the nose should be set well back, and the lower jaw should turn upwards. The neck moderately long, well arched, with a good dewlap. The ears should be small and on the top of the head. Three descriptions of ear are permitted, called "rose," "button," and "tulip." The rose ears fold at the back; the tip laps over outwards, exposing part of the inside; the button ear falls in front, hiding the interior completely; the tulip ear is quite erect, and is allowed to be an undesirable form. Skull, 25; ears, 5; eyes, 5; "stop," 5; shortness of face, 5; chop, 5; nose and jaws, 5; neck, 5.

The chest should be wide and deep, the back short, wide across the shoulders, and not so wide across the loins; ribs round. There should be a slight fall behind the shoulders, and the spine should rise at the loins,

Bulldog "Champion Facey Romford."
Winner of many First Prizes and Championships. The property of Mr. D. Y. Cassels, Hamilton.

falling rapidly to the stern, and well arched. The stern should be moderately thick where it joins the body, and be fine to the point. It should have a decided downward carriage. I prefer a tail of a moderate length, decidedly objecting to a long tail having a curve at the end, commonly called the "ring-tail." The tail should be low in its setting on also. Chest, 5; body, 5; stern, 5.

The fore-legs should be strong, muscular, and straight; they should be short, the elbow well let down. The hind legs should be rather longer in proportion than the fore-legs, so as to raise the loins; and, in direct opposition to the established opinion of connoisseurs, I prefer the hocks to be straight, and that the stifles should not turn out, which must be the case if the hocks approach each other. The fore-feet should be well arched, they should be moderately round, and the toes should be well split up. The feet should turn neither in nor out; they should be small, and the hind feet should be of the same character. Legs and feet, 15.

The coat should be fine and smooth. The colour should be whole or unmixed, and may be red, red-smut, fawn, fawn-smut, fallow, fallow-smut, or blue-fawn, or white, the last being preferred. With all these points and properties he must be symmetrical. His action is rather slovenly, his hind legs not being lifted high as he runs. He varies in weight from 15 lbs. to 60 lbs. Coat, 5; colour, 5.

The **Bull Terrier** is, like the bulldog, almost peculiar to this country, and indeed in the whole family of terriers he is pre-eminent. This breed is known in the hardware and pottery districts, where it is carried to high perfection as the "half-bred" *par excellence,* and Mr. Hinks, of Birmingham, may lay claim to having carried off the highest honours from his competitors with his succession of Madmen, his Puss, Tartar, &c. This dog is used solely for fighting, which is still privately carried on by his patrons, but the breed is equally good for attacking the badger, and other hard-biting vermin, requiring high courage and more quickness and docility than are possessed by the pure bulldog. Hence he is a great favourite as the companion of young men, whether military or civilian, and as he can make himself generally useful, he is popular also with the groom and the workman. The first cross is generally too much like the bulldog, but the second shows in perfection all the attributes required for the purpose I am alluding to. In weight he varies from 9 lbs. up to 35 lbs., or more. In general appearance he resembles the terrier, except that he is wider across his skull, and possesses more strength and stamina.

His head should be long, the muzzle sharp, the jaw level—not underhung, which is a disfigurement, and also prevents a dog punishing his adversary. *The under-jaw should display great power*, and the neck should be long. Head, 25 points; neck and ears, 10.

The chest is wide, the shoulders sloping and powerful, the loin and back strong, the hind quarters and thighs muscular. The tail should be fine and sting-like, but not bare; carried gaily, but not "hooped." Chest, 10; shoulders, 10; loin, 10; tail, 5.

The feet and legs should resemble those of the hound in shape. Value, 10.

The coat throughout is fine and short, and it should lie smoothly, as in a well-dressed race horse. Pure white, with a black nose and eye, is the most approved colour. Next in merit I should place white with coloured ears, or a patch on the eyes. I believe all the best judges entertain a strong preference for the white dog; but in any case the colour should be "whole," that is, unmixed with white, unless the dog be all white, which is, in that case, considered a "whole" colour. If coloured, it should be either red, red-smut (that is, red with black muzzle), fawn or fawn-smut, fallow or fallow-smut, brindled, white, blue-fawn (that is, fawn with blue muzzle), or pied with any of those colours. Coat and colour, 10; symmetry, 10.

A loving and gentle temperament is of great importance.

The family of Pure Terriers is a large one, and includes besides the "toys," the Scotch, Skye, and Dandie Dinmont in Scotland, the Bedlington in the north, and the various strains of smooth terriers in England. Of late years the Scotch broken-haired dog has been by selection converted into an animal possessing a silky and comparatively long and wavy coat, utterly unlike his ancestry. The subdivisions are now almost endless, but the above-mentioned breeds are the leading ones.

The **Smooth English Terrier** (not black and tan) is a very old breed, probably as old as any we have. Possessed of a merry and active temperament, and gifted with a good nose, he is the model of a vermin dog, where there is no badger or otter to attack; but for these he is scarcely fitted in power, and as a rule he will not face them at close quarters. Elegant and graceful in his outline, he shares with the bull terrier the patronage of young men, with whom his companionable qualities make him a favourite indoors as well as out. He may weigh from 6 lbs. to 10 lbs., or even 20 lbs.; but, provided he is large enough for his calling, he cannot be too small. It is an advantage to keep down the size of certain dogs as much as possible, and we ought to consider that two small terriers will do more than double the work of one large dog, whilst they consume no more

The head is narrow, long, and flat. The muzzle must be fine, tapering, sharp, and fox-like; but the jaw must be muscular, and the mouth must *never* be underhung. It is better that the upper jaw should be slightly in excess, if there is the least deviation from a level mouth. The "stop," or indent between the eyes, must be evident and "pronounced." The eye must be sparkling, bright, but not large. The ears round, flat to the head in repose, but raised, although falling over, when the dog is roused. A tulip or prick-ear is a great deformity, and betokens mongrel family. It has been the fashion to crop the ears of terriers for many years, and the eye has become so accustomed to it that many good judges will scarcely look at a terrier unless he has been scientifically cropped. In large towns it is not the fashion to shorten the tail at all when the ears are cut, whilst country sportsmen leave the ears, but shorten the tail. The neck should be long, tapering, and muscular, and clean where it joins the lower jaw. Head, 25; neck, 10.

The ribs must be round, the shoulders deep and well set back, and as powerful as possible, enabling the dog to grapple with his foe or to dig him. The loins must be strong and the back ribs deep. In conformation, his body must be neither high nor wide, but well knit together, *multum in parvo*. Chest, 10; shoulders, 10; loin, 10.

The fore-legs should be straight as arrows; the feet strong, the toes moderately arched and well split, and the

English Terrier.

form of the foot should be round and fox-like. The thighs should be large and muscular, the hocks in a straight line, and the hind legs should be moderately straight also. Value of legs and feet, 10.

The tail must be very fine, with a low carriage, but *not bare;* and when a dog is excited it is carried gaily; 5.

The best colour is white, when used for ratting, as it is more easily distinguishable than any other, and there is

the same advantage as to colour when the dog's services are required for rabbit-hunting. Smooth terriers may be found of other colours—yellow, yellow and white, hound-pied, black, or fawn. A beautiful blue or blue-fawn variety exists, said to be crossed with the Italian greyhound. Brindle colour is a sign of bulldog cross. Coat and colour, 10; symmetry, as in the bull terrier, 10. Whether coloured or white, his coat should be smooth yet hard, and he should be perfectly free from the very least roughness, or anything approaching coarseness of coat, about his muzzle, eyebrows, thighs, or any part of his profile.

The **Black and Tan English Terrier** should have a long fine muzzle, not underhung, but, if anything, the upper jaw projecting over the lower. The skull should be flat and narrow between the ears; the eye must be small and black; the nose black; the ears, if not left on, must be well cropped, erect, and long; if entire, they should be small, not tuliped, and free from any tan behind. The neck tapering, muscular, and well cut under the lower jaw. The shoulders deep and well set back. The loins strong, ribs round, and the back ribs deep, the body well knit together. The legs straight, the feet round and small. The tail must be fine, carried straight, and not curled. The colour, which is a principal point, must be raven black, with rich mahogany tan, well pencilled on each toe; the tan should be clear, and free from any admixture of black. Above the eyes there should be a distinct spot of tan. The body should be black, with a rich tan on the fore-legs half-way up them. The breast should have two distinct marks of tan. The jaw should also be well tanned up the gullet, and the cheek divided, having a small tan spot a little less than that over the eyes. The upper jaw should also be nicely tanned, and run in conformity with the tanning on the lower jaw. The hind legs should be perfectly free from tan on the outside, but on the inside there should be some tan. The vent should have a small tan spot, and there should also be tan half-way up the tail.

The weight varies from 10 lbs. to 25 lbs.

The *points:* Colour, coat, and correct markings, 40;

head, 25; eye, 5; neck, 5; chest, 5; shoulders, 5; feet, 5; loins, 5; tail, 5.

Rough or **Broken-haired Terriers** are no doubt all descended from the broken-haired Scotch dog, with which all must be familiar, but whether the modern silken hair has been developed by crossing with the Maltese, or by selection, is a moot question. In general shape this dog resembles the smooth variety, but he is slightly longer in frame, and not so elegant in his proportions. The chief peculiarity, as I before remarked, is in coat and colour. The roughness of coat about the muzzle and face makes the head look larger, and takes off a good deal from the lively look so remarkable in the smooth dog.

The old-fashioned hard and wiry-coated dog is, I believe, more game than the silky-haired dog now in fashion; but no doubt the latter is a very elegant animal, and well suited for the bar-parlour, where he is extensively patronized. The modern favourite is of a blue colour, with rich fawn (approaching to a tan) legs, the under-parts being all of the latter colour. The tail is carried higher than that of the smooth dog. In the old-fashioned strain the colours are either grizzled, black, with pale tan spots, or generally of a grizzled black-brown, sometimes quite grey and constituting the pepper-and-salt colour. Sometimes the broken-haired dog is white, more or less marked with blue, or some other colour, but the less the better.

There is a great difference of opinion as regards the points of a broken-haired terrier; we will therefore describe the points of the two varieties in most esteem, beginning with those chiefly bred in Lancashire and Yorkshire, as these, up to the present time, have distanced the Scotch terrier at our great shows on account of their taking appearance to the eyes of the general public. In our opinion, however, the Scotch terrier proper is superior in point of usefulness at home and abroad, and when the two are shown together it should be preferred—shape, make, and colour being equal

The points of the Yorkshire dog are the same as regards shape and make as the smooth English terrier; but the coat differs in being long, and of three different shades—that on the back being a blue slate; the face, head, and legs a silky silvery fawn; the whole undermined by short tanned hair. The older the dog the more silvery he gets.

The Scotch dog is also the same in shape. His colour may be pepper or mustard, or pepper and mustard, in each case more or less mixed with salt.

The toy dog of these strains is the same in all but weight, which should not exceed 7 lbs.; the smaller the better.

The estimated value of their *points* is as follows:— Head, 15; neck and ears, 10; shoulders, chest, and loins, 20; feet and legs, 10; colour and coat, 30; symmetry, 10; tail, 5.

The **Skye Terrier**. This dog is, with the exception of the turnspit, and his foreign representative, the barbet, the longest of all dogs in proportion to his height. From the nose to the tip of his tail, when extended, the Skye should measure at least three times its height, and sometimes it is met with three and a half times as long. At the same time its coat is so developed that its shape is really very like the door-mat to which it is so often compared—ears, legs, and tail all merging in one mass, with the exception of the tip of the latter, and of the feet. In a well-coated specimen the eyes are only to be guessed at, and even the nose is often obscured; but generally they are each more or less visible on a close inspection.

The head looks large, from the profusion of hair with which it is invested, but it is not really so. Its shape is not easily got at, but it is somewhat wide, while the neck is unusually long. The eyes, which are from the same cause scarcely visible, are found, on separating the overhanging hair, to be keen, expressive, small, and generally of a dark colour, either black or brown, as are the nose and palate. The ears are of good size, that is, about 3 in. long, clothed thickly with hair, which should mingle with that of the face and neck, and decidedly, in my opinion, should fall, but not quite close to the cheek, owing to the quantity of hair by which they are surrounded. Many breeders, however, prefer the prick-ear, asserting that the strains possessing it are harder and better at vermin. The mouth must be level, with a large and black nose. The body is too much coated to show

Dandie Dinmont Terrier.

its shape, and the form of the shoulder and back ribs can only be ascertained by handling.

The fore-legs are generally more or less bandy; there are no dewclaws, and the feet are not very strong, having a tendency to flatness, and thinness of the soles. Tail long, and carried horizontally, but with a sweep, so that the tip is a little below the level of the back. Weight from 10 lbs. to 18 lbs., the bitches being nearly as heavy as the dogs—perhaps about 2 lbs. less.

The colours most fancied are steel with black tips, fawn with dark brown tips to the ears and tail, dark slaty blue (slightly grizzled, but without any absolute admixture of white), black, and pure fawn—the order we have named being in accordance with the value of each. The hair should be long, straight, and shining like that of the tail of the horse, any appearance of silkiness, woolliness, or curl being to be avoided, excepting on the top of the head, where it may have a slight tendency to the first-named condition.

The *points* are : Coat, 25 ; colour, 20; head, 10 ; ears, 10; length of body, 10; carriage of tail, 10; symmetry, 15.

The **Dandie Dinmont** resembles the Skye terrier in general appearance, but there are several points of great importance by which the two may be distinguished. As stated in the *Field*, and not contradicted, Sir Walter Scott was the first to draw attention to this breed in the second of the Waverley series of novels, in which Dandie Dinmont, of Charlieshope, is introduced as the owner of "auld Pepper and auld Mustard, and young Pepper and young Mustard, and little Pepper and little Mustard," which he had "a' regularly entered, first wi' rottens, then wi' stots or weazels, and then wi' the tods and brocks, and now," as he said, "they fear naething that ever cam' wi' a hairy skin on't." According to this high authority in matters canine, therefore, the dog of his day was a good vermin-killer, and so he remains to this day. The original of this strongly-marked character was a Mr. James Davidson of Hindlee, holding from Lord Douglas a wild farm on the edge of the Teviotdale mountains, bordering closely on Liddesdale. He was an ardent fox-hunter, according to the fashion of the district, which is detailed at length in the twenty-fifth chapter of "Guy Mannering," and which, as Sir Walter remarks, was conducted in a manner to "shock a member of the Pytchley Hunt"—the fox (tod) being coursed by an indefinite number of "large and fierce greyhounds," when driven from his earth by the " terriers, including the whole generation of Pepper and Mustard," together with "mongrel, whelp, and cur of low degree." Excepting, therefore, by tradition, the Dandie Dinmont terrier can only be traced back about three-quarters of a century. Mr. Macdona (of St. Bernard fame) has obtained access to a curious document in Mr. James Davidson's handwriting, which was sent to the Hon. George H. Baillie, of Millerstown, as follows :—

"1800.—Tuggin, from A. Armstrong, reddish and wiry; Tarr, reddish and wire haired, a bitch ; Pepper, shaggy and light, from Dr. Brown, of Borjenwood. The race of Dandies are bred from the two last.—J. D."

Mr. Macdona, in a letter to the *Field*, dated November 2, 1869, concludes "from this, that Dr. Brown, of Borjenwood, gave Mr. Davidson, in the year 1800, Pepper and Tarr, and that this couple were, without doubt, the first parents of all true-bred Dandie Dinmonts, being the original stock from whence all Mr. Davidson's generations of Mustards and Peppers sprang." And in this conclusion I think him perfectly right. Of late years the most celebrated strains have been those of the Duke of Buccleuch, obtained direct from James Davidson; Sir G. Douglas, of Springwood Park; Mr. Stoddart, of Selkirk; Mr. Frain, of The Trews; Mr. M'Dougall, of Cessford; Mr. Somners, of Kelso ; Dr. Brown, of Melrose; Mr. Aitken, of Edinburgh ; Mr. Hugh Purvis, of Leaderfoot; Mr. Nicol Milne, of Faldonside ; and Mr. Bradshaw Smith, of Ecclefechan.

The *points* of the Dandie are as follows :—

Head—Large and long, with immensely strong jaws and teeth, which are quite level, and the nose cut short like a pointer's. The head of the bitch is generally much smaller than that of the dog, so that they may be distinguished by a glance.

Ears—Pendant, from 3 to 4 in. long, and hanging close to the cheek, as the hound's or beagle's, but not so broad or round at the point—more in the shape of an almond or filbert.

Eyes—Full, bright, and very intelligent.

Neck—Well developed and rather short.

Body—Long, but not quite so long as that of a good

Skye, being about 2½ times the height, with low shoulders, and the back slightly curved down behind them, with a corresponding arch of the loin.

Legs—Short, particularly in front, with extraordinary bone and muscle in proportion to the size.

Tail—Slightly curved, and carried over the back in a hound-like manner, with little or no feather on it.

Height—From 10 to 12 in. to top of shoulders; it may be less, but it should not be more.

Coat—A mixture of hardish and soft (but not silky) short hair—what old John Stoddort used to term a " pily coat "—with the head more or less covered with soft and silky hair (which is generally of a lighter colour than that on the body); and the legs and feet partake to a slight extent of the same soft silky hair.

Colour—Either " mustard " (reddish-brown) or "pepper" (bluish-grey), or a combination of both, in which case the back is of the latter colour, while the legs, inside of ears, chest, and under-side of tail are " mustard," verging on a pale tan or fawn-colour.

Weight—From 13 to 18 lbs.

The *points* are: Head, 15; ears, 10; eyes, 5; colour, 20; coat, 20; symmetry, 10; feet and legs, 10; carriage of tail, 10.

Bedlington Terrier.—This is probably one of the most active, plucky, and thoroughly game members of the terrier breed. His origin is involved in some doubt, though it is averred that he is descended from the same source as the Dandie Dinmont. The following are the points claimed for him by the first breeders of the day, and also laid down by the Bedlington Club. The *Head* is not quite ferrety, but wedge-shaped. The *Skull* is high and peaked; the jaws are long and lean, and punishing, with large strong teeth. Many dogs are pig-jawed, but preference should be given to level, strong teeth. The *nose* is well developed, standing out prominently from the jaws. The nose is black in the blue, or blue and tan breeds, and flesh-coloured in the light-coloured dogs. The *Ears* resemble those of the Dandy Dinmont, not being set on low, lying easily on the cheek, being shaped like the filbert, and feathered at the tips. The *Eyes* are small, well placed, singularly bright, and piercing during animation. The *Colour* varies with that of the coat generally, but too much stress should not be laid on this point.

Bedlington Terrier.

The *Neck* is long and strong, and well set on the body, being especially wide at the base. The *Body* is compact, well knit together, somewhat long, and having the appearance of strength, combined with speed. The *Ribs* are somewhat flat, the *Back* short, *Loins* strong and slightly arched, the hind-quarters being slightly elevated above the fore. The *Legs* are straight, rather long, and the muscles hard and well defined. The *Feet* are large, a point of singular distinction. The *Coat* is "woolly," or, according to some, "linty," having a "sprinkling of wiry hairs through it." The *Colour* is blue and tan, red, liver, liver and tan, or sandy. The blue is decided, without inclining to black, and the tan is light. The *Weight* varies from 18 to 25 lbs.; good specimens stand well and firm on apparently long legs, which undoubtedly enhance the general appearance.

The dog which may be cited as an illustration or type of the Bedlington terrier, is "Orme," the property of Mr. John Smith, of Montrose. He has gained upwards of thirty First Prizes, also a Cup, Gold Medals, and two Championships. At home he is a house companion, but away, he is liable to resist handling by strangers. For this fault he on two occasions was put back to a second position. His colour is liver, and show-weight 23 lbs.

The Irish Terrier has been known as a distinct breed for many years, and is now brought to great perfection in all the desired points. As an ordinary country sportsman's dog he is probably not to be surpassed. His general appearance is that of a complete terrier, larger than the rough Scotch terrier, having a shorter body but longer legs than the Skye. He is rough, wild, and bold as a lion, of quick perception, and his unkempt coat completes his character as a truly Irish dog. The following description is the standard laid down by the Irish Terrier Club. The *Head* is long; the skull flat and rather narrow between ears, getting slightly narrower towards the eye; free from wrinkle; stop hardly visible, except in profile. The *Jaw* must be strong and muscular, but not too full in the cheek, and of a good punishing length, but not so fine as a white English terrier's. There should be a slight falling away below the eye, so as not to have a greyhound appearance. Hair on face of same description as on body, but short (about a quarter of an inch long), in appearance almost smooth and straight; a slight beard is the only longish hair (and it is only long in comparison with the rest) that is permissible, and that is characteristic. The *Teeth* should be strong and level, the *Lips* not so tight as a Bull terrier's, but well fitting, showing through the hair their black lining. The *Nose* must be black; the *Eyes* a dark hazel colour, small, not prominent, and full of life, fire, and intelligence; the *Ears*, when uncut, V-shaped, of moderate thickness, set well up on the head, and dropping forward closely to the cheek. The ear must be free of fringe, and the hair thereon shorter and generally darker in colour than on the body. The *Neck* should be of a fair length, and gradually widening towards the shoulders, well carried and free of throatiness. There is generally a sort of frill visible at each side of the neck, running nearly to the corner of the ear, which is looked on as very characteristic. The *Shoulders* must be fine, long, and sloping well into the back; the *Chest* deep and muscular, but neither full nor wide; the *Body* moderately long. The *Back* should be strong and straight, with no appearance of slackness behind the shoulders; the *Loins* broad and powerful, and slightly arched; *Ribs* fairly sprung, rather deep than round, and well ribbed back. *Hind-quarters* well under the dog, should be strong and muscular, the *Thighs* powerful, *Hocks* near the ground; *Stifles* not much bent. *Stern*, generally docked, should be free of fringe or feather, set on pretty high, carried gaily, but not over the back or curled. The *Feet* should be strong, tolerably round, and moderately small; *Toes* arched, and neither turned out nor in; black toe-nails are preferable and most desirable; *Legs* moderately long, well set from the *Shoulders*, perfectly straight, with plenty of bone and muscle; the *Elbow* working freely clear of the sides; *Pasterns* short and straight, hardly noticeable. Both fore and hind legs should be moved straight forward when travelling; the stifles not turned outwardly, the legs free of feather, and covered, like the head, with as hard a texture of coat as body, but not so long. The *Coat* is hard and wiry, free of softness or silkiness, not so long as to hide the outlines of the body, particularly in the hind-quarters, straight and flat, no shagginess, and free of lock or curl. *Colour:* Should be "whole coloured," the most preferable being bright red; next wheaten yellow,

IRISH TERRIER "CHAMPION BREDA MIXER."

Winner of fifty First Prizes, thirteen Kennel Club Championship Prizes and the Irish Terrier Club Thirty Guineas Challenge Cup seven times. The property of Mr. L. F. Wright, Loughall, co. Armagh.

and grey, brindle disqualifying. White sometimes appears on chest and feet; it is more objectionable on the latter than on the chest, as a speck of white on chest is frequently to be seen in all self-coloured breeds. *Size and Symmetry:* Weight in show condition, from 16 lbs. to 24 lbs.—say 16 lbs. to 24 lbs. for bitches, and 18 lbs. to 24 lbs. for dogs. The most desirable weight is 22 lbs. or under, which is a nice stylish and useful size. The dog must present an active, lively, lithe, and wiry appearance, lots of substance, at the same time free of clumsiness; as speed and endurance, as well as power, are very essential. They must be neither "cloddy" nor "cobby," but should be framed on the "lines of speed," showing a graceful "racing outline." *Temperament:* Dogs that are very game are usually surly or snappish. The Irish terrier, as a breed, is an exception, being remarkably good-tempered, notably so with mankind, it being admitted, however, that he is perhaps, a little too ready to resent interference on the part of other dogs. There is a heedless, listless pluck about the Irish terrier which is characteristic, and coupled with the headlong dash, blind to all consequences, with which he rushes at his adversary, has earned for the breed the proud epithet of "The Dare-Devils." When "off duty" they are characterised by a quiet, caress-inviting appearance, and when one sees them endearingly, timidly pushing their heads in their master's hands it is difficult to realise that on occasion, at the "set on," they can prove they have the courage of a lion, and will fight on to the last breath in their bodies. They develop an extraordinary devotion to, and have been known to track their masters almost incredible distances.

Disqualification.—Brindled in colour, nose cherry or flesh coloured; white anywhere is highly objectionable. A grizzly appearance about the muzzle at four and five years old is not considered to be detrimental.

The Welsh Terrier.—This dog has been known for several generations as a distinct breed, and his peculiar adaptation for rabbiting, getting foxes out of the rocks, destroying lesser vermin, etc., has led to a careful system of breeding, as well as training for efficiency. Special strains are carefully preserved, of which full pedigrees are also compiled. Successful shows were first held in Bangor and Carnarvon, since which the breed has sprang into high favour. The following are the points agreed upon by the Welsh Terrier Club. *Head:* The skull should be flat, and rather wider between the ears than the wire-haired fox terrier. The jaw should be powerful, clean cut, rather deeper, and more punishing—giving the head a more muscular appearance than that usually seen on a fox terrier; stop not too defined; fair length from stop to the end of nose, the latter being of a black colour. The *Ear* should be V-shaped, small, not too thin, set on fairly high, carried forward and close to the cheek. The *Eye* should be small, not being deeply set in or protruding out of the skull, of a dark hazel colour, expressive and indicating abundant pluck. The *Neck* should be of a moderate length and thickness, slightly arched, and sloping gracefully into the shoulders. The *Back* should be short, and well ribbed up, the loin strong, good depth, and moderate width of chest. The *Shoulders* should be long, sloping, and well set back. The *Hind-quarters* should be strong, thighs muscular, and of good length, with the hocks moderately straight, well let down, and fair amount of bone. The *Stern* should be set on moderately high, but not too gaily carried. The *Legs* should be straight and muscular, possessing fair amount of bone, with upright and powerful pasterns. The *Feet* should be small, round, and cat-like. The *Coat* should be wiry, hard, very close and abundant. The *Colour* should be black, or grizzle, and tan, free from black pencilling on toes. The *height* at shoulder should be 15 inches for dogs, bitches proportionately less. *Twenty pounds* is considered a fair average weight in working condition, but this may vary a pound or so either way.

The Whippet.—The origin of this dog is given in the closing lines concerning the Italian greyhound at page 93. The whippet is comparatively a recent introduction, being the result of a cross with the terrier and Italian greyhound. Earlier crosses, twenty-five or thirty years ago, were, doubtless, intended to perfect the breeding of the "snap-dog," by adding speed to his qualification of killing the greatest number of rabbits. The later development is evident in the former. He is, therefore, a greyhound in miniature, possessing the elegance and grace of the original ancestry, combined with the pluck, and determination to "hold on," which characterises the typical terrier. The whippet is now a pure bred dog, having secured a place in the "Kennel Stud Book," and is essentially a racing dog. As such he is rapidly coming into increased prominence. He is no less a show dog, sporting dog, or constant companion, and runs in all colours, as black, blue, brindle, or fawn, with a dash of white in some instances. The points are those of a good greyhound, with the exception that the head, comparatively speaking, is not so long or so fine, the prominence of the frontal bones, immediately above the eyes, being the stamp of the terrier breed.

The Old English or Bob-tailed Sheep Dog.—This dog is justly entitled to greater consideration than he has hitherto received among the numerous exhibits at the various dog shows throughout England. His services have been mostly confined to the southern counties, by drovers of sheep and cattle; he is not, therefore, so well known as he should be. Many specimens do not present an inviting appearance, being ill-fed and otherwise badly treated, which severely operate upon all animals, to the prejudice of their intelligence and cleverness. There are, however, among the members of the breed, not only well-shaped, active, and intelligent dogs, but some are really clever, and even beautiful creatures, and it may be inferred that if as much care were bestowed upon him as is given to the Scotch collie, the former would become a close rival for the honours now carried off by the latter.

The Welsh origin of this dog has been strongly maintained, the contending parties having omitted to master the details of their family history. Others have taken up the task, and rescued from oblivion the interesting information that so near a relation as the Grandfather originally introduced the breed from Sussex.

This animal has been long known in Suffolk as the "cow-dog," a service in which he proves himself singularly clever and useful. At milking time he may be seen taking his rest near the farm-steading, and as the cows are turned out singly he ensures their return to the pasture, and selecting another—always one that needs milking—returns with her to the farm, where he remains as before. It is remarkable that in this service the "bobtail" never makes a mistake from first to last in the daily routine.

The query of "tail," or "no tail" has proved a difficulty to many. It is, however, fairly understood that the peculiarity of the breed consists in the production of puppies in the same litter with and *without* tails, others being considered short. In some instances docking is resorted to at an early period, by which even some of the knowing ones have been deceived.

The colour is steel grey, or black and tan, the first being considered the hardier of the two. There are animals which exhibit various shades of blue, blue merle, or grizzle, having white on the face or legs. The *Head* is large, wide across the forehead, the muzzle heavy and somewhat short. The *Eyes* are small, being dark or smutty grey; the wall, or china eye being common to light haired dogs. The *Body* is square, and of large proportions, hind-quarters heavy and round, sloping forwards. The *Coat* is broken, harsh, wavy, and dense throughout. The *Ears* are small, well-set, and covered with wavy hair. The *Limbs* are strong, bony, well furnished with muscle, flat from side to side, and covered with hair to the bottom. The *Feet* are large and round, pads thick and horny, and the claws large and firm. The powers of digestion and assimilation are good, and he is able to subsist on common or coarse food; the constitution is also hardy, bearing exposure to the vicissitudes of weather without serious inconvenience.

Disqualifications.—Soft, and curly coat of a poodle-like character; black and tan, as well as brindled colours.

Noted examples of the class are "Sir Hereward," a winner of numerous first prizes, and his descendants "Sir Tatton," "Sir Coventry," "Sir Peveril," "Dame Rachel," etc.

The Scotch Collie, or Highland Sheep Dog, is a far more graceful animal, and his sense and intelligence are equal to any breed of dogs in the world. Two races are to be found in Scotland—the rough and the smooth. The rough or shaggy-coated collie is the most choice description; for his impenetrable warm thick coat is a good protection to him when his duty calls him to face the storms and mists and snows of the wild mountains, especially when the stragglers of the flock have been covered by the snow-drifts, and he goes in search of them with his master. He has a fine fox-like muzzle; full, expressive, but rather crafty eyes; small ears dropping forward, and the mask of his face is smooth. From the base of the skull the whole of the neck and the entire body are protected by a deep, warm, long coat of various colours—sometimes black with tan points; sometimes sandy, or of various mixed greys, some of which are singularly beautiful and picturesque. There is generally a very fine white line down the forehead, not amounting to a blaze, as in the spaniels. His legs (especially the hind legs, from the hocks) are bare, that is, not feathered; and for many years authorities on the dog have described the collie as having one, or even two, dewclaws on each hind leg, which is indeed generally the case. His neck is long and rather arched; his shoulders are set well back, and are very powerful; the elbow is well let down; the forearm is short; the ankles or pasterns are long, and rather small for his size; and the feet are round, arched, and have excellent thick hard soles; the chest is deep, but rather narrow; he is broad over his back; his loins are well arched; the hips are wide; his thighs are muscular, and he is inclined to go rather wide behind; the tail is very bushy and large, and carried up when he is in motion, and when he is controlling his excitement it is turned over his back.

The Collie Club have arranged the standard of points

as follows: The *Skull* of the collie should be quite flat and rather broad, with fine tapering muzzle of fair length, and mouth the least bit overshot, the *Eyes* widely apart, almond-shaped, and obliquely set in the head; the skin of the head tightly drawn, with no folds at the corners of the mouth; the *Ears* as small as possible, semi-erect when surprised or listening, at other times thrown back and buried in the ruff. The *Neck* should be long, arched, and muscular, the *Shoulders* also long, sloping, and fine at the withers; the *Chest* to be deep and narrow in front, but of fair breadth behind the shoulders; the *Back* to be short and level, and the loin rather long, somewhat arched, and powerful; *Brush* long, " wi' upward swirl " at the end, and normally carried low. The *Fore-legs* should be perfectly straight, with a fair amount of flat bone, the pasterns rather long, springy, and slightly lighter of bone than the rest of the leg; the foot, with toes well arched and compact soles, very thick. The *Hind-quarters* drooping slightly, should be very long from the hip-bones to the hocks, which should be neither turned inwards nor outwards, with stifles well bent. The *Hip-bones* should be wide and rather rugged. The *Coat*, except on legs and head, should be as abundant as possible; the outer coat straight, hard, and rather stiff, the under coat furry and so dense that it should be difficult to find the skin. The *Ruff* and *Frill* especially should be very full. There should be but little feather on the fore-legs, and none below the hocks on the hind-legs. *Colour* immaterial. The dog should be a fair length on the leg, and his movements wiry and graceful; he should not be too small; height of dogs from 22 to 24 inches, bitches from 20 to 22 inches. The greyhound type is objectionable, as there is no brain room in the skull, and with this there is to be found a fatuous expression, and a long powerful jaw. The setter type is also to be avoided, with a pendulous ear, full soft eye, heavily feathered legs, and straight short flag. The smooth collie only differs from the rough in its coat, which should be hard, dense, and quite smooth.

Disqualifications.—Domed skull, high peaked occipital

Rough-coated Collies.

bone, heavy pendulous ears, full soft eyes, heavy feathered legs, short tail.

Competent judges of the collie will scarcely be satisfied with some of the foregoing statements, notably those with reference to the eyes being "widely apart," and "almond shape." Surely the dog with such points would be an oddity, and useless for his calling. For other useful strictures, the reader is referred to the monograph by Dalziel.*

The Smooth Collie is believed to be a separate breed by many fanciers, who fail to see that he is the *facsimile* of the rough-coated dog. His points except the coat are the same, and he therefore needs no special comment. Puppies of the smooth variety are not infrequently met with in the litters of rough-coated collies, over which every care has been exercised. There are, however, two varieties of this dog, which are as widely different in their capabilities as in their outward conformation. In his natural place the former is trained for work among the sheep of the bleak Highland regions, about which he proceeds with a dignity and grace unknown in the other. The Lowland dog finds his service commonly among cows, and he lacks the energy and experience of his aristocratic rival of the Highlands. The head of the Highland collie, taken as a whole, is a perfect study; the set of the ears, and the intelligent gaze of his eyes combine in assuring you "the dog kens what ye are talkin' aboot, and what ye are thinkin' aboot tae." The slightest utterance, or movement of the hand is ample for his quick intelligence, and he bounds away with the speed of the antelope. His attachment to his master is based on his special intelligence, for in this respect he is above all other dogs. We have known a collie to follow his master hundreds of miles, taking his place on the steamboats, visiting the usual places of call, and after an unsuccessful search in distant towns, return home by the same route, tired, hungry, and almost prostrate; and on meeting the object of his solicitude,

* "The Collie." London: E. Upcott Gill,

throw himself at his feet, and yell with delight. A little later he rests on the rug before the blazing fire, his huge paws covering his beloved master's feet, and as he steadily gazes you read in those starlit eyes the petition "Ye'll gang awa nae mair."

The **Pomeranian** or **Spitz**, like the St. Bernard, can scarcely be called a dog of the British Islands, but, like that dog, it is now so common as to be almost naturalized among us. It resembles, in shape of body and head, the Scotch collie, but is a size smaller, carries the tail over the back, and is generally of a pure white colour. The ears also are more pricked, being quite fox or wolf-like in their character. Hence it is often called in France by the name *loulou*. No *points* have been assigned to this breed as yet.

CHAPTER V.

LADIES' TOY DOGS.

King Charles Spaniel—Blenheim Spaniel—Italian Greyhound—Pug—Maltese Dog—Toy Terrier—Poodle.

FASHION changes her toy dogs just as often as her costumes, and the favourite of one year is turned into the streets (metaphorically) the next. Poodles, spaniels, terriers, Italian greyhounds, and pugs, have each had their reign, but at present it would be difficult to determine which has the pre-eminence. As a rule, the short-haired dog makes a better drawing-room pet than his long-coated rival, and especially when his skin is peculiarly free from smell, as is the case with the pug dog and Italian greyhound. Hence it is no wonder that these little animals fetch £30 apiece, though we have known £50 paid for a King Charles spaniel; and this being the highest sum I ever heard of as paid for a toy dog, I shall commence with that breed.

The **King Charles Spaniel** is now always either black and tan without white, or a mixture of these colours in handsome patches, the tan spot over the eye in the latter case being always an important feature. In the time of Charles II., from whom the dog gets his name, the colour, as shown by Vandyck, was liver and white, which colour was in vogue until the present century, when the black and tan superseded it, and is now considered the speciality of the breed. Nor is the modern shortness of face of old standing when carried to the extreme which now prevails. Vandyck's dogs are quite sharp-nosed, and those which I remember early in the present century were at least only half-way on the road to the state in which they are now exhibited, with faces like those of the bulldog. At present the dog should weigh about 7 lbs. (not more than 10 lbs.) Perfection in shape is seldom attained below 7 lbs., but if it can be obtained in smaller compass, so much the better

He should have a round skull and large round prominent eyes, with a deep indentation or "stop" between them. The lower jaw should project beyond the upper, and turn up. Large ears "touching the ground" are highly esteemed, but this is a figurative expression. They must droop close to the head and be thickly coated. The back of all the legs must be densely feathered, and the feet must be almost lost in the feather, which ought to project beyond the nails.

The tail should be carried low, the dog should stand on short legs, and appear compact. Any protrusion of the tongue is most objectionable.

His coat should be silky, straight, very abundant, and of the richest colour. The black should be intense, the tan vivid and rich. The dog should be altogether free from white. He should have tan of this rich red quality on his cheeks and the inner margin of the ear. His lips should be tan, and he should have a spot of the same colour over each eye; the larger this spot is the better. His cheeks should be well tanned, also his chest or "mane," all his legs, his belly, the feather of his haunches, his vent, and the under plumage of his tail.

The following scale of *points* is in general acceptation:—Form of head, 10; nose and formation of jaw, 10; eyes, 10; ears, 10; coat and texture, 10; form and compactness, 10; brilliancy of colour, 10; feather of legs and feet, 10; size and weight, 10; carriage of tail, 10—total, 100.

The **Blenheim Spaniel** was thus described in the *Field* of Sept. 15, 1866:—

"This drawing-room favourite derives his name from the celebrated seat of the Dukes of Marlborough, where he used to be carefully bred; the town of Woodstock being some years ago the fountain-head for pure Blenheim spaniels, which could also be purchased wonderfully small and well marked at Oxford about twenty-five years since.

"It is very difficult indeed to trace the origin of this dog, which judging from Vandyck's pictures, was cherished at Courts in the days of Charles I. Sir Godfrey Kneller, we have heard, has painted small red and white spaniels at the feet of several Court beauties, or nestling in their laps. We are also informed that portraits from his hand are to be seen at Blenheim Palace and Arundel Castle, and that the small 'comforter' of this colour was in favour in the reigns of Charles II., James II., and up to the end of the time of Queen Anne.

"It has been called the 'Marlborough spaniel' by some authors, who assert that it was first crossed with the King Charles, otherwise known as the King James spaniel, by a former Duke of Norfolk, who had a large number of them at Worksop.

"It has been asserted that the same description of dog was a favourite in the time of Henry VIII., that it was much esteemed by Elizabeth, and that the small 'dogg' which was found under the clothes of Mary Queen of Scots after her execution was of this breed. As we have before stated, it is almost impossible to give positive information as to the first origin of the Blenheim; and we incline to the opinion that it sprang from a race of cockers of that colour, for which the first owner of Blenheim was celebrated, and that the small race known by that name derived their origin from in-and-in breeding, and jealousy to preserve the breed.

"Good specimens were the great exception; and about the year 1841 perhaps but two or three *good* specimens existed in the neighbourhood of Blenheim, and of these we can call to mind but one of surpassing excellence, a bitch named Rose, belonging to A. R. Reingle, Esq., of Oxford. This bitch would at the present time bear comparison with anything to be purchased in London, and she quite came up to the description we shall give of a true 'Blenheim.'

"This charming spaniel did not weigh more than $4\frac{1}{2}$ lbs. or 5 lbs. Her head (exquisitely modelled and full of character and intelligence) was in exact proportion to her size. Her coat was soft, silky, shining, luxuriant, and of transparent whiteness, except where it was stained in patches with the genuine rich 'Blenheim orange,' whilst her feet and legs were almost lost in the exuberant feather of her 'mane,' body, and thighs.

"At the time Rose was in her glory we were receiving instructions from her owner, and possessed many opportunities of marking her beauty and intelligence—two properties which are not always found together in pet spaniels.

"The Blenheim is at the present time rare, but, compared with the King Charles, it does not command a large price. About a year ago it was with the greatest difficulty we procured one; although of perfect form and exceedingly diminutive, only £15 was asked for it, whilst a King Charles of equal excellence would have been cheap at double the money.

"The points of the Blenheim do not differ from those of the King Charles. The main difference consists in the colour and markings, and in the texture of the hair, which may be more waved in the Blenheim than in the other breed. He should have the same round skull, the same prominent, large, round eyes, weeping and wet at the corner, and leaving a wet trace down the cheek. He must also have the deep stop, the projecting lower jaw,' and the short black nose. He should have large, well-coated ears; but we must not expect to find them so dense or so deep and large as in the King Charles. He must be compact, well coated, and the feather of his legs and thighs must be profuse. His tail should be bushy, 'well flagged,' and carried low. He should not exceed 5 lbs. in weight; and if he weighs 8 lbs. or 9 lbs. he is of very little value.

"His head should be well marked, a white streak should run down his skull, and his lips and chin should be white, freckled with red. In the centre of this white blaze, or rather in the centre of his forehead, he should have the 'spot' about the size of and as round as a sixpence. His chest must be exceedingly well coated; and to this point of beauty great attention should be directed by any judge, as the 'mane' has always been a great point in Blenheims.

"The markings of the body are not of very great importance, provided there is no preponderance of either colour, and that both are distinct or clear. Freckled legs are not in favour; and although a few spots would not prejudice a judge, the fewer of these spots the better.

"The 'red' should be brilliant, and of a yellow or golden hue, by no means approaching the deep sienna stain of the black-tan spaniel or Gordon setter; and many admirable specimens of breeding are of a positively sandy tone. This colour is not, however, *Blenheim colour*, which ought to be rich, pure, and defined. The well-bred animal is lively in temperament, but is more capricious and snappish than the King Charles; and occasionally it forms deep and lasting attachments to those with whom it associates."

I give the *points* of the Blenheim thus:—Form of head, 15; eyes and ears, 15; coat, 10; compactness and form, 10; brilliant colour and spots, 20; feather of legs and feet, 10; size and weight, 10; and tail and its position, 10 —total, 100.

The **Italian Greyhound.**—All authorities unite in the opinion that this beautiful little dog must be an English smooth greyhound in everything but size, which is tantamount to stating that it must be one of the most graceful, or, perhaps, the most graceful and racing-looking creature on the face of the earth.

Bewick gives no engraving of the Italian greyhound, which is to be regretted; and without doubt he would have given one if a specimen could have been procured.

In Italy it has always been a favourite, and we gather from the pictures of Antoine Watteau, the celebrated French painter, that it was much esteemed by the lords and ladies of his country at the close of the seventeenth or at the beginning of the eighteenth century; but they were known and in the hands of the rich—as graceful and perhaps as small as at the present time—in Milan in the fifteenth and sixteenth centuries.

Hogarth has represented a pair of dogs, somewhat of the breed, in one of his pictures of "Marriage à la Mode," and this dog occasionally appears in the portraits of our old English families; but as we have before observed, it has always been scarce, and it is exceedingly delicate and hard to rear.

It is neither more nor less than a small greyhound, for which Italy was celebrated, and which perhaps was originally bred as a distinct breed. It must have become dwarfed from climate or constant "in-breeding," but it has never been in any way deformed by the means adopted to decrease its size.

The external form of the Italian exactly corresponds with that of the smooth English greyhound. I will observe that the head should be wide behind, and larger in circumference if measured over the ears than over the eyebrows. The jaw should be very lean, with a good muscular development of the cheek. The eye of the Italian variety, however, should not be so large or full as that of the English dog.

It has been settled that the ear of the Italian should be exceedingly small, and falling flat, except when the animal is animated. It may then be slightly raised, but never pricked.

Blue and fawn are the favourite colours; the latter should be of an auburn hue. Various colours, however, are fashionable for a time, and then fancy changes. At one time cream-coloured dogs commanded the highest price, then white with black nose. At one time black muzzles were in vogue, and we believe they are preferred at the present time, and party-coloured dogs are not thought much of. When these dogs are self-coloured, they should be free from any white, and this may be predicated of every description of dog or hound. Fawn dogs should have black toe-nails. All of the breed should have very glossy coats and a compact form. The tail should be very fine, and though coated, and not bare or showing the caudal vertebræ, it should be void of all roughness.

The weight must not exceed 8 lbs. or 9 lbs., and the dog is valuable in proportion as he weighs less than this. Specimens have been bred, which, at maturity, did not reach 5 lbs., but they were very delicate and shy. Some of the best shaped and most perfect greyhounds of this description have reached from 14 lbs. to 18 lbs., and at this weight they are certainly more robust than the more valuable dwarfs, occasionally becoming fat and losing the beautiful lines of their kind. The bitches are much less than the dogs.

Some very charming specimens have been shown in London. We have a lively recollection of Mrs. Burke's Silver, Dr. Palmer's Garibaldi, and Mr. Hugh Hanly's Psyche. Some very good ones have also appeared at all our metropolitan exhibitions. But at the present moment it would be exceedingly difficult to obtain a first-class specimen, and I have no hesitation in saying it is the rarest dog of the day.

It has been crossed in Staffordshire with the small bull terrier with advantage, and the produce displayed no delicacy and lost none of its courage. I have seen many of these in "the black country." They were slate-coloured or blue-tanned, and very like the blue terrier known in London as the "Blue Peter," which I suspect is bred in a similar manner.

Although the pure Italian greyhound is generally delicate and nervous, it now and then displays wonderful affection and fidelity, and we remember hearing that a celebrated bitch of the breed, named Fly, the property of the same gentleman who possessed the Blenheim Rose, once jumped from a third-story window into the street to follow her master, and alighted without injury.

) This dog was used as a model by more than one sculptor, and we believe that she was the original of the celebrated and artistic model in parian published by the artist potter of the day. The *points* of this animal are of course identical with those of the smooth English greyhound, but some preference in marks must be given for the fashionable colour at the time when the award is made. They are, therefore, as follows:—Head, 15; neck, 5; legs and feet, 15; shoulders, 10; hind quarters, 15; back, 10; symmetry, 10; tail, 5; colour and coat, 10; size, 5.

The **Pug Dog** is now again in fashion, but between the years 1836–46 it was the rarest breed in Great Britain. About the year 1843 one or two specimens were obtained by a member of the Willoughly family, and, under his fostering care, admirable examples were produced. The old and absurd system of cropping off the whole of the ears prevailed, and this cruelty was excused because it occasioned that wrinkling and puckering of the forehead considered essential in a pug dog. The barbarous fashion was continued simply because it had been followed in the days of our grandfathers and great-grandfathers, at any rate up to the year 1804, when the dog was the rage; and very beautiful specimens thus mutilated have been exhibited at our modern dog shows. Within the last few years this unhappy custom has been on the wane, and where expediency cannot be pleaded, owing to the dog's occupation, we trust such torture will be abandoned.

The pug, it is said, derives his name from a Greek word which forms the root of the Latin *pugnus*, a fist, as his profile closely resembles a man's hand when tightly clenched. This is open to question. It is more likely to have arisen from a study of the countenance, as well as general appearance of the animal. The jet-black muzzle, or mask, secured for him the term "carlin," from the resemblance to a harlequin who was famous in France during the middle of last century. Previously the breed was known in that country as "doguins" and "roquets," names still retained in various parts. The breed was carefully propagated, and highly esteemed during many years, exclusively as parlour pets, many wealthy families having their specially pure and celebrated "pugs." Such was the rage of fashion that no lady was seen abroad without her pet, and when the owner sat for his or her portrait, that of the pug occupied a prominent place in the foreground. The old English breed was distinguished by a black patch on the head, known as the "black velvet," but the best breeds of to-day are destitute of the mark. In Holland, and Italy also, the breed has been highly prized, but in symmetry, colour, and special marking, the dogs are entirely behind in all points of excellence. The Dutch dogs are large, coarse, dull, and heavy, with crooked legs, those of Italy being spoiled by impure crosses. The pug is a perfect aristocrat in all his ways, especially in the presence of other dogs, but at heart he is minus the pluck of our terriers. He nevertheless makes an excellent pet, and settles down most admirably in the ways of ease and luxury.

Some years ago a strain of all black pugs was introduced, it is said, by the late Lady Brassey, some of which were exhibited, showing the characteristics of the breed. As a contrast to these, others have been produced almost or altogether white.

The origin of the black pug has been ascribed to various sources. In one instance it is said to be the result of pure accident, being a "sport," descended from an unusually dark coloured strain owned by a working fancier in the north of London. Setting aside various improbabilities, it is certain that Lady Brassey owned several of these dogs, and although at the time it was kept a close secret, it now seems to be well known that they were Chinese or "Peking" pugs, obtained by her during her memorable voyage in the "Sunbeam." There is now, therefore, no doubt that by subsequent mating a distinct breed has been produced, with, however, the tendency in some instances among individual members to be grey instead of black. The present development of the breed is largely due to three individuals—viz., Mrs. Fiefield, of Eastleigh, Southampton, Miss "Mortivals," (Miss M. D. Robinson), Takeley, Essex, and Mr. A. Bond of Gravesend.

The black pug is somewhat altered by breeding in this country. He stands on shorter legs and is thickly set or "cobby" in appearance, while the head and face in conformation possess the characteristics of our ordinary pug-dog. Judging from the experience of the past, it is not unlikely that he will perpetuate a true type, notwithstanding some of the adverse criticisms which have been launched against him.

Lord Willoughby d'Eresby, Mr. Morrison, of Walham Green, the late Mr. H. Gilbert, Mr. John Anderson, Mr. Jardine, Mr. Hinks (the owner of Madman, the celebrated bull terrier), and Mr. Henry Brown, of Gilling Lodge, Haverstock Hill, one of the most reliable breeders of valuable dogs, and certainly one of the best judges in England of toy dogs—all these and many others have bred and exhibited beautiful specimens of the old English pug dog; and we may gather from the favour the dog has met from high quarters that the breed is in no danger of extinction.

The true English pug should be of a fawn or nutty-colour, devoid of any smut approaching *blackness*. Clearness and purity of colour are essential, so as to render the various markings (which I shall proceed to describe) as clear and sharp in outline as possible. The dog should stand on short legs, as straight and well made as a foxhound, but with long "hare feet," the toes well split up. His head should be round, and the forehead high and monkey-like; nose short, teeth level, jaw square. The eye should be full and black; the ears are small, silky, black, and close to the head. A black mole should be clearly marked on each cheek, with three hairs in each. The mark should be black and positively marked with well-developed wrinkles in the skin; the neck should be strong and thick, devoid of all loose or puckered skin. The chest should be broad, the back and loins wide and

Maltese.

strong, and a black line or "trace" should run down the back to the end of the tail. The tail should be tightly curled over the side or hip, having a second curl, and the point coming out. The ribs should be round—this is a great point, as a ragged or narrow dog of this description is considered deformed.

It will be seen that compact form, pure colour, and

PUG "PRIMROSE KNIGHT."
Winner of many Prizes. The property of Miss Stewart, Southwick, N.B.

distinct marking form the principal points in these dogs; but perhaps hardly any toy dog requires a more experienced eye. As all "toys" are beautiful by comparison, no one can form a correct estimate of a dog's relative value unless he is pretty well informed upon the subject, and the rivalry of breeders leads to one excellent example giving place to another.

A narrow or pointed nose is a very great disfigurement; so is a woolly or dead coat. The coat should be sleek and shining, short, and soft to the touch. Round feet are also bad, so are white toes, or indeed, white anywhere. If the black of the mask melts gradually into grey, and is softened until it mingles with the fawn, the dog loses much of its value.

The *points* of a pug we give below:—Head, 10; ears, 10; pure colour, 15; distinct mask, 10; black trace, 10; cheek moles, 5; quality of coat, 10; curl of tail, 10; compactness, 10; hare feet, 10—total, 100.

The **Maltese Dog** resembles in general appearance a diminutive Skye terrier, differing chiefly in being of much less size, shorter in the back, and far more silky in coat, which should be of the purest white. Most of the breed are very animated in expression, and in every way are well adapted to be made drawing-room pets. Mr. Mandeville, of London, has of late years carried all before him at the various shows, and indeed, has had little opposition, so completely have the claims of his strain been recognised.

This pretty, diminutive animal has long been an especial favourite as a pet or parlour dog, but by some strange absurdity has been commonly spoken of as a terrier, of whose blood not a drop flows in his veins. His pedigree is long, stretching away far back in the annals of the ancient races. Few, if any, older variety exists. History associates them with the high-born dames of Greece and Rome, who lavished large sums on the importation of the Maltese lap-dog. What they were in those days it is impossible to say, as to form, size, colour, coat, and actual weight. Records are strangely wanting, even in the original home of his birth. Nothing of the breed, as we know it at this day, exists in the Island of Malta. As a drawing-room pet, it would be impossible to find a dog so thoroughly adapted for the purpose. Besides being diminutive, he is even-tempered, sagacious, and firm in his attachment. No breed of dog is more cleanly in his habits. He is surprisingly intelligent, rapidly discovers the mind of his teacher, and easily becomes proficient in various feats. He is full of life and spirits, moves with the alertness and grace of the squirrel, and by his innocent cunning and clever antics proves himself an indispensable companion. One of the most perfect dogs of this breed is said to be "Prince Lillywhite," by "Prince Leopold," ex "Queenie." He is the property of Mrs. Watts, of Antwerp House, 48 Lordship Road, Stoke Newington, N.

The *points* are as follows:—Head, closely resembles that of the Skye terrier, but the hair covering the face is more flossy. The general coat is as long also, but more transparent and soft, sometimes running into a fine species of wool; tail carried over the back, but very short with a brush of silky hair. Colour white, with an occasional patch of fawn. Weight, not more than 6 lbs. or 7 lbs., and as much less as possible.

The *points* are:—Colour, 30; coat, 30; nose and eyes, 20; tail and carriage, 15; symmetry, 5.

The **Toy Terrier.**—Each variety of the terrier when bred less than 5, or even 7 lbs., is considered to belong to the toys. If black and tan, the colours should be very distinct and rich, without a speck of white, and on the tan each toe should be pencilled with a fine streak of black, reaching to the knee. This is a point greatly insisted on by fanciers. In other respects the description of this dog already given will apply. Blue and fawn smooth terriers are also prized highly, but they are not so handsome in my opinion as the black and tan. Smooth white terriers should be without a speck of colour; but they show too much of the pink colour of the skin for my taste. These dogs have generally their ears clipped, with tails left perfect, but some people prefer both left as Nature provides them. The rough blue fawn, silky coat terrier, makes a very pretty toy dog, and so does the dwarf bull terrier—both resembling the larger breeds in all points. The Italian greyhound, crossed with the terrier or spaniel, is often passed off as the pure toy terrier, especially the latter, which may be known by the full eye peculiar to the spaniel breed.

The Poodle.—This dog is not unlike the terrier in general conformation, very intelligent, and quick in learning various tricks. In temper he is apt to exhibit peevishness, and even to bite. The colour is black or white, the coat being curly, and, when not cropped, grows inordinately from head to stern, reaching even to the ground. This peculiarity affords opportunity for many owners to practise "trimming" or "clipping," portions here and there being entirely removed, while others are allowed to remain like tufts, circlets on the limbs, or robe-like folds reaching to the ground. The general appearance is then supposed to be greatly enhanced, particularly if the animal is used by the peripatetic player or street conjuror, whose performances admit of ample scope for showing the tricksy capabilities of the animal. The following are the points laid down by the Poodle Club:

The Perfect Black Poodle.—*The General Appearance* is that of a strong, active, and very intelligent dog; well built, and perfectly coated with curls or long ropy "cords." *Head:* Long; the skull large and plenty of room for brain power; wide between the ears and a slight peak; the parts over the eyes well arched; the whole thickly covered with curls or cords. *Muzzle:* Long (but not "snipey"), strong, square, and deep; the "stop" should be defined, but not to a very great extent. The *teeth* should be perfectly level, strong, and white. *Eyes:* Small, dark, and bright, with a very intelligent expression; they should be set at right angles with the line of the face. *Nose:* Large, and perfectly black in colour, with wide open nostrils. *Ears:* Very long, close to the cheek, low set on, and well covered with long ringlets or "curls." *Neck:* Well proportioned, and very strong, to admit of the head being carried high and with dignity. *Chest:* Fairly deep, but not too wide; strong, and well covered with muscles. *Legs:* Forelegs perfectly straight, very muscular, and "set on racing lines;" they should be long enough to raise the body from the ground, but without legginess. Hind legs very muscular, fairly bent, with the hocks well let down. *Feet:* Large, strong, and rather wide, but standing well on the toes, and of good shape; the nails perfectly black, and the pads very strong and hard. *Back:* Short, with body well ribbed up; the loins very strong and muscular, but without fat. *Tail:* Carried at an angle of 45 degrees, having long ringlets or cords hanging down. *Coat:* Thick and strong. If corded, hanging in long, ropy "cords"; if curly, the curls close and thick. *Weight:* Large, 60 lbs.; medium, 40 lbs.; small, 20 lbs. and under.

The Perfect Red Poodle.—*All the foregoing points hold good for this variety, with the following exceptions:*— *Eyes:* Yellow, and free from black rims round the eyelids. *Nose:* Liver colour. *Nails:* Liver colour. *Back:* The ticks (spots) on back should be red or liver, and the whole body should be free from black ticks.

CHAPTER VI.

GENERAL MANAGEMENT OF THE DOG

General management of Dogs—Of Whelps—Dressing—Kennels— Management of pet Dogs.

GENERAL REMARKS.—The management of the greyhound and foxhound as to their kennel management, feeding, exercise, and training, belongs rather to a treatise on sport than to this little book. We therefore refer our readers for information on this subject to *British Rural Sports*, by Stonehenge. Of the treatment necessary for the pointers, setters, spaniels, retrievers, and Newfoundland, we must say a few words.

All these dogs are, in the usual way, chained up to a wooden kennel, with a length of chain which allows of no exercise; and the only advantage which they have over neglected hounds is, that they are generally kept clean for the sake of appearances. But too often they are fed irregularly and on improper food, and almost invariably proper exercise is denied them. For these dogs Indian meal is by far the cheapest and the best kind of food, and with greaves it will keep them in good health, if they are only sufficiently exercised every day. But in many cases horseflesh, being at times very cheap, is given raw, and often unmixed with vegetable food; and the master is then surprised if an eruption appears over the bodies of his dogs, when the chief reason for wonder is that any ever escape, with such a diet to stimulate and inflame their blood, and nothing to carry it off. This improper feeding and neglect of exercise are fertile sources of madness, and should be avoided by all who value their own safety; but besides this motive, which some may perhaps disregard, there is another, which every sportsman will carefully consider, namely, that dogs so mismanaged are almost always deficient in nose. It is very often said that there is no scent for pointers or setters early in the season, but quite as frequently they have not come to their noses, and it is only after a fortnight's work that they carry off the stimulating results of bad feeding. No sporting dog ought ever to be neglected, for he will seldom entirely regain his health, and without a full share of that commodity he will not be capable of making out a scent. Servants, therefore, ought to be well watched during the spring and summer, that the dogs may be attended to by them; and if they do their duty there will be very little reason to complain of birds flushed, or of sore feet, or knocking-up. Sporting dogs (not including greyhounds) will seldom exercise themselves at a fast pace unless they are allowed to hunt; and as this is impossible in the summer, they should be taken out with a man on horseback once or twice a week on the road. Very little flesh should be given them, which is only wanted when they have severe work, and can seldom then be procured. Greaves, with meal, and occasionally potatoes, form the best food; carrots, cabbages, or turnips should be given once or twice a week; and a dose or two of castor oil, salts, or jalap will do good two or three times in the summer, or an aloetic ball.

Management of Whelps.

Coursing will equally apply to other sporting dogs. Few people will take the full amount of trouble which should be bestowed on whelps, but it will suffice if the whelps are sent into the country to be reared at the butcher's, or the tanner's, or at the small wayside public house. When milk or buttermilk can be obtained, it is a good article to rear all whelps upon; but it is seldom afforded to ordinary dogs. The accidents likely to occur in whelping are alluded to in the part on the diseases of the dog.

Dressing.

Dressing with a mixture of sulphur and train oil is very generally adopted every year with sporting dogs, and if they are mismanaged in their feeding, it is absolutely necessary; if, however, they are clean in their skins, it is not required. Soft soap and soda kills their fleas, and white precipitate, ticks; but the latter should only be used with a muzzle on, to guard against its being taken into the stomach by the tongue. Carbolic acid, diluted with twenty or thirty times its bulk of water, likewise kills fleas, but it also requires a muzzle.

Kennels.

Sporting dogs, as, for example, pointers or setters, are often kept in such numbers as to require a kennel or kennels. When such is the case, an open yard paved with glazed tiles or blue bricks must be added, but it is better not covered in. The lodging-room must be in proportion to the number of dogs, but it is better not to have more than three or four together. The whole of this part should be boarded and raised 18 in. or 2 ft., with a lining of board 1 ft. high, to keep the backs of the dogs from the wall. An opening 3 ft. high and 2 ft. wide is left for the dogs to go in and out, and this should be provided with a wooden door, hinged at the top, and kept partly open by Λ-shaped sides, so as to allow the dog to jump up and down freely, and yet keeping the wind and rain from entering. This is a wonderful improvement on kennel doors, which I introduced, and which ought to be generally adopted, as it is the only plan by which kennel beds can be kept clean, and at the same time airy, without admitting the rain and wind. When the bed is to be removed, the door with its sides is lifted up, and the attendant easily enters.

Management of Pet Dogs.

The food of pet dogs is almost always too heating in its nature, considering that they are generally deprived of a proper amount of exercise.

I am sometimes induced for the sake of brevity to recommend correspondents to diet their dogs as they do their children. But unfortunately the latter are also often crammed with all sorts of improper articles of food; and I should perhaps be less liable to mislead my readers if I advised them to give their dogs the same kind of food which they would think right for the children of their acquaintances. Theory and practice are often widely separated, and many a mother is so weak as to allow her own child to tease her into giving creams and pastry, which she would, "on principle," refuse to another not holding the same power over her maternal feelings. We all know how well bachelors' wives and old maids' children are managed, and therefore I would in a few words wind up the general principles of managing pet dogs by suggesting that, if the plans so often recommended by the wise virgins of this world for feeding their nephews and nieces are carried out in favour of pet dogs, a great improvement will be effected in their health and appearance.

To begin with the beginning, however, I will suppose that a puppy six weeks old, and of a breed not exceeding 15 lbs. weight, is presented to one of my readers. What is to be done? First of all, if the weather is not decidedly warm, let it be provided with a warm basket lined with some woollen material, which must be kept scrupulously clean. The little animal must on no account be permitted to have the opportunity of lying on a stone floor, which is a fertile source of disease; bare wood, however, is better than carpet, and oilcloth superior to either on the score of cleanliness. In the winter season the apartment should have a fire, but it is not desirable that the puppy should lie basking close to it, though this is far better than the other extreme. Even in the severest cold a gleam of sunshine does young creatures good, and the puppy should, if possible, be allowed to obtain it through a window in the winter, or without that protection in the summer. It will take exercise enough in playing with a ball of worsted or other materials indoors until it is ten weeks old; but after that time a daily run in the garden or paddock will be of great service, extending to an hour or an hour and a half, but not so as to overtax its limbs. After this age, two or three hours a day, divided into periods of not more than an hour each, will be of service; but it is very seldom that young pet dogs can reckon upon this amount of exercise, and, indeed, it is not by any means necessary to their healthy growth. Until after the tenth week, cow's milk is almost essential to the health of the puppy. It should be boiled and thickened at first with fine wheat flour, and after the eighth week with a mixture of coarse wheat flour and oatmeal. The flour should be gradually increased in quantity, at first making the milk of the thickness of cream, and towards the last adding meal in quantity sufficient to make a spoon stand up in it. If the bowels are relaxed, the oatmeal should be diminished, or if confined, increased. This food, varied with broth made from the scraps of the table, and thickened in the same way, will suffice up to the tenth or twelfth week, after which a little meat, with bread, potatoes, and some green vegetables, may be mixed together and gradually introduced as the regular and staple food. The quantity per day will of course vary according to the size of the puppy; but, as an approximation to the proper weight required, it may be laid down that for each pound the puppy weighs an ounce of moderately solid food will be sufficient. From the time of weaning up to the tenth week it should be fed four times a day; then up to four months, three times; and afterwards twice until full-grown, when a single feed will, in our opinion, conduce to its health, though many prefer going on with the morning and evening supply. When the puppy is full-grown, meat, bread, and vegetables (either potatoes, carrots, cabbage, cauliflower, or parsnips), in equal proportions, will form the proper diet, care being taken to avoid bread made with much alum in it. Dog-biscuits, if sound, answer well for pet dogs; but the quantity required is so small that in most houses the scraps of the bread-basket are quite sufficient. Bones should be supplied daily, for without them not only are the teeth liable to become covered with tartar, but the digestion is impaired for want of a sufficient secretion of saliva.

If the above quality and quantity of food and exercise are given in combination with the protection from cold recommended, the pet puppy will seldom require any medical treatment. Sometimes, in spite of the most careful management, it will be attacked by distemper contracted from some passing dog infected with it; but with this exception, which will not often occur, it may be anticipated that the properly treated pet dog will pass through life without submitting to the attacks of this disease, which is dire in its effects upon this division of the canine race. If care is taken to add oatmeal and green vegetables to the food in quantity sufficient to keep the bowels from being confined, no aperient will ever be required; but sometimes this precaution is neglected, and then recourse must be had either to castor oil or the compound rhubarb pill—the dose being one drop of the former or half a grain of the latter to each pound the puppy weighs. If the oil is stirred up with some milk, the puppy will take it readily enough, and no drenching is required; but care should be taken that the quality is good, and that the oil is not the rank stuff sometimes used in kennels of sporting dogs. The compound rhubarb pill may be given by opening the mouth with the left hand, and then dropping in the pill. It must be boldly pushed well down the throat as far as the finger will reach, no danger being risked in effecting this simple process. If the liver is not acting (which may be known by the absence of the natural gingerbread colour of the evacutions), from half a grain to a grain of blue pill may be added to either dose, and repeated if necessary every day or every other day till the desired effect is produced.

Very young puppies should not be washed even in the summer season, as they are very liable to chill. After they are three months old, however, a bath of warm water, with or without soap, will do good rather than harm, provided that care be taken to dry them well afterwards. For white dogs, white soap is required to give full effect to this operation; and it may be either curd or white soft soap, whichever is preferred, the latter being most effective in cleaning the coat. Long-haired dogs, such as spaniels, the Maltese and Skye terriers, require combing and brushing until they are dry, which should be done in the winter before a fire; and in the latter breeds the coat should be parted down the back with the comb in the most regular manner. If the hair has become matted, a long soaking will be necessary, the comb being used while the part of the dog submitted to its teeth is kept under water, which will greatly facilitate the unrolling of the tangled fibres. After the coat is dry, where great brilliancy is demanded, a very slight dressing of hair-oil may be allowed occasionally; but the brush is the best polisher, and when "elbow-grease" is not spared, a better effect will be produced than by bear's grease at half-a-crown a pot.

With the exception of fleas, pet dogs ought never to be infested with any vermin. Sometimes, however, they catch from others either lice or the ticks which infest the canine race. The appearance of the first two parasites is well known to every one; but the tick is not among the things commonly presented to the eye, and we may therefore mention that it may be known by its spider-like shape, and by its close adhesion to the skin by means of its legs, with which it digs into the surface. In size it varies from that of the head of a small pin to the magnitude of a small grain of wheat, but not being so long in proportion to its width. The colour changes with that of the dog, and with the quantity of blood imbibed, which always gives a greater or less tint of bluish red; but in very young ticks the colour is a pearly grey. In destroying fleas, the best remedy is the insect-destroying powder sold by Butler and M'Culloch, of Covent Garden, and by Keating, of St. Paul's Churchyard, which may be well rubbed in without fear of consequences. Lice and ticks require a stronger drug to destroy them, and this should be used with more care, as, being a mercurial preparation, it is liable to be absorbed if the skin is wetted, and then produces serious mischief, accompanied by salivation; or, if the dog is allowed to lick himself, this effect is still more likely to follow. The dog should therefore be kept carefully from all wet for at least twelve hours, and during the application of the remedy it should either be carefully watched and prevented by the hand from licking itself, or it should be muzzled. The remedy is white precipitate, in powder, well rubbed into the roots of the hair over the whole body, and left on for six hours, after which it should be brushed out. At the expiration of the week the application should be repeated, and possibly it may be required a third time; but this is seldom needed.

CHAPTER VII.

DISEASES OF THE DOG.

General Observations — Health and Disease — Pathology — Fever: Simple, Symptomatic and Specific — Inflammation — Abscess — Serous Cyst — Prevention of Disease — Classification of Disease.

THE public health is largely determined by the condition of our domestic animals, notably those which minister to the wants of mankind as a provision for daily food. Although the dog does not figure in the general influences exerted in that direction, he is in other respects, as the close companion of mankind, capable of developing somewhat dismal consequences. To maintain a uniform standard of health is an absolute necessity; otherwise, not that only, but the lives of the human population are laid under serious peril.

The knowledge acquired by companionship with our domestic animals is first evident in our judgment of their being in health. Subsequently, and often by mere intuition, we discover the antithesis, and acquire the power to interpret the sign language of disorder and disease. The "Bloom of Health" is a state which the experienced in canine lore comprehend at a glance. The clear bright eye, sleek coat, maintenance of general function, cool, moist, and sweet odour of the mouth and breath, dewy state of the muzzle and general vivacity, present a spectacle on which a true lover of the lower animals will gaze with unwearied delight. On the other hand, the signs of disorder are readily comprehended by similar intelligence. They are recognised by their being the reverse of health and spirits. The animal is dull, heavy and listless, the coat, having lost its sleek and glossy appearance, is more or less dull, dry, harsh, or staring, and probably fouled by accumulations of scurf and dirt which the creature does not care to remove. The mouth is probably hot, foul, and dry, or slimy, and the breath fœtid. The functions of secretion and excretion are irregular or suspended, and the fæces are hard, small, irregular, and probably offensive; the urine is also deficient, highly coloured, and emits an odour not consistent with health. To these may be added coldness of the ears and legs, a hot, dry muzzle, &c., all of which suffer more or less modification or intensity with specific additions enforced by the various organs involved.

With regard to *appetite or taste*, the dog is not a clean animal. Designed by Nature as the scavenger of the earth, he devours the most disgusting filth with obvious enjoyment, and digests his dainty morsel without suffering systemic disturbance. Notwithstanding, he lays claim to the possession of a depraved appetite under disease, and, to satisfy the morbid demand, hesitates not to swallow sticks, stones, sand, paper, rags, and the filthiest of decomposing material, even human excrement, or that of other dogs as well as his own.

The department of science which determines the state of an animal under disease, and defines its nature, is known as *Pathology*. In order to realise the various morbid conditions which are comprehended within a given word, the practitioner resorts to numerous methods of observation, specific testing, and comparison of the several signs exhibited by the suffering animal. The *usual* signs of disturbance are first carefully noted, and often by negative forms of examination he may decide which organs are free from morbid disturbance, while others exhibit special indications which lead conclusively to their identification with some unusual process. This property of acquiring information during life is greatly assisted by examination after death, the morbid processes revealed by *Pathological Anatomy* being highly useful in turning the attention of the practitioner to the diseased organs during life.

In the *treatment of disease* the department of *Materia Medica*, or the nature, actions, uses and doses of medicines, as well as their legitimate combinations affords a vast amount of usefulness. In ignorant hands medicines often prove as so many violent poisons; great care and sound judgment are therefore essential in all cases, but especially when the amateur aspires to the office of physician and surgeon.

As a preliminary to the study of general diseases, we turn to a consideration of *fever, inflammation*, &c.

Fever, as understood by the practitioner, consists of a general disturbance of the vital functions, in which the system is bordering on a state of more serious derangement, which, if not checked, is eventually located in some important organ, and *confirmed disease* is the inevitable result. Three kinds of fever are recognised—viz., *Simple* or *ephemeral*, *Symptomatic* or *sympathetic*, and *Specific*.

Simple Fever is defined as the short-lived, or ephemeral disturbance common to highly-fed and pampered animals, taking little or no out-door exercise, and subjected to a close, warm atmosphere, and soft downy beds. All the animal functions, as respiration, circulation, temperature, &c., are accelerated, and a hot, dry mouth is associated with constipation and diminished secretions generally. Such conditions are by continuous occurrence developed into serious diseases, and should be met with the needful remedies, as more frequent exercise in the open air, a less stimulating diet, and the substitution of laxative materials. This form of disorder is too frequently neglected, the result being that local or general states of a congestive nature are induced, followed by slow and insidious structural changes in important organs, which finally end in serious disease or death.

Sympathetic or Symptomatic Fever is a form of aggravated disturbance of the system consequent upon the development of disease in some important organ, or set of organs, and may be thus defined: severe accidents, such as fracture of one or more limbs, ribs, &c., producing violent shock, the whole system is seriously disturbed, and by nervous sympathy the functions are deranged or suspended. In such cases the lungs as a rule suffer acutely by congestion or engorgement with blood, or they are inflamed, and the disease being violent the effects upon the system, already influenced by the initial shock, is more than it can bear, death arising, not from the result of the original injury, but from the impediment raised within the circulatory system. In other words, the *constitutional disturbance* in its magnitude and severity is the cause of death, and being the indication of the serious nature of the original injury, it is understood as being *symptomatic* in its real nature.

Specific Fever is a similar, but more frequently a milder, form of constitutional disturbance, resulting from some form of animal poison within the system, and propagated by contact with other subjects of the disease. Contagious fevers supply the needed examples, which differ from the subjects in the preceding class in their slow and insidious nature as a rule, the absence of violent shock, and few sudden deaths.

Treatment of Fever.—The rule is embodied in the apt expression: "Remove the cause and the effects will cease." This is an easy procedure with *Simple Fever*. Change of diet, lodging, a supply of fresh air, light, and water; more frequent exercise, cleanliness, friction to the skin, &c., will usually effect the desirable changes; or when the causes have been long applied, a moderate purgative, or a dose of alkaline medicine, is probably effectual. As regards *Symptomatic Fever* the case is widely different. The causes are more powerful and destructive. We cannot replace arteries, veins, and nerves, as well as muscular and other tissues destroyed or disorganised by violence in one form or other, or forces of the most subtle character which wait upon injury and disease in all their fulness and potency for evil.

Inflammation.—The infallible signs are *heat, pain, redness,* and *swelling*. The first and second are usually evident, but owing to the dense covering of hair in many animals, redness and swelling are not so readily observed. In small pet animals, with light-coloured or white coats and thin skin, the difficulties are not so great. Inflammation is the result of violent causes, consisting of an increase of blood in the affected part, with more or less suspension of function in the contiguous structures, as well as in the integral parts of the blood itself. *Acute Inflammation* is characterised by severity and activity; it is *atonic* or *subacute*, when by reason of low vital force it proves slow or tardy. Closely allied to this state is a peculiarity of the circulation, common to the larger organs having abundant vessels and elastic tissue, known as *Congestion*. It is sudden in its origin and departure, sometimes attended with dropsical states, and is probably confined to the venous system.

Inflammation terminates in various ways—viz., *Resolution*, or gradual decline, the parts shortly regaining their original state; in *suppuration*, or the formation of *pus*, in some cases discharged from the surface of membranes, as in catarrh, or otherwise collected within a cavity between muscles, or in deep-seated tissues, when it is known as an *abscess;* in *effusion* from the surface of membranes, as water (serum), or mucus, or by lymph within or between structures inflamed, by which permanent union, thickening and enlargement is the result. Inflammation is further distinguished by the structures involved : thus, we have *serous* and *mucous* inflammation, as the serous and mucous membranes are implicated ; when the substance of organs is the seat, it is known as *parenchymatous ;* if it seizes the ligaments, tendons, and coverings of joints, it is *rheumatic ;* and inflammation of the skin and deeper-seated tissues is termed *erysipelatous*.

Treatment of Inflammation may be *local* or *general*. The former consists of liberating the vessels of the affected parts by *scarification* or slight incisions across the surface by means of a small lancet, as in conjunctival ophthalmia, or by means of blisters, the hot iron, &c., in the case of important organs. *General treatment* consists of attacking the system by internal remedies known to be efficacious in controlling the circulation and nervous force.

Abscess.—The collection of *pus*, or matter, within a cavity in soft parts of the body, is termed an *abscess*. The signs are heat, unusual tenderness, and defined swelling ; and as the process of pus formation matures, the swelling and tenderness are confined to the central part, which becomes first moist, then denuded of hair, and, later, by internal absorption or ulceration of the skin; the contents, now become fluid, are readily felt by the fingers. Internal pressure, the result of pus formation, and the action of contiguous muscles, &c., now causes the abscess to bulge outwards, and ultimately forces the skin at the weakest part, when the contents are evacuated.

Treatment.—The maturation of an abscess often causes much pain and systemic disturbance, and to avoid this the surgeon, after investigation, detecting the presence of pus, hastens the process of recovery by plunging a lancet through the point where maturation is evident. Thus, as a rule, ends the malady. With the evacuation of the contents healing proceeds rapidly and safely, all that is required being the usual means of cleanliness to prevent the accumulation of dried pus or dirt around the orifice. In the case of deep-seated abscesses, or those situate below or between muscles some distance from the surface, much judgment and skill are required in order to decide upon the exact locality, and the requisite form of surgical treatment which can neither be understood nor practised by an amateur, and, therefore, calls for no farther comment here.

Serous Cyst, otherwise known as **Serous Abscess**, is mostly located superficially, and is the result of blows, falls, or severe local pressure. It is not of frequent occurrence in the dog, neither serious in its nature nor consequences. The contents being *serum* or a red-coloured fluid, having the density of water or thereabouts, the produce of the blood-vessels involved in the injury, the accumulation is regulated by the surface involved. Absorption of the contents is also delayed by the formation of a dense lining membrane of cellular tissue, and the swelling may remain for weeks or months.

Treatment consists of liberating the contents of the sac by means of a lancet or curved bistoury. The former is plunged through the centre, and the orifice widened as the instrument is withdrawn. The bistoury is preferable, being passed through the skin on one side and across to the opposite, when it emerges; it is then turned edge upwards, and the whole skin between the two points is divided. Pressure is next applied by means of a pad of soft tow, &c., saturated with some healing fluid, and renewed from time to time as cleaning is carried out.

Prevention of Disease.—This is a department of social economics which is regarded more frequently as Utopian than real, or possible, from the circumstance of its introduction within recent years. The usual plan has been for every man to do that which seemeth right in his own eyes, a legacy which we have come to regard as sacred, and not to be interfered with by others. This excessive liberty is the cause of our towns and villages being infested by numbers of dogs, whose sole use and purpose is to annoy the inhabitants by their furious barkings, and numerous attacks on the person, especially of children, and on other dogs under enforced control. Besides this, the animals breed indiscriminately, and the progeny are a nondescript race, which "walk in the ways of their forefathers," or when opportunity serves they are ruthlessly drowned in some river or ditch, where the bodies lie rotting and polluting the water and atmosphere to the great disgust of pedestrians seeking open air exercise. *Like produces like.* Thus all the defects of race are handed down by the careless mating of animals, including the idiosyncrasies of their nature, which in most cases determine the hereditary latency of disease. If we desire strong and healthy animals, the parents must be sound. *Regularity of Feeding* is also an important item. Without this, the process of digestion is interfered with, and the assimilative powers weakened, by which nutritive material is imperfectly transformed, more frequently proving deleterious than nourishing or sustaining. *Fresh Air and Cleanliness* have a large share in the maintenance of health. The effect of the former on the blood is to facilitate the process of combustion or formation of animal heat. Thus, not only the rich principles of food, but the deleterious portions, with the effete or waste products of the body are burned and suitably transformed to ensure their expulsion by the proper channels from the system. The effect of cleanliness is to promote the movement of fresh air. Foul and dark habitations interfere with true ventilation. The system breathes the poison thus generated, which acts as a powerful sedative on all the functions of animal life, predisposing it to diseased conditions. The system, in other words, acts like a sponge, and constantly imbibing impure elements, becomes fertile soil in which the seeds of disease may find the needful sustenance of their nature. *Regular Exercise in the Open Air*, apart from actual work, is essential for the promotion of organic function, many varieties of which are going on incessantly, besides eating and drinking. Food and exercise produce waste, the latter being mainly essential in the process of eliminating the waste, as the result of consumption of the first. *Systematic Feeding* is also essential. The character of the food should vary with work and rest. When animals come from hard work to partial or complete idleness, the food should be suitably changed. Rich aliment as flesh, should be replaced by smaller allowances, the usual bulk being supplied by adding vegetables, as boiled greens or potatoes, &c. Linseed mucilage may be suitably added to meal, porridge, &c., when the fæces are dry and hard. If they should become darkcoloured, or black, and offensive, which may arise from the ingestion of raw, decaying animal food, as dead rabbits, &c., a dose of the castor-oil mixture, or simply raw linseed oil, should be given, containing 5 to 60 drops of the "Sanitas Fluid." The *Abuse of Medicines* is a constant source of ill health in many establishments. Proper food, water, and rest, will often do more good than medicines, which should never be given without a clear knowledge of the requirements of the case and their suitability for it. *Frequent and Indiscriminate Drugging* is the basis on which blatant quackery thrives. Those who practise the first are responsible for the latter, and have no cause to complain when their malady becomes intolerable. Lastly, *the means of promoting health* includes the use of good and reliable antiseptics, the effect of which is the destruction of offensive odours, which act powerfully through the medium of respiration, and subsequent absorption by the blood. Our experience of "Sanitas" preparations is such that we confidently recommend them as especially suitable for kennel use in a variety of ways, as specified in the directions which accompany the various forms.

Classification of Disease.—In order to present the subject in a simple and comprehensive form, we have arranged the maladies of the dog, as far as possible, in accordance with their supposed nature and causes: thus, many are conveniently included under the head of Blood Diseases; others as due to Specific, or Contagious elements; while the majority, probably arising from interference with normal organic function, injury, &c., are more conveniently dealt with in their respective classes.

CHAPTER VIII.

MATERIA MEDICA.

The Dispensing of Medicines—Nursing—Doses of Medicines—Alteratives—Anodynes—Antiseptics—Antispasmodics—Aperients—Astringents—Blisters—Caustics—Clysters, Enemas, or Injections—Cordials—Demulcents—Diaphoretics—Digestives—Diuretics—Electuaries—Embrocations or Liniments—Emetics—Expectorants—Febrifuges—Fomentations—Hypodermic Injections—Inhalations—Lotions—Ointments—External Parasiticides—Poultices—Stimulants—Stomachics—Styptics—Tonics—Worm Medicines: Internal Parasiticides.

THE continuation, as well as the proportions of remedies for the treatment of disease, are details which demand careful attention. In ignorance of the exact nature and action, &c., of drugs on the animal body, strange and often baneful compounds are prescribed. By simple mixture they may become inert, or possibly a deadly poison. The truth should be kept in view by all who prescribe without the needful intelligence which a lengthened study of the subject provides.

The following are examples of each class of remedies suitable for the dog, and to render the plan of admixture as well as administration intelligible, reliable formulæ are given, from which the reader may suitably make choice.

The Dispensing of Medicines.—Canine pharmacy is a department of no little importance. Next to the selection of suitable remedies ranks the judicious compounding and admixture, an art which can only be acquired by great experience of the nature and properties of drugs.

Medicines are prescribed in several forms—viz., the *bolus*, or *pill*, *electuary* and *draught*. These are administered by the mouth. In some cases it is advisable to administer remedies in the form of *enemas*, or by *subcutaneous injections* (see p. 132).

The *bolus*, or *pill*, is a compound of two or more remedies, which, after being reduced to fine powder, are worked into a plastic mass by means of honey, treacle, &c., to the requisite size, and subsequently covered with fine paper. The latter is often indispensable in order to prevent nausea, which may cause rejection of the dose. The *form of the pill* may be cylindrical, or spherical. In the first the paper is rolled on to the mass and tucked in at the ends. A spherical pill is placed in the middle of a small square of thin or tissue paper, when the circumferent edges are drawn together and twisted to a point.

To *administer a pill* the dog is taken on the knee, supported by the left arm placed across the shoulder, while the left hand seizes the lower jaw, the thumb and fingers being pressed on each side of the mouth. This has the effect in most cases of separating the jaws, when the lower is quickly and firmly grasped, and simultaneously the pill, held between the thumb and forefinger of the right hand, is passed to the back of the tongue. At the same moment the grasp of the lower jaw is removed, and the fingers and thumb secure both upper and lower jaws with firmness, yet without absolute punishment. The result as a rule is that the dog swallows almost immediately the jaws are approximated. If he fails to do so a few gentle passes of the forefinger over the front of the nostrils will hasten the needed result. Older dogs often become experienced patients in deception, sometimes feigning to swallow, and on their release will walk to a distance and calmly eject the pill, not simply once, but frequently. Some practitioners seize the jaws from above by the left hand, and press the cheeks on each side into the mouth, thus causing the animal to separate the jaws. It is obvious that only small dogs can be thus treated. Large animals are usually held between the knees, while assistants, by means of a tape or cord looped behind the tusks, forcibly separate the jaws.

The *Electuary* is a semi-soft or pasty preparation, the base of which is honey, treacle, &c., containing the needful remedy. Successive portions are placed on the tongue, which the creature seldom dislikes, and during the consequent insalivation pass to the stomach (see p. 128).

The *Draught*.—This is a fluid mixture containing the requisite quantity of each remedy, the whole of which is to be given as one dose. A *mixture* is usually understood to be two, three, or more doses, for the apportionment of which specific directions are given.

To *administer a draught* the operator proceeds as follows: Fairly manageable animals are taken on the knee by an assistant, who steadies the head by means of the left hand, the thumb being placed across the nose, and the fingers beneath the lower branches. The operator inserts one finger of the left hand into the angle of the cheek of the *right* side, and drawing it away from the teeth a suitable pouch is formed, into which the fluid is poured in successive quantities as the animal swallows. Small and even some large dogs are often successfully managed by practitioners without any assistance. The medicine, being prepared, is put into a one or twoounce bottle, and manipulated by the right hand. The dog is raised to the knees, encircled by the left arm, and the nose firmly held by the left hand. The mouth of the bottle is placed within the angle of the lip of the *right* side, when the thumb presses from the outside, the effect being to capture the cheek, draw it from the teeth, and form a pouch, into which the fluid is gently poured in successive quantities as the animal swallows. By care and tact many dogs may be treated for severe illness during lengthened periods without tiring or rendering them obstinate or vicious.

Nursing.—The importance of careful nursing cannot be overstated. The term, although of acknowledged scope, is minus one important essential. Plenty of food, water, warmth, or ventilation, cleanliness, &c., are liberally conceded, but the creature mopes and pines, making no progress; some, indeed, die, because the surroundings are ungenial. Perhaps the attendant is not so studious of the state and requirements of the patient as he should be, neglect and coarse treatment having the effect of rendering the sufferer absolutely miserable. We have a somewhat extensive and vivid experience of the value of gentleness and kindness to canine patients. They are exceedingly susceptible to kindly treatment, and frequently yield obedience to a firm and salutary discipline, the effects of which are evident in the memory of the animal during long subsequent periods.

In the various formulæ now to be considered, the maximum or full dose is intended for mature dogs of the Setter and Retriever class; one-half for other breeds half their size and weight, and one-third, one-fourth, or even one-sixth, &c., for puppies and the breeds of corresponding diminutive proportions.

The Bloodhound, St. Bernard, Mastiff and the like, will require double, three-fourths, or one-half in addition to the proportions laid down for Setters, size and age being considered.

Alteratives.—A variety of substances are included under the term which is neither precise nor commendable. It is usually understood to refer to remedies which restore healthy functions to organs previously disordered. If the definition be correct, *all* remedies are alteratives.

1. Sublimed sulphur, 5 grs.; powdered nitre or saltpetre, 1 gr.; linseed meal, 1 or 2 grs.; lard or palm-oil, sufficient to incorporate the whole as a pill.

The above ingredients may be given in form of a

draught, in which case the lard or palm-oil is omitted, and the dry powders are mixed in a tablespoonful of linseed tea or thin gruel.

2. Æthiops mineral, 2 to 5 grs.; powdered ginger, ½ to 1 gr.; powdered rhubarb, 1 to 3 grs. Mix, and form a pill with syrup, to be given every evening.

3. Plummer's pill, 2 to 5 grs.; extract of hemlock, 2 to 5 grs. Mix, and give every night.

Such remedies are usually made use of during slight febrile conditions, attended with defective appetite, slight liver disorder, &c.

Anodynes.—These are remedies which allay pain, and soothe the nervous system. In this way they remove spasm, as in colic, diarrhœa, tetanus, &c. Opium, belladonna, hyoscyamus, &c., are chief examples.

1. For *Simple Diarrhœa.*—Prepared chalk, 2 drms.; aromatic confection, 1 drm.; tincture of opium, 5 to 8 drms.; rice water, or cool flour gruel, 8 oz. Mix. Dose, two tablespoonfuls after each fluid evacuation.

2. *Continued Diarrhœa.*—Dilute sulphuric acid, 3 drms.; tincture of opium, 2 drms.; compound tincture of bark, 1 oz.; water, 6½ oz. Mix. Two tablespoonfuls every four hours.

3. Castor or linseed oil, 2 oz.; tincture of opium, 1 oz. Mix by agitation. Dose, a tablespoonful night and morning during the diarrhœa.

4. Powdered opium, ½ to 2 grs.; prepared chalk, 5 to 10 grs.; catechu, 5 grs.; powdered ginger and powdered carraway seeds, of each, 1 to 3 grs. Mix, and form a pill with simple syrup, and give every three hours.

5. "Sanitas" Fluid in doses of 10 to 30 or 80 drops, in cold whey, flour gruel, mixed with the usual medicine, is an invaluable agent in the protracted forms of diarrhœa attended with offensive odours.

6. For *Cramps or Spasms.*—Powdered opium, ½ to 2 grs.; spirit of chloroform 10 to 20 drops; camphor 3 to 10 grs. Mix, and give in a tablespoonful of glycerine.

Antiseptics.—Antiseptics, or Antiputrescents, are agents which prevent the septic or putrescent stage, and thus arrest or destroy the noxious odours which are the result of putrefaction. They are largely called for in maintaining the purity of dwellings where the lower animals are retained, especially when contagious diseases are present, or offensive effluvia arise from the bad state of the floor or drains, and to cleanse woodwork, &c., fouled by animal discharges. When used for the latter purposes they are known as *deodorisers* or *disinfectants*.

1. "*Sanitas*" *Oil* stands pre-eminent for service in any of the above-named departments when used in accordance with the simple instructions furnished with each supply. It has also a useful place in the treatment of some internal diseases attended with putrid discharges, as diarrhœa, metritis, cystitis, &c. For this purpose, and also for promoting the healing of wounds, "Sanitas" Oil has been employed in the following form :

2. *Antiseptic Mixture.*—"Sanitas" Oil, 2 parts ; glycerine, 4 parts ; olive oil, 6 parts. Mix, and agitate thoroughly, and keep in a well-corked bottle.

3. "*Sanitas*" *Fluid* is even more portable for many purposes, needing only admixture with water or glycerine for internal or external use.

4. *Condy's Fluid* is also effective when applied as directed.

5. Any of the mineral acids, as sulphuric, nitric, muriatic, or acetic, diluted with 100 parts of water, form useful antiseptic lotions for wounds and chronic discharges.

6. Chloride of zinc, 3 grs.; distilled water, 1 oz. To form a lotion, or as No. 8.

7. Lunar caustic, 5 grs. ; distilled water, 1 oz. To form a lotion, or as No. 8.

8. Solution of sulphurous acid applied by the spray producer, or as a lotion.

Antispasmodics.—Medicines of this class are also anodynes (which see). They have the property of allaying spasm or cramp ; hence the name.

1. Tincture of opium and sulphuric ether, of each, 5 to 60 drops; camphor mixture, $1\frac{1}{2}$ drms. to 1 oz. Mix, and give every two hours, during the attack.

2. *Injection.*—Tincture of opium, tincture of belladonna,

Aperients.—Aperients are mild, gentle purges. They are also known as *laxatives;* and when required in powerful form are termed *cathartics*.

1. *A Mild Oleaginous Purge.*—Castor oil, 4 drms. to 1½ fluid oz. N.B.—For young dogs equal parts of castor and linseed oil forms the best purgative.

2. *Castor Oil Mixture.*—Castor oil, 3 parts; syrup of buckthorn, 2 parts; syrup of white poppies, 1 part. Dose, 1 dessert to 1 tablespoonful. Shake well before administration.

3. *Active Aperient.*—Powdered jalap, 1 to 3 or 4 scruples; calomel ½ to 2 grs.

4. *Blue, or Liver Pill.*—Blue pill, 5 grs.; powdered colchicum, 6 grs.; extract of colocynth, 10 grs. Full dose.

5. *Liver Pill, No. 2.*—Blue pill, 5 grs.; compound extract of colocynth, 10 grs.; oil of peppermint, or oil of cloves, 3 to 6 drops.

Astringents.—Medicines of this class constrict animal tissue, acting directly when applied to the part, or remotely when administered by the mouth or rectum.

1. *Mixtures for Internal Use.*—Tincture of opium, 25 drops; powdered catechu, 15 grs.; flour or powdered starch, 2 drms. Mix, and administer promptly.

2. Powdered opium, 3 grs.; powdered alum, 10 to 15 grs.; ground ginger, 20 grs.; strong tea, 2 fluid ozs.

Dissolve the alum in the tea, and add the other ingredients.

Nos. 1 and 2 are useful in protracted diarrhœa, &c. When the evacuations are offensive, 5 to 10 drops to 1 teaspoonful of "Sanitas" fluid may be added.

Astringent Boluses for the dog useful in—

3. *Diabetes or Hæmorrhage.*—Powdered opium, 2 to 3 grs.; gallic acid, 4 to 6 grs.; alum, 5 to 10 grs.; powdered bark, 10 grs. Linseed meal, enough to form a bulus, to be given to a large dog (or divided for a small one) two or three times a day.

4. Nitrate of silver, ½ gr. Crumb of bread, enough to make a small pill, to be given twice a day, or divided according to the size of the dog.

5. *Astringent Wash for the Eyes.*—Sulphate of zinc, 5 to 8 grs.; water, 2 oz. Mix.

6. Goulard extract, 1 drm.; water, 1 oz. Mix.

7. Nitrate of silver, 2 to 8 grs.; water, 1 oz. Mix.

8. *Wash for the Penis.*—Sulphate of zinc, 6 to 10 grs.; water, 1 oz. Mix.

9. Chloride of zinc, ½ to 1½ gr.; water, 1 oz. Mix.

10. *Astringent Ointment for Piles.*—Gallic acid, 10 grs.; goulard extract, 15 drops; lard, 1 oz. Mix.

Blisters.—Blisters are irritant applications designed to produce inflammatory action in the skin. Their action, when continued, is attended with the formation of vesicles, or bladders, by which deeper-seated disease is overcome. They are also known as *counter-irritants*. Prompt rising of the blister is essential to successful treatment; if these results are delayed or absent, the original disease proves refractory, and fatal issues may be expected.

1. *Fluid Blister.*—Olive oil, 20 parts; powdered cantharides, 1 part. Mix, and heat in a water bath for 2 hours, then stand aside to cool. The fluid is then separated by straining through fine muslin, after which add 2 drms. of oil of origanum. Apply a small quantity, and rub well into the skin before the application is repeated, otherwise the fluid will gravitate to lower portions and produce unnecessary irritation.

2. *Blistering Ointment.*—Powdered cantharides, 1 part; pure lard, 8 parts. Mix. This should be prepared sometime before use.

3. Powerful and immediate action, when called for in severe inflammation of important organs, may be induced by the application of a rag saturated in spirit of turpentine, or solution of ammonia, which should be covered with a piece of oil-skin or paper, and closely applied.

4. *Mild Blister Ointment* (counter-irritant).—Hog's lard, 4 oz.; Venice turpentine, 1 oz.; powdered cantharides, 6 drms. Mix, and spread.

5. *Stronger Blister Ointment* (counter-irritant).—Spirit

of turpentine, 1 oz.; hog's lard, 4 oz.; powdered cantharides, 1 oz. Mix, and spread.

6. *Very Strong Blister* (counter-irritant).—Strong mercurial ointment, 4 oz.; oil of origanum, ½ oz.; finely-powdered euphorbium, 3 drms.; powdered cantharides, ½ oz. Mix, and spread.

7. *Rapidly Acting Blister* (counter-irritant).—Best flour of mustard, 8 oz., made into a paste with water. Add spirit of turpentine, 2 oz.; strong liquid of ammonia, 1 oz. This is to be well rubbed into the chest, belly, or back, in cases of acute inflammation.

8. *Sweating Blister.*—Strong mercurial ointment, 2 oz.; oil of origanum, 2 drms.: corrosive sublimate, 2 drms.; cantharides powdered, 3 drms. Mix, and rub in with the hand.

9. *Tincture of Iodine*, which should be painted on with a brush daily, until it causes the cuticle to exfoliate. It may then be omitted for a few days, to be resumed after that interval.

Caustics.—Substances capable of exerting chemical action on the living tissues are known as caustics, such action being simply burning or decomposition. The most familiar example is the *actual* or *potential cautery*, or heated iron. Chemical agents as caustic soda, caustic potash, and lunar caustic, or nitrate of silver, are also variously employed. The general use is to stimulate indolent wounds, repress luxuriant granulations, also removing tumours, or parts destroyed by sloughing, and arresting the flow of blood from injured vessels.

1. *Caustic Potash* is conveniently sold in sticks or pencils, and requires a suitable holder for operating with it. Its action is prompt and powerful, but being liable to become fluid when exposed to the atmosphere, its use is sometimes limited.

2. *Lunar Caustic*, or nitrate of silver, is by far the most manageable, and effective. It is sold in pencil form, and also requires a holder of silver or platinum for its preservation.

3. Sulphate of copper, burnt alum, verdigris, red precipitate, and corrosive sublimate are used in powder as

dry caustics. The last is often a dangerous remedy in the hands of unskilled persons.

4. Muriate, or butyr of antimony, is a powerful caustic, useful for fungoid growths, &c. The addition of water effectually destroys it. When dilution is needed, tincture of myrrh is the proper agent.

5. Sulphuric, nitric, muriatic, and acetic acids are also powerful caustics, and with No. 4, are usually applied by means of a small mop of cotton wool.

Caustic Lotions are made of any required degree of strength, by the addition of water as follows:

6. Nitrate of silver, 3 to 15 grs. per ounce.

7. Corrosive sublimate, 3 to 10 grs.; muriatic acid, $\frac{1}{2}$ fluid drm.; cold distilled water, $7\frac{1}{2}$ fluid drms. An effective remedy for fistulous sinuses, indolent tumours, &c.

8. Sulphate of copper, 3 to 6 drms.; sulphuric acid, $\frac{1}{2}$ fluid drm.; water, one pint.

9. Chloride of zinc, 3 to 5 grs.; muriatic acid, 3 to 5 drops; distilled water, 1 fluid oz.

Caustic Ointments find their base in hog's lard, vaseline, cocoa butter, &c.

10. Verdigris, finely powdered, 1 to 3 or 4 oz. of one or other of the bases named.

11. Sulphate of copper, finely powdered, 1 oz.; to 3 or 4.

12. Burnt alum, 1 oz. to 3 or 4. Mix, in each case causing thorough incorporation.

Clysters, Enemas or Injections.—Two kinds of clyster are in common use, fluid and gaseous. The first are used to unload the rectum, remove obstruction, relieve spasm, and promote intestinal action in debility; also to convey nutritious fluids to the bowels during the process of wasting disease; gaseous enemas are effective in allaying spasm, as in colic, &c.

1. *Warm fluid clysters* are constituted as follows: They are used at a temperature of 90° to 100° F. Soft, or hard soap, 2 drms. Cover the soap with boiling water, and when the former is dissolved, add sufficient cold to secure the above-named temperatures. Inject a teacupful as required.

2. Common salt may be substituted for the soap when a direct irritant action is required.

3. *Medicated enemas* consist of some remedy added to warm water, beef-tea, linseed mucilage, &c.

4. Flour, oatmeal, gruel, or beef-tea, 4 or 5 fluid ozs., spirits of nitrous ether, 2 to 4 drms. Useful when the animal is unable to take food.

5. Tincture of opium, 1 fluid oz.; powdered catechu, 4 drms.; solution of starch, as used in the laundry,

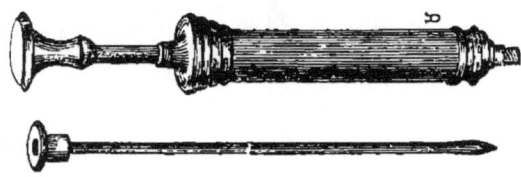

Enema Syringe.

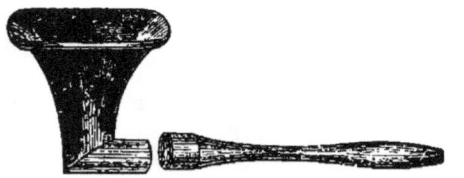

Enema Funnel.

thickened by boiling, 1 pint. Mix, and inject one-fourth part as needful in persistent diarrhœa, dysentery, &c.

6. *Gaseous Enema.*—In some instances the fumes of burning opium are useful as a means of reducing spasm in colic and other affections of the bowels, but in all cases the treatment calls for the greatest care.

Enema Funnel.—Various forms of apparatus are used for administering an enema, the simplest being the common funnel shown in figure annexed. The pipe, first smeared with simple lard, oil, or soap, is carefully passed within the intestine to the extent of two inches. The bowl being upwards is filled with successive portions of the fluid, which readily disappear with a gurgling sound. In some instances a syringe, a cut of which is also given, is made use of, the fluid being passed into the intestines by means of pressure. Both instruments are to be obtained from Messrs. Arnold & Sons, 31, West Smithfield, E.C.

Cordials.—The various warm aromatic seeds, ginger, pepper, &c., are included in this term; also fluids, as nitric ether, &c., in certain instances. The seeds are employed in the form of powder to assist the action of mineral tonics in recovery from severe illness; and the latter is added to enemas to assist the general action when needful, or given by the mouth with tincture of cardamoms.

1. *Cordial Pills.*—Powdered carraway seeds, $1\frac{1}{2}$ drms.; ginger, 20 to 40 grs.; oil of cloves, 3 to 8 drops. Mix. Make 10 to 20 pills.

2. *Cordial Drench.*—Tincture of cardamoms, 1 drm.; aromatic spirits of ammonia, 1 drm.; infusion of gentian, 1 drm.; camphor mixture, 1 oz. Mix. Divide into doses of 1 or 2 drms., as needful, and give in linseed mucilage. *See* Demulcents.

3. Liquorice powder, $\frac{1}{2}$ oz.; gum ammoniacum, 3 drms.; balsam of Tolu, $1\frac{1}{2}$ drm.; powdered squill, 1 drm. Linseed meal and boiling water, enough to form into a mass, and make into 12 or 24 pills, or draughts as No. 2.

Demulcents. — These are a useful class of agents, although destitute of any specific medicinal action. They are, more correctly speaking, foods, which, containing a large amount of mucilage, render them useful as mechanical agents in providing a thick smooth protective covering to irritable and inflamed tissues, notably the intestinal mucous membrane, and those lining the lungs, kidneys, bladder, &c.

1. *Linseed Mucilage.*—Linseed, 4 oz.; cold water, 1 quart. Mix, cover up and set aside, frequently agitating. In twenty-four hours it is ready for use. Add warm water as required.

2. The above quantities may be boiled to expedite the bursting of the seeds, and used when cool.

3. Marshmallows, a double handful; boiling water, 1 quart. Strain, and use when cool.

4. Gum arabic, finely powdered, 4 oz.; water, 1 pint. Mix, and agitate frequently, until a mucilage is formed, and administer 2 to 4 oz. for a dose.

Diaphoretics.—The power of promoting transpiration from the skin of the dog, as in man or the horse, is a matter of extreme doubt. The only reliable method of accelerating the normal functions is by a judicious use of stimulants, as ammonia, assisted by warm clothing or the vapour bath.

Digestives.—These are agents used to promote the discharge of pus, in stimulating the tardy or chronic action of wounds, and thus promote healing. They are also used for smearing setons with a view of hastening desirable suppuration. In canine surgery they are not largely made use of, simple resin or cantharidine ointment being all that is required.

Diuretics.—Medicines which exert their beneficial effect by stimulus of the kidneys are known as diuretics. They reduce the watery parts of the blood and thus promote absorption, by which dropsical states are removed. They also exert a sedative effect on the circulation, the object of which is to reduce the tendency to fever and inflammation.

1. *Bolus.*—Nitrate of potash, 1 drm.; extract of gentian, sufficient to make a paste. Divide into 6, 8 or 10 pills, as may be required.

2. *Draught.*—Dissolve the required dose of nitrate of potash in 1 or 2 oz. of linseed mucilage.

Electuaries.—Electuaries are syrupy concoctions for conveying medicines to the mouth for sustaining local action. They slowly dissolve, and are carried by the tongue to all parts of the cavity, exerting a beneficial action when movement of the jaws is painful, or the animal is unable to swallow.

1. Muriate of ammonia, 1 drm.; camphor, 1 drm.; gum kino, 1 drm. Pulverise separately, and further triturate the whole to an impalpable powder, then add treacle sufficient to form a soft paste. Dose, half a teaspoonful placed on the tongue three or four times a day.

2. Powdered catechu, 1 drm.; linseed meal, 1 drm.; honey or treacle sufficient. Mix, and use as directed for No. 1.

Further remedies may be alternated with the foregoing —viz., tannic acid, powdered galls powdered alum, boracic acid, &c. &c.

Embrocations or Liniments.—These preparations are for *external use only*, and should be distinctly labelled as such, as powerful poisons are in some instances incorporated. They are designed to reduce pain, inflammation or swelling, especially old standing enlargements.

1. *Stimulating.*— Olive oil, 4 oz.; liquor ammonia, 1½ fluid drm.; oil of origanum, 1 drm. Mix. Apply with friction.

2. *Sedative.*—Tincture of opium, 1 fluid oz.; tincture of belladonna, 1 fluid drm.; olive oil, ½ pint. Apply with gentleness to the affected parts.

3. *Soothing and Stimulating.*—Soap liniment (opodeldoc) 4 fluid oz.; tincture of opium ½ oz. Apply with gentle friction to enlarged joints in the latter part of the acute stages of inflammation.

4. For *Dispersing Enlargements.* — Add to No. 3 tincture of iodine 1 oz., and agitate thoroughly. Apply, as required, with smart friction.

5. *Mustard Embrocation.*—Best flour of mustard, 6 oz.; liquor of ammonia, 1½ oz.; oil of turpentine, 1½ oz. Mix with sufficient water to form a thin paste.

6. *Stimulating Embrocation.*—Camphor, ½ oz.; oil of turpentine and spirit of wine, of each 1½ oz. Mix.

7. *Sweating Embrocation for Windgalls, &c.*—Strong mercurial ointment, 2 oz.; camphor, ½ oz.; oil of rosemary, 2 drms.; spirit of turpentine, 1 oz. Mix.

8. *Another, but stronger.*—Strong mercurial ointment, 2 oz.; oil of bay, 1 oz.; oil of origanum, ½ oz.; powdered cantharides, ½ oz. Mix.

9. *A most Active Sweating Embrocation.*—Red iodide of mercury, ½ to 1 drm.; powdered arnica leaves, 1 drm.; soap liniment, 2 oz. Mix.

N.B.—This must be repeated until a blister is raised,

which usually takes two or three applications. It may then be omitted for a week.

Emetics.—Emetics are sometimes required for the dog, though not so often as is commonly supposed. Vomiting is a natural process in that animal, and seldom wants provoking; indeed, if emetics are often had recourse to, his stomach becomes so irritable that neither medicine nor food will remain on it. Hence their administration should be carefully kept within the bounds of absolute necessity.

Under proper regulations emetics have a useful place in canine medicine. They greatly assist other remedies or measures by the facility with which they cause rejection of the contents of the stomach, and produce a direct sedative effect on the system, which proves beneficial in active diseases as pneumonia, hepatitis, enteritis, &c.

Prescriptions.—1. Tartar emetic, $\frac{1}{2}$ to 1 gr.; powdered ipecacuanha, 4 to 5 grs. Mix, and dissolve in a little water, to be given as a drench, and to be followed by 2 to 8 oz., of lukewarm water, in a quarter of an hour.

2. *Common Salt Emetic.*—A teaspoonful of salt and half this quantity of mustard are to be dissolved in half a pint of warm water, and given as a drench.

Expectorants.—Remedies of this class are employed to assist or relieve the lungs by promoting discharge from the mucous lining of the air passages, in which office they prove eminently useful. They restrain irritation and thus remove the cough which it occasions, promote tranquillity, affording rest and comfort to jaded spirits, and greatly facilitate recovery.

1. *Bolus.*—Carbonate of ammonia, finely powdered, 1 drm.; gum asafœtida, 1 drm.; extract of belladonna, 12 grains. Pulverise the ammonia and gum separately, using to the latter a few drops of spirit of wine, then mix and triturate together, finally rubbing in the extract with linseed meal and treacle to form a paste. Divide into 12, 18, or 24 pills according to the size of the patient.

2 Carbonate of ammonia, and carbonate of potash,

of each 1 drm., finely powdered; extract of belladonna, 12 grs.; powdered squills, 1 drm. Mix by trituration, and work into a paste with careful and small additions of oxymel squills. Divide into pills as directed for No. 1.

3. *Draught.*—Spirit of nitrous ether, or aromatic spirit of ammonia, 1 or 2 drms.; oxymel squills, 2 drms.; tincture of belladonna, 1 drm. Mix, add 7 drms. of linseed mucilage, and agitate thoroughly. Dose, ½ to 1 drm. (30 to 60 drops).

4. Ipecacuanha powder, 1 to 1½ gr.; powdered rhubarb, 1 to 3 grs.; compound squill pill, 1 to 2 grs.; powdered opium, ½ to 1 gr. Linseed meal and water, enough to make a bolus, to be given night and morning.

5. Ipecacuanha powder and powdered opium, of each a grain. Confection enough to make a pill, to be given every six hours.

6. *An Expectorant Mixture for Chronic Cough.*—Friar's balsam, 10 to 15 drops; syrup of poppies, 1 drm.; diluted sulphuric acid, 5 to 10 drops; mucilage, ½ oz.; water, ½ oz. Mix, and give two or three times a day.

7. *An Expectorant in Recent Cough.*— Tincture of lobelia, 10 to 15 drops; almond emulsion, 1 oz.; extract of conium, 2 to 3 grs.; ipecacuanha wine, 5 to 10 drops. Mix, and give two or three times a day.

Febrifuges.—Fever medicines or febrifuges comprise a large number of substances having more or less direct influence upon the heart and circulation, probably through the nervous system, and the excretory channels. They reduce existing febrile states by neutralising or destroying the causes, rendering the process of inflammation less powerful under their presence and action.

1. *Bolus.*—Nitrate of potash, 1 drachm; camphor, 15 grains; digitalis, 12 grains. Reduce each separately to powder, and afterwards triturate together, adding 1 drachm of linseed meal, and treacle sufficient to make the mass. Divide into 12, 18 or 24 pills as needful.

2. Substitute 12 grains of extract of belladonna for the digitalis in No. 1.

3. Calomel, 1 to 3 grs.; digitalis, ½ gr.; nitre, 3 to 5 grs. Confection to form a pill, to be given every night.

4. Nitre, 3 to 5 grs.; tartar emetic, ⅛th gr. Confection to form a pill, to be given night and morning.

5. *Fever Mixture.*—Nitre, 1 drm.; sweet spirit of nitre, 3 drms.; mindererus spirit, 1 oz.; camphor mixture, 6½ oz. Mix, and give two tablespoonfuls every six hours.

6. Solution of the acetate of ammonia, 2 drms.; tincture of belladonna, 1 drm.; sulphuric ether, 1 drm.; linseed mucilage, 4 drms. Dose, 60, 30, 15, or 10 drops several times daily.

Fomentations.—In canine therapeutics this class of remedy has no special advantages. Far better results are produced by carefully immersing the sufferer in a warm bath not higher than 76° F., the head being supported above the fluid. This is a useful proceeding in cases of internal spasm, nervous affections and other functional disorders requiring soothing and sedative treatment. On removal from the bath, which should not be continued longer than ten or fifteen minutes at the most, the patient should be quickly dried, at least as far as all means will allow, and enveloped in a blanket and other coverings to protect him from cold until he is quite dry. When the hot bath proves too much, causing a disposition to faint, or show any signs of distress by panting, &c., he should be quickly removed, and revived by 5, 10 or 15 drops of the aromatic spirits of ammonia.

Hypodermic or Subcutaneous Injections.—The advantages of this method of treating disease in the lower animals are such as to commend the practice in numerous instances. It is not only cleanly, as waste is entirely avoided, but the speediest results are secured, and animal suffering frequently subdued, if not totally arrested, with remarkable promptitude and permanence. By means of a suitable syringe, provided with a tubular needle, the administration is thus effected. A fold of the skin, seized by the left hand, is raised from the body, and the point of the needle is passed through the first layer, parallel with the structures beneath. The fold is then released, and spread or smoothed by the hand, when the piston is pushed home, and the fluid permeates the interstices of the connective tissue. Absorption is rapid, and the physiological action of the remedy is often immediately demonstrated, especially when powerful agents are made use of.

It is essential to remind the reader that the greatest attention will be necessary, in order to avoid an overdose, or too frequent repetition. The remedies should be carefully prepared solutions, and the exact degree of strength must be ascertained. Indifference towards these precautions will result in bitter regret and disappointment.

Inhalations.—The class of remedies useful as inhalations have not as yet been put to an extended use. *Warm vapour* is very helpful in catarrhs by promoting discharges from the nostrils and frontal sinuses. *Medicated inhalations* are conducive also towards arresting the progress of disease in catarrhs, especially those of an influenzal or purpura type, "Sanitas" oil, or the fluid, eucalyptol, &c., being added to the vapour, or used by means of the *spray distributor*.

The *inhalation of chloroform* may be now so successfully administered as to be considered as near perfection as possible. Humane proprietors will have no difficulty in meeting with humane surgeons who successfully conduct operations by means of this agent, thus reducing many to the least possible degree of suffering or danger.

Lotions.—Lotions are usually solutions of one or more remedies in water, and their principal uses are for the healing of wounds, or the application of cold and sedative influences to parts under inflammatory action. They have but a limited use in canine practice, as the natural habit of the animal to lick the part so treated forbids the use of sufficiently potent remedies. *When it is desirable to adopt such, the animal must necessarily be muzzled*, the possibility of using the tongue being absolutely prevented.

1. Cold water *constantly applied* is efficacious to inflamed limbs, &c.

2. Solution of the acetate of ammonia, 4 fluid oz.; spirit of wine, 4 fluid oz.; water, one pint. Apply as No. 1.

3. *Lotions for Sprains.*—Tincture of arnica, 2 fluid oz.; spirit of wine, 6 fluid oz. Mix. Apply a *thin* bandage to the affected part, and keep it constantly wet with the lotion to ensure cold by evaporation.

4. Goulard's extract of lead, 2 fluid oz.; dilute acetic acid, 2 fluid oz.; distilled water, 1 pint. Apply as No. 1.

N.B. The dog must be muzzled to prevent his licking the application.

5. *Healing Lotion for Wounds.*—Sulphate of zinc. ¾ oz.; sugar of lead, 1 oz.; soft water, 1 quart. Shake well before using, and dash the fluid upon the wound direct from the bottle. Muzzle the dog.

6. *Cooling Lotion in Bruises or Cuts.*—Extract of lead, 1 drm.; tincture of arnica, ⅓ to 1 drm.; water, ½ pint. Mix, and apply constantly by means of a sponge.

7. *Cooling Lotion in Stiffness from Bruises or Work.*—Tincture of arnica, 1 drm.; spirit of wine, 7 drms. Mix, and rub well into the part, before the fire, with the hand.

8. *Lotion for the Eyes.*—Sulphate of zinc, 20 to 25 grs.; water, 6 oz. Mix.

9. *Very Strong One, and only to be Dropped in.*—Nitrate of silver, 5 to 8 grs.; distilled water, 1 oz. Mix, and use with a camel-hair brush.

10. *For Internal Canker.*—Nitrate of silver, 10 grs.; distilled water, 1 oz. Mix, and drop in every night.

Ointments.—Unguents, or Ointments, are soft compositions finding their base in pure hog's lard, with which some special curative remedy is incorporated, examples of which will be found under Anodynes, Astringents, Blisters, &c. They are easily applied, and as a rule remarkably effective, the emollient action of the grease, combined with needful friction, being conducive to the free absorption of the remedy which gives the essential character to the compound.

1. *Ointment for Mange.*—Iodide of sulphur, 1 drm.; pure lard, 10 drms. Mix, and apply with moderate friction. Being non-poisonous, there is no fear of danger from absorption, or being licked by the patient.

2. Green iodide of mercury, 1 drm.; lard, 10 drms.

Mix, and apply as directed for No. 1. In this case the animal must be carefully muzzled to prevent licking.

Parasiticides.—The agents of this class are such as possess the power of destroying parasites. Of those common to the dog, two kinds are recognised—viz., *External*, or those infesting the skin, and *Internal*, or those common to the digestive organs, and included under the familiar title of Worms.

External Applications for Mange.—1. Sublimed sulphur, 8 oz.; whale oil, 8 fluid oz.; oil of tar, and blue, or mercurial ointment, of each ½ fluid oz. The whole should be thoroughly mixed before use.

2. Whale oil, 6 fluid oz.; oil of turpentine, 1 fluid oz.; sulphur ointment, 6 oz. Mix. The above are for mild cases only.

3. Creasote, 1½ fluid oz.; rectified spirit of wine, 15 fluid oz.; water, 11 to 14 fluid oz. (Gamgee.)

4. Balsam of Peru, 1 oz.; alcohol (spirit of wine), 4 fluid oz. (Fleming.) An effective and very safe remedy, especially adapted for house dogs.

N.B. The above remedies are useful for sarcoptic mange. The following are especially prepared for follicular mange.

1. Olive oil, 14 fluid oz.; creasote, 1 fluid oz.; liquor potassæ, 1 fluid oz. Mix, and agitate thoroughly. Apply by means of a piece of rag to all diseased parts every third day, the dog having been thoroughly washed and dried a few hours before dressing. (Hunting.)

2. Balsam of Peru, 1 part, dissolved in 30 parts of alcohol. (Fleming.)

3. Nut oil, oil of tar, and spirit of turpentine, equal parts, well shaken together. (Mayhew.)

Carbolic Acid Preparation.—Take carbolic acid (No. 5 preparation), 1 oz.; soft soap, 1 oz.; water, 2 pints. Put the soap into the water, and boil until it dissolves, after which add the acid, and the moment the fluid boils remove and set aside to cool. Use 1 part to 40 for local applications, and 1 to 50 for extended use.

For Fleas and Lice.—Oil of aniseed, 1 fluid oz.; glycerine, 1 fluid oz.; spirit of wine, 2 fluid drms.; olive oil, 4 fluid oz. Mix, and apply thoroughly to the skin and hair, placing the dog meanwhile on a temporary bed. After a few hours wash with warm water and "Sanitas" dog soap.

For remedies for **Internal Parasites**, *see* WORM MEDICINES.

Poultices.—The remarks already made in reference to lotions apply also to poultices. The best substitute, under the restrictions of a fine wire muzzle, is *spongio-piline*. A piece of suitable size is selected, dipped in *hot water*, partially wrung out, and rapidly bound upon and around the limb if possible. For renewal, a second piece is required, that the attendant may immediately replace the fresh, hot covering, on the removal of the first. This material is made in various degrees of thickness, thus presenting a most effective and cleanly method of applying the best means for promoting suppuration in the case of abscess, or as a fomentation to injured parts.

Medicated poultices also claim our notice. Their object is the application of some remedial agent as well as heat, for which purpose *spongio-piline* is eminently useful, cleanly and effective. The arrangement consists of cutting the *spongio-piline* to a size suitable for an entire covering to the affected parts, after which it is plunged into hot or cold water, as required, and quickly pressed to remove superfluous fluid. It is next spread out and saturated with the remedy, and applied to the affected parts without delay. When the application is to be hot, the remedy should also be heated by admixture, as with water of suitable temperature. Heat or cold, to prove serviceable, must be continuous to the well-ascertained end of the operation. The reverse brings inevitable disaster and disappointment.

Purgatives, *see* Aperients.

Stimulants.—By this term is understood those substances which excite the action of the whole nervous and vascular systems; almost all medicines are stimulants to some part or other, as, for instance, aperients, which stimulate the lining of the bowels, but to the general system are lowering. On the other hand, stimulants, so called, excite and raise the action of the brain and heart.

1. *Stimulating Mixture.*—Aromatic spirit of ammonia, 1 oz.; tincture of cardamoms, 1 oz.; camphor mixture, 6 oz. Mix, and give two table-spoonfuls every six hours.

Stomachics.—Stomachics are medicines given to improve the tone of the stomach when impaired by bad management or disease.

1. *Stomachic Bolus.*—Extract of gentian, 6 to 8 grs.; powdered rhubarb, 2 to 3 grs. Mix, and give twice a day.

2. *Stomachic Mixture.*—Tincture of cardamoms, $\frac{1}{2}$ to 1 oz.; infusion of cascarilla, 7 oz.; carbonate of soda, $\frac{1}{2}$ drm. Mix: give one or two table-spoonfuls twice a day.

Styptics.—Styptics are remedies which have a tendency to stop the flow of blood either from internal or external surfaces. They are used either by the mouth, or to the part itself in the shape of lotions, &c.; or the actual cautery, which is always the best in external bleeding.

Internal Styptics.—1. *For Bloody Urine, or Bleeding from the Lungs.*—Superacetate of lead, 12 to 14 grs.; tincture of matico, $\frac{1}{2}$ to 1 oz.; vinegar, 2 drms.; water, $7\frac{1}{2}$ oz. Mix; give two table-spoonfuls two or three times a day to a full-sized dog.

Tonics.—Tonics augment the vigour of the whole body permanently, whilst stimulants only act for a short time. They are chiefly useful after low fever.

1. *Tonic Pills.*—Sulphate of quinine, 1 to 3 grs.; ginger, 2 to 3 grs. Extract of gentian, enough to form a bolus, to be given twice a day.

2. *Tonic Mixture.*—Compound tincture of bark, 1 oz.; decoction of yellow bark, 7 oz. Mix, and give two table-spoonfuls twice or thrice a day.

Worm Medicines (Parasiticides).—Worm medicines, or vermifuges, are given in order to expel worms, which they do partly from their specific action upon the parasite itself, and partly by their purgative qualities, which all ought to possess, or to be followed by medicines of that class.

1. *For Worms Generally.*—Two drachms of powdered

areca nut to be given mixed up in water as a drench, and followed by a dose of castor oil. This is the dose for a very large dog. It may be regulated for all sizes by giving 2 grains of the nut for each pound the dog weighs.

2. *Medicines for Round-Worm.*—Infusion of Indian pink, 1 to 3 table-spoonfuls, on an empty stomach.

3. Santonine, 3 to 4 or 5 grs.; jalap, 5 to 10 grs.; powdered ginger, 3 to 5 grs.; extract of gentian to make a pill.

4. *For Tapeworm.*—Kousso, 2 to 4 drms.; lemon juice, $\frac{1}{2}$ oz. Mix, and give as a drench, with the addition of a little water, on an empty stomach. This should be followed by a dose of castor oil eight hours after.

5. *For Tapeworm* (another plan).—Root of male fern, 1 to 4 drms.; powdered jalap, 15 grs. Liquorice powder or linseed meal enough to form a bolus with water.

6. Oil of male shield fern, 20 drops; sulphuric ether, 60 drops; oil of turpentine, 30 drops. Mix. Add the white of one egg; 2 drams of glycerine, and beat together. When thoroughly incorporated administer to the dog when the stomach is empty.

CHAPTER IX.

BLOOD DISEASES.

Plethora—Obesity—Anæmia—Rheumatism—Rickets or Rachitis—Inter-breeding—Crooked or Bandy-legs—Leuchæmia—Jaundice—Uræmia—Apnœa.

THE blood in its circulation or movement through the numberless vessels of the body is exceedingly liable to deterioration by admixture with various foreign substances. The vital constitution is more or less depleted, and when the causes are continued, it fails to nourish the body in its integral parts; or the excess of foreign materials, although strictly speaking they are food elements, but insufficiently elaborated, may induce severe general disorder; still worse results may follow the not infrequent decay or degeneration of such food elements, which are retained in consequence of the attendant inability of the system at the time to expel them. Suspension of function more or less, is a constant sequel to over-repletion. The system suffers frequently, but regains the power to throw off the offender; at length it fails to recoup itself, vital stamina is impaired, and the next attack has removed the conditions from the area of simple disorder. Vital action is impaired by reason of structural decay or permanent change, and the conditions are those of disease, with the possibility that the changes are not only of permanent duration, but functions essential to life are seriously interfered with or destroyed, and the end, sooner or later, is death. Such conditions are recognised in one or other of the following forms.

Plethora or fulness of blood, consists of an excess of nutritious elements derived from the food, which, circulating through the body, gives rise to rapid growth and development known as "blooming condition." The absence of needful exercise largely favours these states and renders the consequences dangerous. Overfed, obese, and inactive dogs are the usual subjects.

Symptoms.—In addition to the conditions already named, the animal exhibits a generally bloated appearance; the skin is hot, dry, and red. The mucous membranes are also injected, or highly coloured. The mouth is dry, or slimy, breath faint, or disagreeable, bowels constipated, urine highly coloured, and probably offensive. The creature is indolent, drowsy, tires on the least exertion; the artery is full, and the circulation unusually accelerated, imparts a strong resistance to the finger, and the general temperature is increased.

Treatment.—Reduce the blood pabulum by purgatives occasionally. Change the food, substituting a less quantity, of less nutritious quality, and especially institute regular exercise to stimulate the natural functions of waste, decay, and expulsion of the effete products.

Obesity.—Following hard upon the conditions of Plethora is the disposition to accumulate fat. The degrees of this are various, culminating in a state of superlative inability, associated with positive ugliness. Internally the organs are surrounded by accumulations of fat, which impede the essential functions, and often cause sudden death. Even the muscles are replaced by fat, and the animal is a trouble if not a torture to himself.

The *Causes* are those enumerated under Plethora, a discontinuance of which must be ensured before curative measures can be successful.

Treatment.—Avoid the causes which generate Plethora. Institute gentle exercise, gradually increased as the effects are fruitful. Substitute a less fattening diet. In spite of these measures some cases refuse to yield even to the exhibition of strong medicine of an aperient character. In such an event regular doses of iodine should be given in conjunction with aperient medicines at stated intervals.

Anæmia.—*Deficiency of Blood.*—This definition indicates the exact reverse of the state known as Plethora. The deficiency applies to the *pabulum* or rich elements needful for building up the body. It is the disease of badly fed dogs, especially puppies, in which the organisation lacks vigour and development. It is the outcome of overcrowding, bad smells, *want of light and fresh air*, especially when unsuitable, or unnutritious and indigestible food is supplied.

Symptoms.—Weakness, often amounting to prostration, precarious appetite, indisposition to rise, generally depressed spirits, cold limbs, which sometimes swell, pallid membranes, staring coat, scanty excretions, with general inability for any exertion. The mouth is cool and the gums with the tongue are remarkably pale. Diarrhœa usually supervenes and terminates fatally.

Treatment.—Remove the cause. Supply good food *judiciously*, together with fresh air, water, etc. Treat the diarrhœa by means of half or quarter doses of oil and laudanum, and when successfully arrested, commence carefully with a course of iron tonics with quinine in small doses.

Rheumatism.—This disease owes its origin to the state of the blood as the result of impaired digestion and assimilation: it is charged with elements inimical to its constitution, an arrest of certain functions being the cause of their accumulation and retention within the organism. The disease exhibits a preference for particular tissue, such as the joints and ligaments, when it is known as articular rheumatism; and in the muscles, especially their terminations and attachments by tendons. The latter form producing much stiffness of the body, especially, has been known for generations as the "chest-founder" of the old farriers, and lumbago of more recent days. In sporting dogs the disease appears as the result of cold and damp quarters, hence the term "kennel-lameness."

Two forms are observed, the acute and chronic, the first, as a rule, subsiding into the latter, assuming persistent and incurable states, extremely liable to aggravation by adverse states of the temperature and moisture of the air. The acute form is also liable to become periodic, and heart complications, as valvular disease, of a serious and fatal nature are common.

Symptoms.—In the acute articular form the joints are hot, swollen, and intensely painful. Movement causes intense agony, which the sufferer avoids, but yelps piteously when forced to change his position.

In the muscular form or "chest-founder," the sufferer is more or less unable to advance the forelegs, or move the shoulders, which are stiff, the whole of the limbs being carried in a piece, and with extreme care. The sufferer objects to being handled, and yells loudly when the limbs are manipulated, especially if abducted or moved away from the body. Considerable fever is present.

In lumbar rheumatism the same objection to movement is evident. The back is arched upwards, the feet being near together, movement in any direction causing intense agony, and as a result, the creature refuses to be disturbed, and pressure, or forced movement rouses his anger by the intense pain which attends the least change of position.

Constitutional disturbance is severe in each of the forms, the temperature being increased, the pulse rapid, hard, and sharply defined, respiration accelerated, tongue coated with mucus, breath foul, bowels constipated, and the urine deficient, depositing a sediment on cooling. The same tendency to move from one part or go out to another as seen in the human subject, characterises the disease in canine sufferers, and an intensely inflamed joint may be apparently sound in a few hours, the disease being transferred with all its severity to another. The erratic nature of the disease is particularly striking, and serves an important purpose in correct diagnosis.

Treatment.—The bowels should be moved in the earliest stages, assisted by enemas. Give the fever bolus No. 1, page 131, or one of the draughts there prescribed. In the early stages of extreme constitutional disturbance one or two minims of Fleming's tincture of aconite may replace the belladonna. It, however, requires great care, and must not be continued too long. In addition, and between the other remedies, 20 or 30 grains of the bicarbonate of potash or soda may be given in half or one ounce of water.

In the chronic form, the disease appears to be milder. There is less pain and little disposition to move from one part to another. Deformity of limb is common and is associated with enlargement, which suffers aggravation in changes of weather. In this instance a modification in the essentials of treatment is called for, the most useful remedies being salicylic acid and colchicum, or iodide of potassium with the carbonate of soda, or potash. Blisters, and setons to the affected joints are sometimes serviceable.

As damp and cold are undoubtedly active agents in the development of the disease, prevention depends on the adoption of warm, dry, and airy quarters; and when dogs are washed, to ensure they are carefully dried subsequently by friction with towels, &c., being quickly removed to sheltered places, free from direct draughts, and having a normal temperature.

The complication, valvular disease of the heart, will be referred to under diseases of the circulatory system in Chapter XII.

Rickets or **Rachitis.**—The deformities which characterise this affection are the evidences of an abnormal state of the digestive and assimilative functions. Flesh and fat may be greedily partaken of, but the power to convert earthy or calcareous matters into true, solid bone structure is absent. The disease is not so common or widespread as generally supposed. Many crooked, bow, or bandy legged dogs, especially whelps, are met with, but these form a totally distinct class, often deriving their characteristics from the irregularities of their mongrel descent. The ricketty whelp is sickly, weak, and ailing, always morbid, and rarely worth the trouble which the apparent gravity of the case demands.

The *symptoms* are briefly as follow. The bones are the seat of the principal abnormalities, swellings of variable size being present on the limbs, sometimes in connection with the joints, attended with more or less inflammatory action, pain, and lameness. The latter is so pronounced in some cases as to render the animal incapable of rising from the bed. The legs are thus deformed by bends, or twists, the weight of the body being instrumental in their production. Bulging of the facial bones, or jaws is also somewhat common. The spine and ribs are more rarely affected, but the same want of earthy material is evident with more or less softening after death. The coat stares, the flanks are hollow, the loins narrow, and the whole vertebræ develop the razor back appearance. The mucous membrane and the "white" of the eye, are singularly pale, and the creature as a whole is a miserable and profitless being.

Treatment.—Success attends only upon those cases in which the disease is of a recent or slight nature, and when fresh air, light, suitable food and freedom from cold and damp are ensured. The food should contain the elements necessary for bone formation, as lime water, finely ground bones or egg shells, good oatmeal porridge forming the medium as well as the bulk of the daily food. Cod-liver oil, glycerine, or linseed oil should be variously alternated with the foregoing to promote assimilation, and impart warmth. Additional advantages will be derived from daily, but suitable and gentle exercise. As a general medicine, the following may be advantageous:—Cod-liver oil, or linseed oil, and lime water, of each 8 fluid ounces; solution of dialised iron, one fluid ounce; aromatic spirit of ammonia, one fluid ounce. Mix the oil and lime water together and shake well; next add the ammonia and again agitate; finally put in the iron solution and mix. The *dose* should vary from one teaspoonful to a tablespoonful twice a day, age and size of the patient being considered.

It remains to be stated with emphasis that *ricketty dogs should not be used for breeding purposes.* Male and female alike hand down the defects and hereditary taint, which effectually frustrate the designs of the owner to improve his animals through that means.

Inter-breeding, or breeding from animals of close consanguinity is also set down as the cause or origin of rickets as well as many other diseases. This is undoubtedly true when one or both parents are unsound from existing disease. We need to remember that a close system of in-breeding has given us our famous flocks and herds, as well as unrivalled studs of the finest horses. A true system of in-breeding is based on careful selection of the healthiest as well as the best formed animals, and the results are inevitably favourable, even with animals of close consanguinity. Health, hardihood, vigour, conformation, &c., are fortunately as hereditary as the taint of scrofula, or any other specific disease, the value of the progeny being in direct ratio to the soundness or otherwise of the parents.

Crooked or Bandy Legs are peculiarly common to some breeds of dogs, and of late years the deformity has gradually come to be esteemed as a peculiarity of breed. The Dachshund and Basset Hound are of this class.

It is not improbable that originally the defect, for such it must be considered, had its origin in the hereditary transmission of a weakly constitution, and later in attenuation of form and physical development. The absence of sound judgment in the selection and mating of canine animals is evident in the various deformities of the heavier breeds, as the Mastiff and St. Bernard. The system of feeding also, as inducing weight of body while sacrificing the essentials of the bony skeleton is probably the immediate cause. What we would think of the builder who places his superstructure on an inferior foundation? The breeding from animals possessing heavy carcases set on inferior legs, composed of deficient osseous material is a practice of similar kind, having the same inevitable results.

Leuchæmia or **Leucocythæmia**, otherwise *white blood*, or *white cell blood*, is described as occuring in canine and other animals, as well as the human subject. As its name implies, the corpuscles of the blood are white, the characteristic red or crimson colour being absent as a result of disease in the blood-producing organs—viz., the spleen, lymphatic glands, or spinal marrow.

Dogs and cats suffer most of all domestic animals, usually at or about the middle, or in advanced life. The cause appears to be due to engorgement of the spleen with blood, and later to its becoming thickened, hard, and anæmic, finally involving other organs as the liver, kidneys, etc., and ending in death.

The disease is identified with difficulty, examination of the blood during life being the only reliable test. The outlines of a cure have not yet been defined.

Jaundice or *Icterus*, is essentially a disease of the blood owing to retention of bile products, and indicated by a deep yellow colour of the tissues. As the original cause is disease of the liver, the subject will be suitably considered in connection with the several maladies of that rgan. (See Chapter XIII.)

Uræmia is the state of blood poisoning by retention of elements which should be expelled by the kidneys. The skin exhales a strong and sickly odour of urine in fully developed cases, the mouth being slimy and equally offensive, and the fæces are small, hard, glazed with mucus, and emits the same disagreeable odour. The end soon comes on. Dulness is followed by insensibility, the animal lies stretched on the side, and life gradually passes away. Uræmia may be due to disease of the kidneys, but as a rule it is the result of obscure causes, without special disease of those organs.

Apnœa.—This is a form of blood-poisoning arising from an arrest of the functions of the skin. It is mainly due to the use of large quantities of resinous ointments and other agents which prevent due transpiration. Among horses and sheep the disease is more or less prevalent, but in dogs, as the skin is less active, this form of disease is not so common.

CHAPTER X.

SPECIFIC AND CONTAGIOUS DISEASES.

Anthrax—Cholera—Diphtheria—Distemper—Eczema Epizoötica—Glanders—Measles—Rabies—Relapsing Fever—Septicæmia—Tuberculosis—Variola or Small Pox.

The specific diseases of the blood in canine animals have received much greater attention in later years, and close observation has been rewarded by the recognition of various forms from which the system of the dog was believed to be practically exempt. This may possibly be due to the extension of the causes, the majority of which bear close relation to our international relations with other countries of the world. They present a wide field for study, especially in their relation to the diseases of mankind, and in a few years hence the present list may be considerably extended and enriched by further discoveries, removing many difficulties we now experience.

Anthrax, or **Charbon,** otherwise coal, derives its

name from the dark coloured or black state of the blood.

The usual form of infection is by means of the flesh of cattle which have died of the disease, or when the dog has been allowed to forage among the excrement of those suffering from the intestinal form. The disease has appeared with violence among foxhounds, from which the losses have been serious, but as a rule dogs resist the poison better than cattle.

Symptoms.—The intestinal form of the malady is most common. It commences by violent colic, during which the bowels are moved, the evacuations being mixed with blood. Vomition is likewise severe, the contents of the stomach being largely mixed with blood. Recovery is more common in the dog than among cattle. In some instances the lymphatic glands about the throat and neck rapidly swell, with local tumefaction and serous infiltration of the surrounding tissues, which greatly interfere with respiration. The skin and parts thus implicated, together with the membrane of the mouth, and tongue, is spotted with blood effused beneath, and shortly becomes gangrenous; viscid saliva copiously flows from the mouth, and the bowels discharge fluid fæces largely mixed with blood. The affected animal usually dies within three to five days, or recovery is betokened within that time. As a result of the contagion entering by the mouth, the buccal membrane lining the whole cavity is often studded with blebs or pustules, which occasion severe fever and irritation. Such states are believed by the ignorant to be the result of an encounter with a toad, snake, &c. It is said that a dog affected with anthrax will convey the disease by attacking with his teeth. If this is correct, may we not suppose it is due to the presence of blood or other matter on which the animal has fed previously? If it is proved to be conveyed by the saliva, or discharges from the blebs, &c., in his mouth, we realise the formidable nature of the complaint, and the need for the greatest caution.

Treatment must be regulated by the attendant circumstances. The milder forms, and only when the dog is valuable, should be treated, as great risk is imminent from the conveyance of fatal blood-poisoning. The care of the patient properly rests with a qualified veterinary surgeon. "Sanitas" disinfectants should be largely made use of for purifying the litter, floor, &c., fouled by the discharges, and as a wash for the mouth, nothing answers better than "Sanitas" fluid diluted with an equal bulk of water. One or two fluid drachms with one ounce of cold water will form an excellent medicine, which may be given several times daily; and a fluid injection, say two to four ounces of tepid water containing one teaspoonful, will materially aid in correcting the offensive dejections. Otherwise the warmth and general comfort of the animals must be ensured.

Cholera.—The communication of cholera to the dog or cat may not be improbable. Both these animals in their association with mankind run serious risk during an outbreak of the disease. They may partake of the malady by their disposition to seek delicate morsels from the evacuations or vomited matters; they may also become carriers of contagion, and spread the disease far and wide among the population of the district. With regard to the first, the evidences of cholera in either dog or cat are by no means clear. During visitations of the plague in certain countries, cats and dogs have suffered extensively from an epizoötic form of disease which has been recognised at the least as of a choleraic nature, and exceedingly fatal even after a few hours. The chief symptoms were severe vomiting, &c., with violent as well as profuse diarrhœa; the animal appeared to be suddenly reduced, having a "pinched" or wasted appearance, and the eyes, sunk deep in the orbits, added considerably to the woebegone or dejected condition. After death the internal evidences very closely agreed with those witnessed in the human subject. It has, however, been carefully ascertained that notwithstanding the great similarity in the post-mortem appearances, the true choleraic poison was probably not present.

Diphtheria.—Prominently among the discoveries of

recent years is the susceptibility of dogs to diphtheria. The *cause* is ascertained to rest with the defective state of the drainage, the gases from which are inhaled, or by the access of *putrilage* to the system, the medium being the food. By nature the dog is surprisingly immune as to many putrid forms of disease, as he is almost the only scavenger in many countries; yet it appears to be possible for the system to become susceptible as the animal is exposed to the operation of causes while under constrained or domestic conditions. My late friend Professor Robertson, in his extended observations was enabled to witness the effects of the disease in a number of horses, as well as a kennel of greyhounds, and I give the results of his experience in the following observations.

Some of the cases were characterised by high fever at the outset, when the inflammation was acute, the mouth, fauces, tonsils and palate being of a dark red colour, tense, smooth, and glistening, as a result of distension from sub-cellular infiltration. The gland structures were swollen and tender, which rendered swallowing difficult or impossible. The early signs were increase of temperature, accelerated pulse and respiration, and when this increased functional activity subsided, the animal was depressed, and listless from a want of muscular energy. The end of the disease was betokened by emesis, diarrhœa and death. In those surviving twenty-four hours were the characteristic grey coagulable exudate, sometimes arranged in spots or stripes, but always adherent to the mucous membrane; more frequently the exudation was glossy, tenacious, soft, and devoid of structural arrangement, or granular material was thickly deposited in some parts, or almost absent in others.

In another form there was less fever, and the power of swallowing was only slight.

In the third form the disease was principally located in the nasal passages, being characterised by dulness, and fever of a low type, with sore throat, sanious discharge from the nostrils, and a similar fluid, mingled with saliva, flowed over the tongue when the mouth was examined.

Of the few which recovered, one became blind of both eyes from infiltration of the layers of the cornea, but ultimately sight was restored. Another, affected a fortnight later, was seized with clonic spasms of the muscles of the face and cervical region, followed in a few days by paraplegia. After a tedious convalescence this animal recovered his full nervous power.

Examination of the drains proved them to be full of filth, which had percolated through the floor of the kennels, and escape of effluvia took place through a perforated grating, conditions which fully accounted for the fatality.

Other writers have noticed the occurrence of diphtheria in dogs from the consumption of the excreta of human patients under the disease. And Professor Law also alludes to croup as occurring in the dog, probably due to the confinement within buildings to which mephitic vapours have gained more or less constant access.

Distemper.—In the list of canine ailments distemper probably ranks first in importance, prevalence, severity, and fatality. It is a specific disease, and usually believed to be closely associated with early life, a peculiarity which may, to some extent, be responsible for its fatality. In later years the belief in a contagion by which it is carried from one animal to another, has included it among the highly infectious maladies, yet some who accept the theory of its being "self-generated," also admit that many dogs safely pass through the vicissitudes of life without contracting the disease. It is also in evidence that one attack does not always ensure immunity from a second, or even a third. Various attempts have been made to establish identity with various diseases of other animals and the human subject, which, it is almost needless to state, have failed. In our student days, we assisted in the inoculation of numerous dogs as a preventive, the belief of our teacher in that day being that the disease resembled small pox of the human subject.

Nature.—The evidences gained by a careful study of the disease are decidedly in favour of its being dependent upon an altered condition of the blood, leading to an asthenic or debility of a peculiarly low type. It may be located at one time in a special set of organs, and during a succeeding attack the manifestations are removed to a totally distant part: thus, at one time it is wholly catarrhal, and in other instances it proves to be either pulmonary, intestinal, hepatic, or cerebro-spinal, all of which may suffer modification in their special characteristics under various circumstances.

Causes.—Contact with diseased animals is perhaps the chief. The exciting causes are those which by inducing debility, impoverishment of the blood, &c., favour the attack, such as bad or insufficient food, damp, overcrowded, or ill-ventilated dwellings, over-feeding, want of exercise, &c. &c. Worms and teething also contribute their share in reducing the natural stamina of the system. As we are assured of the demonstration of a special disease producing bacterium of micrococcus characters, we may content ourselves in the inevitable assurance of the contagious cause under all circumstances.

Symptoms.—The most recent views of the nature of this disease are that, primarily, it is a specific form of catarrh, in which the mucous membrane of the air passages, or the upper alimentary track, as far as the stomach, are involved, degenerating, as already stated, into one or other of the forms of pneumonia, hepatic or bilious, enteric or intestinal, and cerebro-spinal or nervous disease.

The earliest signs of disorder are dulness, lassitude, snuffling or slight husk, or coughing fit, at the close of which the animal attempts to vomit. Somewhat later he is found trembling, with staring coat, a fit of shivers ushering in a subsequent stage. The pulse and temperature are increased, the latter rising to 104° or 105° F. The respiration soon becomes accelerated, and the mucous membranes slightly reddened, which provokes a watery discharge from the eyes and nostrils, and a frequent blowing of air from the latter. In a few hours the watery discharges become muco-purulent, or partly mucus and pus, the mouth is hot, and the tongue coated with dirty-looking mucus. Shortly the throat is inflamed and sore, outward pressure causing pain and coughing, the urine scanty and highly coloured, bowels constipated, legs and ears cold, and appetite very capricious, any attempt to swallow provoking vomition. In mild cases these signs prevail some days, and the patient may recover, or the change may be in the development of severe complications, often ending in some incurable form of disease, or death within a few days.

There are also conditions which merge from the simple catarrh at the outset, which we must now notice. The disease may appear to be mainly located in the nose, eyes, &c. The discharges grow exceedingly thick and tenacious, accumulating around the eyelids, on the face below, and about the nostrils and lips. The eyelids are closed and even united by the hardened discharge, and the breathing is impeded by similar accumulations in the nostrils, relief in either case being gained only by careful soaking with warm water, and removal of the encrustations. Blood circulation and supply are deficient, the result of which is that the parts affected are not nourished; the discharges are offensive, and contain blood, the result of ulceration, which appears in the form of numerous sores on the nostrils, lips, and even the gums, tongue, &c. The eyes are likewise involved, opaque spots first appearing on the eyeballs, and by subsequent ulceration or abscess, perforate the tissues and the aqueous humour escapes. In those cases which recover, the process of repair is wonderfully rapid and effective, the eye being ultimately clear and sight unimpaired. Similar results are not uncommon with respect to the general state of disease. The animal is fearfully prostrated, and each day is thought to be his last. A few hours decides the issue of the case, and he suddenly pulls himself together, enters on the path to recovery, and in a few days is convalescent. In other cases, and in the earlier stages, improvement is suddenly apparent by the absence of all the severe symptoms; shortly, however, he appears weak in the back, is unusually excitable, and at length the worst that can befall him is seen in the evidence of epileptic fits, St. Vitus's dance, or paralysis. Sometimes, owing to brain complication, the sufferer engages in a continual walking in one direction, and in the form of a circle, evidently in a state of stupor or partial insensibility, which terminates in complete coma and death.

The Respiratory or Pulmonary form of Distemper is essentially that of *Bronchitis* of a low and aggravated character, the post-mortem evidences being those common to the usual disease of that name, but associated with general specific blood derangement. (*See* Bronchitis.)

In the *Biliary* or *Hepatic form* jaundice is conspicuous by the yellow colour pervading the tissues generally. The tinge, more or less intense, is seen to great advantage in the mucous membranes of the mouth, tongue, nostrils, eyelids, eyeball, the haw, vulva, and rectum. It is associated with intense depression, a feature which adds considerable difficulty in combating the associated blood poison and its destructive effects. (*See* Jaundice.)

Enteric or *Intestinal Distemper* is principally confined to younger dogs and puppies, which are peculiarly liable in their immature state of physical development to contract a state of blood disease, even under the least favourable circumstances. Worms in the intestines, also teething, often prove exceedingly trying to these creatures, and under their continued effects, without due care as to suitable food, exercise according to capacity, comfortable quarters, &c., the causes of blood derangement are not far distant.

In ordinary *Distemper* the tendency to a loose state of the bowels is general, thus completing the list of signs which are characteristic of blood diseases. A state of looseness is often present from the first, the fæces being laden with mucus shed by the lining membrane of the bowels. Further action induces congestion of the tissues, which is followed by rupture of the minute vessels; blood oozes, and being irritant as well as an animal poison, causes stoppage and sloughing, when an ulcer forms, another source of bleeding; thus the fæces soon become dark-coloured, or black, emitting an offensive odour. Severe colic accompanies the changes referred to, and great depression is evident, the pulse is now running down, temperature declines rapidly, and the animal dies in agony. When this is the case a portion of the intestine may be observed, on post-mortem examination, to be firmly contracted, congested, and probably infiltrated, as well as ulcerated. Some cases do not proceed thus far, death arising from blood-poisoning and coma.

Eczema of a severe form is another serious complication. Innumerable pustules form over the body, or perhaps only over the surface of the belly, some of which are so small as to resemble the puncture by a pin; others are larger and well defined, while a third form consists of a confluence or union of these which raise the cuticle over a wide area as a large swelling. The system then suffers violently from pain, shock, and an enormous drain, and from this period the patient becomes weaker, and finally dies in the majority of cases. In milder forms the pustules mature, burst and discharge their contents, which proves the welfare of the system, but in the severe states the poison is re-absorbed, to the great detriment of the circulation.

Treatment.—This is of two kinds, *preventive* and *remedial*. With regard to the first, vaccination or inoculation with the eye or nasal discharges, has been set forth as all sufficient. Upwards of forty years ago we had the privilege of assisting the late Professor Barlow, of Edinburgh, in a great number of trials for the sole purpose of testing the value and usefulness, if any, of the operation. It is almost needless to state the results were *nil*, and to the present day that experience has been repeatedly verified. If, however, we regard the presence of bacteria as the sole cause, the use of cultivated fluids may solve the mystery. Let the sick be rigidly kept apart from the healthy, observing all necessary rules of sanitation, with a judicious employment of antiseptics of known value, of which "Sanitas" preparations take leading rank. This caution is of the utmost importance in dealing with the profuse discharges from the eyes and nostrils, as well as the fæces, &c. The former should be frequently and carefully removed *to avoid purulent infection*, using the most gentle means, as the ulcerated skin is exceedingly sensitive, and irritation causes intense agony. For this purpose one part of "Sanitas" Fluid to four or five of water will sweeten and soothe the parts. An injection of the same should be used when diarrhœa makes its appearance; and a draught composed of ten, twenty, to sixty drops in water may be given by the mouth.

It is good practice to administer an emetic in the earliest stages, for which form No. 1 or 2 will be useful. A laxative judiciously follows the emetic when the effects have subsided, its action being facilitated by an enema of warm water only. Airy, but warm, dry quarters are absolutely essential, and feeding must be of the most careful kind, in order to avoid constipation or diarrhœa by direct overloading of the stomach, or irritation from unsuitable or indigestible aliment. Stimulants, as No. 1, will be found useful when debility is evident; or when the cough comes on, expectorant bolus or draughts will be called for. In either case the addition of one grain of the sulphate of quinine will be useful against threatened depression.

The insertion of a seton in front of the chest for sore throat or bronchitis is often recommended in the very early stages; afterwards they may prove worse than useless. The seton is also recommended when the eyes are implicated. In this case it is placed at the back of the neck, behind the ears. Opacity of the cornea may be caused by general cloudiness or by small circular spots or depressions, the commencement of ulceration. For these a small quantity of oxide of zinc or calomel is laid on the tip of the finger and held opposite the eye, the lids being separated, and the powder is blown upon the cornea.

The various complications of Distemper, such as

Bronchitis, Enteritic diarrhœa, Jaundice, Eczema, &c., will be dealt with under these heads.

As long as the disease can be confined to the catarrhal stages we have found as a rule the appropriate measures to be fairly successful. It is, therefore, impossible to lay undue stress on the importance of thorough cleanliness, an unremitting use of disinfectants for the floor, &c., of the habitation, with antiseptic dressings for the various points of discharge. In clearing the latter small pieces of soft rag should be used with extreme gentleness, and at the end of the operation consigned to the fire. The attendant also should wash the hands frequently, and always after operating on the patient, the "Sanitas" Fluid being used as directed.

A Malignant form of Distemper occasionally makes its appearance, the general manifestations being those of extreme debility, diphtheria (which see) and severe skin eruption. In such cases little or no good can be done unless the appropriate medical treatment is adopted at the outset. (*See also* Eczema Epizoötica.)

Eczema Epizootica, one of the scourges of the bovine race, is known to be transmissible to the dog and the cat, the medium of conveyance being the milk of diseased cattle. It is very probable that as this disease appears in conjunction with diphtheria as a malignant form of distemper, the source in all probability is the milk from dairies where not only diseased cattle are present, but the water used for washing the utensils, &c., is polluted with sewage. (*See* Diphtheria.)

Glanders.—The dog is highly susceptible of the poison of glanders, which may be communicated in cohabitation, by direct inoculation, spreading the matter on open wounds, or injecting it within the veins. In the latter instance, the operation being carefully performed, the induced disease generally proves fatal; in the other instances, it is thought the effect of the operation is to create immunity from subsequent attacks. This, however, is not sufficiently demonstrated to be set down as an admitted fact. Glanders in the dog is not marked, as in the horse, by chancrous sores on the nasal membrane, &c., yet bloody discharges are common, associated with dropsical swellings of the head and eyes, the membrane of the latter being acutely reddened. More or less fever is also present with lung disturbance and a lingering death, the illness in fatal cases extending over several months. Spontaneous recoveries are, however, quite common.

Measles.—The transmission of this disease from the human subject is set down as quite possible, a case having actually occurred in a pet dog which was allowed to lick the hand of a child affected with measles in a severe form. The animal sickened in twelve days, a discharge from the nose appeared shortly after, and in four days died from resulting congestion of the throat and air passages generally. (*Veterinary Journal*, 1876.)

Rabies.—From whatever aspect we view this disease, there can be but one, the *inevitable* conclusion that it is one of the most dangerous and formidable, the possibilities of which are fearful to contemplate. The number of human victims who are said to succumb to the effects of the poison is not the only horror which comes of its prevalence, however large the quotation may be. In the minds of those who are called to minister to the sufferer, no description can portray the amount of mental agony and utter dismay they undergo while unable to offer the least assistance calculated to assuage the bodily sufferings, or impart solace to the distracted mind. From this point of view it is not surprising that, by general consent, we regard the mention of rabies as synonymous with general prevalence, the cry of "mad dog" having an electrical effect upon a whole population. Nervous subjects, especially those who know little or indeed nothing of rabies, at the mere mention of the name often work themselves into a fearful state of apprehension, not unfrequently attended with serious consequences. Such being the case, it is high time that all interested in canine pets should become acquainted with the general characters of the disease, the usual mode of origin, possibility of communication to other animals as well as ourselves, in order that means for its delimitation at least may be secured if we cannot immediately suppress its existence.

Rabid dogs, it has often been said, exhibit method in their madness. A state of fury is uncommon or at least associated only with certain forms of the disease; in many cases the creature is perfectly docile, the owner himself having not even the vestige of a suspicion against his pet. Rabid dogs have been known to fondle, caress, and lick the hands of their owners as on other occasions, which in some instances have proved fatal, the virus from the saliva gaining entrance to the system through a scratch or other slight form of wound. They show their intense dislike to other dogs in preference to human beings as a rule; even in sleep they rise and violently rush at the object of their fury, which exists only in their disordered imagination; they will also snap as at flies, or other unseen objects, and from apparently sound sleep suddenly rising to the attack have been known to fall exhausted by the effort. The desire for freedom is peculiarly manifested, often with a degree of cunning for which even the dog would scarcely be credited. Once free he commences his wanderings, often covering immense distances, and when unmolested returns to his lair completely prostrate, or partially paralysed, and in a short time wholly so. It is rare that he attempts violence during this remarkable journey, but when provoked is apt to commit fearful havoc. The wisest course, therefore, when a dog is "on the march" and correctly recognised, is to give him possession of the road, as in all probability he will never molest any person. *His evident desire is to get away from the disease*, and to this end he devotes himself with a concentration of will that is remarkable in the brute creation.

In the *furious stages* the dog is inclined to make sudden attacks, the victim receiving one or more grips, and probably thrown down or rolled over, the march being resumed in search of others. Thus, in the space of a single night, not only dogs, but a large number of sheep are bitten, and being unobserved, the circumstance has favoured the surmise that the disease had a spontaneous origin. The disposition to bite is evidently due to the condition of the brain, amounting not only to a loss of the normal sensation, but also to mental aberration. This is shown sometimes by apparent violence in the attack as well as seizure, shortly relinquishing his hold after a harmless grip, then turning to resume his way as if nothing had happened.

In the form known as *dumb rabies* the lower jaw drops from paralysis, the tongue hangs loose and becomes of a dark purple hue, the throat also swells. The eyes are dull, heavy and affected with strabismus or squinting, in some cases the pupils being turned towards the nose.

As a result of previous violence the head is often swollen, and the teeth are broken; the lips and tongue are likewise swollen and lacerated from the violence of attack on other animals or objects, as well as in unsuccessful attempts to gain his liberty. *Perverted taste* is evident from the very earliest period of the disease, which causes the sufferer to take up all kinds of foreign bodies, large accumulations of which are found in his stomach after death. Vomition, sometimes expelling blood, is present only in the early stages, after which paralysis sets in followed by death. The fondness for urine is deemed a sure evidence of rabies. Sexual excitement is often intense before other really diagnostic signs are recognised; sometimes also the desire to lick the genitals of other dogs. Fever is present and increases with the development of the disease. There is a bright red or lurid appearance in the eyes, probably with squinting of both, pus accumulates in the angles, and a discharge flows from the nostrils. As the disease advances the breathing is loud and hollow, and in subsequent stages it is performed mainly through the nostrils. The voice is also peculiarly affected: the howl of a mad dog is an experience which will never be effaced from memory. It is utterly impossible to convey its characters by any selection of terms. It must be heard to be really understood. Confined to his cage or otherwise secure he sits on his haunches, the muzzle directed upwards or resting his head on the wall, he attempts an abortive kind of bark which curiously develops into a succession of equally abortive howls. This is most common at night after the routine of bustle and noise is stilled, and is consonant with the usual recuperative efforts of the system at this season, which have the tendency to aggravate existing disease. At this stage also signs of local irritation may be present, the cause being the cicatrix of a former wound inflicted by another dog suffering from the disease. He licks at first, but eventually bites or even tears the skin which at this part exhibits the gangrenous stage. This is the inoculation point, which, as a result of the introduction of the virus heals but imperfectly, and is subject to the consequences of irritation and ulceration, one of Nature's efforts to rid herself of the poison. The issues are constantly fatal, death taking place from two or three days in some of the most acute cases, or it is otherwise delayed until about the seventh day.

The *Post-mortem Appearances* in fully developed cases are remarkable. The body very shortly enters into a state of decay. At the back of the mouth, and within the stomach, foreign bodies of the most strange character are found, as sticks, stones, dirt, fæces, bits of iron, tin, leather, &c. The back of the tongue and the mouth, with the lining membranes of the windpipe, also those of the pharynx and larynx, are highly congested and streaky, particularly about the epiglottis, and the vocal chords are not uncommonly ulcerated. The salivary glands are involved in the general congestion, which extends to the stomach and intestines, portions of which exhibit patches of extravasated blood, some of which have already entered on the ulcerative stage. As a result of this process within the stomach, considerable effusion 'n the form of a coffee-coloured fluid—abnormal blood material—is present in addition to the usual heterogeneous accumulations. Blood spots are found upon the heart, pleura, peritoneum, and elsewhere. The spleen, liver, and lymphatic glands generally are enlarged by congestion; also the substance of the brain, medulla, and spinal chord with their several coverings. In addition, there are indications understood only by the scientist, assisted by a powerful microscope,

Specific and Contagious Diseases. 161

&c., without which no investigation can be said to be complete.

In *animals recently bitten by a rabid dog, and summarily destroyed*, the post-mortem appearances afford no evidence of rabies. The simple reason for this is that sufficient time has not been allowed for the development of the actual disease. Without disease there can be no alteration or destruction of tissue. For similar reasons the *inoculation test* is equally barren of positive indications. The subsequent appearance of cerebral symptoms in the inoculated victim is no proof whatever.

The *bite of a healthy dog* is regarded by many nervous and timid persons as the probable communication of rabies. This is impossible. Even if rabies developed at a later stage in the same animal, the subject of the bite is perfectly safe. If this were otherwise, the writer would have never penned these lines. The healthy animal, however angry and furious he may be towards strangers, cannot induce or develop within his system the poison of rabies, *he must first receive it, the usual source being some other rabid animal*. Under the exercise of fear engendered in ignorance of the above fact, the biting dog is labelled "mad," pursuit instantly commences, he is run down and killed, and there is the end of him. But the sufferer lives on in doubt and fear, harassed, tormented, and can never be consoled, probably the end being long delayed, without the least sign of the canine disorder. *The mistake occurs in the haste to kill the dog.* Had he been spared, his death or survival, either of which could be ascertained in all probability within a week at the most, would reveal the true state of the case.

Another popular error exists in the belief that rabid dogs have a great *aversion to water*. There is no such fear as far as our observation has been conducted. We have witnessed animals in both forms of the disease endeavour to slake the burning thirst, which they were unable to accomplish, owing to the want of nervous power which is present from the first, but especially developed in the mute or dumb form. With these truths in evidence it is incorrect to speak of a rabid dog as being affected with hydrophobia, or the human subject as being rabid. The dread of water applies to the latter, in whom the disease is correctly hydrophobia.

Frothing or foaming at the mouth is also believed in as a sure sign of rabies. It is a certain condition of this disease that the secretion of foam, or large quantities of saliva worked into innumerable air bubbles, is often impossible, by reason of the congested state of the blood-vessels and the salivary glands.

The *fits of epilepsy* have frequently been mistaken for rabies. It is almost needless to state that rabid dogs do not become unconscious and fall, as is common with the epileptic sufferer, or the young dog in distemper.

There are, doubtless, other conditions which may resemble, more or less, certain stages of rabies, but on careful consideration it will be found they are unassociated with the disease. *Hasty conclusions must be carefully avoided, and in the absence of absolute proof it is a wise proceeding to withhold decisive judgment; place the suspected animal in a secure cage, room, &c., and wait the issue of a systematic course of observation.*

With regard to *curative methods* and remedies suggested, their name is legion and the results of their application *nil*. The *truly rabid dog should be summarily destroyed before he commits any damage,* unless some special reason exists for sparing his life. The body should be burned as the only safe and expeditious method of destroying the virus also, thus limiting the possibilities of spreading the disease. Thorough cleansing and disinfection of yards, kennels, beds, baskets, &c. &c., occupied by the sufferers (the object being the destruction of any saliva) should follow, and as an efficient agent black ashes in boiling water cannot be surpassed. Its great drawback is its effectual removal of paint from woodwork; where this is an objection, strong soap solution with crude "Sanitas" will answer effectually. Those who engage in this work should first see they have no open sores or scratches on their hands, &c., and in all cases the *first washings* should be accomplished by means of brushes having long handles; subsequent courses may be carried out with scrub brush, flannel, &c. The drains also demand attention; effectual flushing by large volumes of a strong solution of black ashes, boiling if possible, will be eminently useful, and in its absence a strong mixture of crude "Sanitas" with water will be equally effective. The recurrence of subsequent cases, be it remembered, will in all probability be due to some lurking virus, and that which proves dangerous to the dog may be equally fatal to the human subject; effectual cleansing must therefore be insisted upon; a few shillings spent at this time may save many pounds later on and prevent serious loss and discomfiture.

The *seizure of a mad dog* is often a most difficult proceeding even with the most fearless. When confined to a stable or other building he should be approached from above if possible and, by cautious movements, seized by the lasso, which, on being pulled tightly, will strangulate the victim; this is often preferable to shooting; the liability of a marksman to miss the vital spot renders death less certain, while the creature is seriously alarmed and roused to violence. When at large the lasso may also be useful, providing the operator is well up to the business, which needs to be done determinedly, fearlessly, and above all quietly. For this purpose the lasso should be attached to a stout stick at the end of which the loop is arranged; the operator grasps the stick as well as the returning cord, and following the dog, projects the loop over and beyond his head; immediately the cord surrounds the neck it is pulled by one hand, the other holding the stick steadily, the dog is securely arrested, and if necessary at once strangled. Iron pincers, formed to encircle the neck, are likewise useful if available at the time. This, however, is the great difficulty, and in a sudden emergency men and others who witness the escapades of rabid dogs, work themselves into an excitement which often paralyses their judgment as well as efforts, and the worst thing is probably done. Seriously aggravated by the treatment, the dog becomes violent, and bites right and left. Presence of mind, cool judgment, and quiet movements are best calculated to secure the victim; he may be cajoled into a building, yard, or enclosure, and there be summarily dealt with.

Prevention of rabies.—Various means have been suggested for this purpose, and to the present day the record is an admission of disappointment. Absolute extermination of the canine race would not secure the stamping out of the disease, as other animals, notably the fox and cat in this country, contribute to the perpetuation of the virus, not among themselves alone, as they are undoubtedly answerable for the sudden appearance of the malady among straying dogs in localities where it has not previously been seen for long periods. *Homeless and mongrel dogs* should be regularly seized and summarily consigned to the lethal chamber. The *uncertain or indefinite period of incubation of the disease*, suggests the detention of many animals in a dog's home should be conducted with great care, otherwise the mingling of various breeds may ensure the propagation of rabies when they return to liberty. For similar reasons *quarantine*, unless the animals are isolated from the first and retained over six months, would likewise prove a mistake. An efficient system of prevention must sooner or later receive the consideration of our Government with the view of their taking over the direct control. A serious matter of this kind should not be left to the hesitating policy of local authorities. It is a matter of surprise and regret that the fell disease should have escaped the attention of the legislature when framing the Contagious Diseases (Animals) Acts, by which the movement of dogs could be effectually controlled. Probably our rulers in their zeal for the chase were oblivious of the denizen of the town, whose nocturnal slumbers are disturbed by the miserable and worthless curs which render night miserable by their cry. The tax is systematically evaded by many who, scarcely knowing the source of their next meal, harbour the nondescript wanderers and mongrels which form the subjects of a constant trade. The *local muzzling order*, we believe, is a mistake, and produces a needless irritation among well-meaning and law-abiding owners. The muzzle is a *cruel torture to most dogs;* its general utility is questionable. The really spirited fellows obstinately refuse to appear in public when so distinguished; others, docile and often useless creatures, take to it quietly, and knowingly put up their heads to passing strangers inviting its removal. The honest boys of the locality are swift to comply with Fido's request, and hang the trapping on the owner's railings or throw it into the area; but the ubiquitous arab, with an eye to business, hands it to the marine store dealer for "a consideration," a large trade in these articles having been done during the rabies scare of 1895 and early months of 1896. Meanwhile Fido's owner is summoned to the police court and is released on payment of a fine, minus the assurance of a speedy abatement of the nuisance.

The wearing of a collar securely locked, on which the name and address of the owner is legibly engraved, serves useful purposes, as the restoration of straying animals to their proper owners, and the means of learning whether the tax is paid. A further security would be ensured by the collar bearing the County initials, or device, and registration number. This should be somewhat ornamental and light, and supplied free with the licence. Dogs thus furnished, and secured by a suitable chain or leather leader, might be allowed, at all times and with perfect safety, to take outdoor exercise under the care of their owners, &c.

Dogs at large in public places need special care. (*See* Balanitis.) The general adoption of a suitable leader is not only a useful training to follow and keep close to the owner, but an efficient safeguard against the unprovoked and savage attacks of jealous animals, which the muzzle does not prevent. It is remarkable, especially in towns, how few are the dogs which, by absence of training, do not disgrace their liberty by their brutality, often encouraged by their owners, who are oblivious of the panic, or otherwise prolific in abuse when reasonably appealed to. This cannot be said of dogs used for sport, as the foxhound, setter, pointer, &c., which are broken to work.

Besides the seizing and destruction of homeless curs and cats, which need especial watchfulness, why should we hesitate to include the fox? Surely when he is known to be "on the mad march," it would be safe to bring him down before he commits any serious damage. The farmer sees such an animal now and again, his errand being the spreading of the virus of rabies by means of his bite, and on he goes again with a business purpose, until he dies from exhaustion. Powder and shot accurately applied have a strictly legitimate use in this direction. A grain of prevention is worth a hundredweight of cure.

Regulations to these ends properly enforced, aided by useful information printed on the back of the annual Dog Licence, would prevent many mistakes, and bring the disease within a small and manageable compass.

After all, rabies is not so prevalent, except in the disordered imagination of persons ignorant of the disease, as is generally believed. Among the three hundred thousand dogs which have passed through the home at Battersea in twenty years, the Manager informed Dr. Gordon Stables that he had never seen one suffering from rabies. The majority of animals destroyed for supposed rabies are doubtless epileptics, and such results are inevitable so long as policemen rank as scientists in such matters.

The Pasteurian System.—The utterly futile nature of remedies propounded for the cure of hydrophobia in the human subject has led to diligent search for others. The great difficulty which confronts the practitioner is the extremely rapid and fatal course after *direct* inoculation. In utter defiance of the physiological action of remedies the fell disease proceeds without deviation, and the inevitable end in death cannot be averted. Thus far internal remedies have failed, but the fact has stimulated research in other directions. The disease has been studied from other aspects. Its existence is believed by some to depend upon the presence of a microbe, but Pasteur, whose investigations have been extensive, has not endorsed the view. His efforts were directed towards sterilising the poison within the system of the person bitten by the mad dog. Briefly, the operation consists of inoculation with a specific virus which has been cultivated by transmission through other animals, as the ape, until it is deprived of its power to induce rabies, while it renders the individual immune or proof against the disease. In order to ensure the greatest results, frequent inoculation of the same patient is sometimes resorted to, many thousands of persons said to be bitten by rabid dogs having been submitted to the test, with, however, variable success. In the state of present experience it is obvious that the end is not attained, yet in the interest of suffering humanity, as well as the brute creation, the issue of further investigation in other directions is eagerly looked for, and with the fervent hope that the inevitable end will be an irreversible good.

The Treatment of Rabies.—In *La Presse Veterinaire* for December 1895, M. Pourtale invites special attention to his treatment of rabies in the dog, which he states has afforded "absolutely positive results." He employs a mixture of sulphate of soda, chloral hydrate, and decoction of linseed which calms the attacks, and produces a purgative, as well as refreshing action. Enemas of similar character are also used. Recovery, it is said, occurs in eight days generally; and from his experience, M. Pourtale is persuaded that if the treatment is applied to the human subject affected with hydrophobia it would bring about his recovery.

Septicæmia, or *Blood Poisoning*. In the evident enjoyment of putrid offal and decomposing filth of various kinds, the dog exhibits a remarkable immunity from disease of a fatal character. If, however, he should happen to imbibe the elements of decomposing flesh by means of a wound, the results are more serious. Varying, of course, with the amount of inoculation, he may succumb to an attack of fever of a severe typhoid nature, marked by speedy collapse, or, under less severe blood impregnation, he surprisingly recovers after acute as well as profuse diarrhœa, attended by repulsive odours. This form of septicæmia is most commonly observed in females, when, in protracted parturition, the fœtus is undergoing decomposition, and the lining membrane of the uterus or womb has been removed by abrasion or laceration, &c. Inoculation is thus complete, and the usual symptoms are observed in about eighteen or twenty hours. The usual signs, as dropsy of the tissues with the never-failing blood spots, are sufficient to mark the character of the case. The animal tissues also pass into speedy decomposition. During life the creature becomes weak, loses power, and at length is dull, unable to stand, becomes unconscious and dies from exhaustion. The *Treatment* should be prompt and energetic. Antiseptic lotion, as the "Sanitas" Fluid, chloride of zinc, or perchloride of mercury solutions are the most useful. The first only is non-poisonous to the dog. The uterus or womb should be carefully and repeatedly washed out by the solutions, which should be used at a temperature of 99° or 100° F. *Internally*, tonics of a stimulating nature are particularly called for.

Tuberculosis.—True pulmonary consumption, due to the presence of the tubercular bacillus, has only recently been definitely recognised in the dog. A variety of *false tuberculosis* has long been observed, consisting of irregular-shaped masses, the *débris* of altered tissue, enclosing small worms which have migrated thither by means of the blood. Such, however, have not developed the serious conditions of true phthisis. The question of its existence in the dog is no longer a matter of doubt as set forth by Professor Stockman in the *Veterinarian* for August 1896. The subject was a Scotch terrier, two years old, which had been in poor health upwards of two months, with rapid loss of condition. The symptoms consisted of great debility, difficult breathing, and temperature 103° F. Percussion revealed no dulness, and auscultation failed to detect abnormal sounds. As small round worms passed from the bowels, it was thought the animal might be suffering from verminous anæmia, and he was treated accordingly. The persistent chest trouble induced the Professor and several colleagues to concentrate attention upon the organs of respiration, but with negative results. Temporary amendment followed the use of tonics, the temperature falling to 101°. Shortly, the digestion was disturbed; fluctuating tubercular tumours were discovered in the abdomen, and on testing the lungs the sibilant râle was distinctly heard. There was no cough, and still the chest was elastic and without dulness on percussion. An injection of tuberculin was made at 1 P.M. At 11.30 P.M. the temperature had fallen to 99° F., and at 12.30 A.M. it was 98° F. Shortly afterwards the animal died. An examination revealed the presence of tubercular nodules in the lungs, varying in size from a pin's head to larger areas, but they were firm, thus accounting for the absence of râles. Bacilli were found in the mucus of the bronchial tubes, and the tubercular areas consisted mainly of epithelioid and spindle-shaped cells. A few bacilli were also found. The stage of caseation does not appear to have commenced. Miliary tubercles studded the mentum, liver, and spleen. The mesenteric glands were enlarged, hard, and fibrous, and in one a large abscess existed. A few bacilli were also found. The absence of caseation, or cheesy degeneration, so common in this disease, is fully accounted for by the action which resulted in the free development of fibrous tissue around the diseased points. The Professor concludes with a suggestion as to the value of tuberculin as a diagnostic in this disease of the dog.

Variola or *Small pox* in canine animals closely resembles the form usually observed in mankind as well as the sheep; one of the means of its introduction being the consumption of the flesh of sheep dying of the disease. It appears in the usual forms of mildness or malignancy; it may be discrete or separate, confluent or running together, and in further stages are those of erythema, nodule, vesicle or bladder, and pustule, the latter assuming the flat or concave surface from the usual internal changes. Subsequently desquamation proceeds, leaving hairless spots, which are hollow or concave scars or "pits." The thin skin of the belly and insides of the fore-arms or thighs are especially invaded.

The *Symptoms*, in addition to those already enumerated, consist of febrile disturbance from the first, which moderates as the pustules cease to form and indicates a tendency to decline. This is the usual or benign condition. Other forms exhibit a tendency to induce *bronchitis, pneumonia* or *broncho-pneumonia*, in which extensive pustular discharges flow from the nostrils, with cough, mucous râle, &c., and in fatal cases stertorous breathing. In the *Intestinal form* profuse bilious and often offensive evacuations take place. All the forms are attended with extremely fœtid breath and excretions, the skin also emitting the same unpleasant odour. Young dogs are especially liable to contract the disease in which mortality is always the greatest, the various stages being developed and merging into each other with remarkable rapidity.

Treatment of the patient comprises diligent and careful nursing, with mild febrifuges, stimulants and tonics. In warm or mild weather the eruption proceeds most favourably, particularly if the animal is sheltered from draughts, but cold winds and exposure generally checks the process of pus-formation, and leads to fatal terminations by implication of important internal organs. Animals recovering from variola are stated to be free from future attacks of the disease.

CHAPTER XI.

DISEASES OF THE RESPIRATORY SYSTEM.

Catarrh or Coryza—Ozæna—Parasitic Ozæna—Epistaxis—Polypus—Laryngitis—Aphonia—Snoring—Bronchitis—Pneumonia—Pleurisy—Parasitic or Verminous Bronchitis—Chronic Cough—Asthma.

Catarrh or Coryza.—Common cold in the head is the colloquial term for this affection. It consists of congestion of the lining mucous membrane of the nasal cavities, which, after some sensation of *stuffiness* or slight suffocation, develops the usual symptoms. The causes are exposure to cold draughts, severe cold weather, particularly east winds, after the comforts of close and warm quarters.

The *Symptoms* consist of fever more or less severe in proportion to the intensity of the congestion, which is attended by a discharge, first of a watery nature, but later becoming opaque, white and thick, as mucus and pus is mixed with it, the attendant irritation causing the animal to snuffle and snort, with attempts to eject the accumulations. A watery discharge flows from the eyes, and this also becomes purulent. Extension of these conditions to the sinuses of the head produces heaviness with dulness, with noisy respiration or "snuffling"; difficulty of swallowing and breathing, with cough, may also arise from the throat (pharynx and larynx) being involved, when the fluids or food partaken of return by the nostrils.

Treatment.—In mild cases removal of the causes usually suffices for cure. Advanced and severe forms must be met by expectorant draught No. 3 or Bolus No. 1 or 2. Support the strength by nutritious food of a laxative nature. Frequent steaming of the nostrils is highly useful. Avoid purgatives and emetics. The early use of tonics is essential.

Ozæna.—This term implies a chronic and often offensive discharge from the nostrils, the result of continued or neglected nasal catarrh, and occasionally it is caused by a polypus, portions of vomited aliment, or pus from the lining membrane. (*See* Polypus.)

The *Signs* are a constant discharge of bad-smelling pus from the nostrils, sometimes bloody, loud snuffling and dulness of the spirits. The disease is also due to a certain conformation, having contracted nasal chambers, as seen in pugs and bulldogs.

Treatment.—The nostrils must be kept clean, and the passages frequently washed out by syringing with "Sanitas" Fluid, solution of the chloride of zinc, or permanganate of potash.

Ozæna due to Parasites is somewhat common in

the dog. The offender is a formidable-looking object, a representation of which is given in the accompanying figure. It is the mature form of the parasite common to man, the horse, and other animals indigenous to various parts of Europe, in which it occupies the digestive organs, &c., and is known as the *Pentactoma denticulatum*. Dogs frequenting butchers' shops, slaughter-houses, and horse-slaughterers' yards gain access to the viscera which contain the parasite. It is taken to the mouth, where it attaches itself by powerful hooklets, and eventually crawls to the nostrils; some indeed pass direct, first attaching themselves to the outer side of the lips, &c. Armed with formidable and powerful hooks, they set up violent irritation as they migrate to and from the various passages, causing the sufferer to push his nose into the soil, or rub it with his feet; he also sneezes, champs the jaws, rolls violently on the ground, or passes into a violent convulsive fit, in one of which he sometimes dies. The parasite requires twelve months to develop, during which it thus tortures the dog whenever from any cause it is obliged to change its quarters by cold or frost, of which it appears to be peculiarly susceptible. The effects of its residence in the nasal chambers of the dog are inflammation, thickening, and probably ulceration of the lining membrane, with more or less disease of the turbinated bones, and even harder structures.

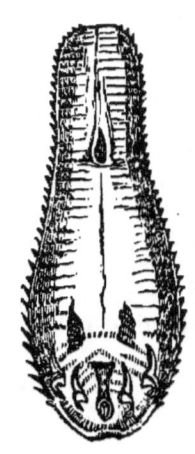

Pentastoma Denticulatum
(after Küchenmeister).

Treatment.—Inhalation of various volatile substances, fluids, &c., as iodine, chloroform, chlorine gas, tobacco smoke alone or combined with other agents. The application of iodoform may be effectual. Sometimes these are useless, as the parasite is located within one of the sinuses. When such is the case, and the exact position is made out, the cavity may be opened with the trephine, when the intruder is dislodged by direct application and destroyed.

Epistaxis, or *Bleeding from the Nostrils*, sometimes arises from plethora during hot weather. It is more common in hot countries than Britain. Blows or falls, by which the bones forming the cavities are subjected to shock communicated to the lining membrane, are common causes. (*See* Polypus.)

Treatment.—Cold water externally; astringent injections into the nostrils, and perfect quietude are essential.

Polypus, or *Tumour in the Nostrils*, is a morbid fibrous growth, covered by a continuation of the nasal membrane, and is sometimes observed from the exterior or front of the nostrils; it may also extend backwards to the pharynx. Its presence is denoted by more or less interference with breathing, ozæna, or hæmorrhage, which may be slight, or issuing in a stream.

Treatment consists of removal by ligature or excision, to determine which the veterinary surgeon is indispensable.

Laryngitis, or *Sore Throat*, is often a troublesome affection in some dogs. As the result of extreme change from the warm fireside to a seat in an open vehicle during cold or damp weather. Yard dogs and dogs at shows, constantly barking and running the length of the chain, suffer from the disease in an aggravated form. (*See* Aphonia.) The adjacent glands sometimes swell considerably, which renders swallowing not only difficult but painful. Food and liquids taken into the mouth return by the nostrils, and cause great inconvenience. The saliva, which is secreted largely and mixed with mucus from the inflamed membranes, has a fœtid odour, and flows in a continuous stream from the lips. The breath is also offensive, and respiration more or less disturbed; the heart-beats are rapid and forcible, the eyes are dull and discharging fluid. Cough is frequent and depressing, feet and ears probably cold, and bowels confined. The voice is lost, and replaced by a hoarse and feeble attempt, often interrupted by cough. As the signs are likely to be mistaken for choking, or the fixing of a bone between the molars, a special examination of the mouth should always be made; or the disease may be confounded with "dumb rabies" in which the mouth cannot remain closed.

Treatment.—Wash or gargle the mouth frequently with astringent lotion of tannic acid, alum, boracic acid, &c., or use one of the electuaries. Relieve the tumefaction of the throat by means of hot fomentations. Spongio piline as described under Poultices. Do not attempt to give food or medicine by the mouth, but support the system by injections of beef tea or mutton broth free from fat, in which half a drachm or more of nitrous ether may be given. With diminution of the sore throat, appetite will return, when food may be given by the mouth in small portions, carefully prepared, until the symptoms have disappeared. In some severe cases the attendant swelling necessitates the opening of the windpipe to admit of respiration; blisters may also be required to hasten suppuration in the glands, or to reduce the irritation in the throat, the use of which must be adopted only after careful consideration of the existing conditions.

Aphonia, or *Loss of the Voice*, is a state in which the bark is reduced to a rough and husky kind of sound, resembling a forcible expiration. The vocal chords being inflamed and relaxed from incessant barking, the sudden shocks from the collar in running violently to the end of the chain also bruise the larynx, which aggravates the complaint. Aphonia arises in conjunction with laryngitis, which see.

Snoring proceeds from a relaxed state of the laryngeal or throat apparatus, as induced by cold in which the vocal chords and velum palati are involved. It is removed by the remedies prescribed for laryngitis; but when it occurs in pet dogs highly fed and pampered, taking little or no exercise, the *treatment* must consist of a reduced diet, regular exertion, gentle cathartics, and subsequently tonics.

Inflammation of the Organs of Respiration contained within the chest of the dog is not usually, as in larger animals, confined to one in particular. The general tendency is for all to participate, while the intensity of disease is resident in one in particular—at least this has been our experience, which is confirmed by other observers. It will, therefore, be more convenient as well as consonant with the view, to consider the several affections as a whole, giving prominence to special manifestations and conditions which may serve to render the elucidation complete. There is also much in common with reference to the needful treatment of the affections which will be given in usual course.

The *first indications*, as a rule, are those of fever more or less severe. He pants and blows, being teased by a constant cough, the ears and extremities are cold, the coat in smooth dogs stands loose and staring, and fits of shivers recur at intervals of greater or less duration. The cause is not far to seek; undue exposure to cold in some form or other is satisfactorily made out, and this probably not long after previous attacks of sore throat, nasal catarrh, &c. The systemic disturbance is now located in some part in particular, and there the chief manifestations will be found, while the whole of the respiratory organs will afford evidences of sympathetic derangement.

Bronchitis, or Inflammation of the Bronchial Tubes, is denoted by accelerated but *even* respiration, a cough, probably dry at first but becoming moist, and attended with a discharge of mucus from the nose, as well as from the lungs during the act. As congestion of the lesser tubes within the lungs proceeds, the ejected fluid is also tinged with blood, the cough is severe and frequent, and a wheezing or hissing accompanies the respirations; the mouth, tongue, and nose are dry as well as hot, and the expired air is likewise indicative of a heated state of the lungs; the pulse is accelerated, the heart-beats felt at the chest are strong in the early stages, and the temperature, as shown by the thermometer placed in the rectum, is high, probably 103° or 104° F. Auscultation furnishes the mucous rattle as soon as the disease is established. From this point recovery is denoted by a cessation of the severity of all symptoms, and the creature every hour becomes "more like himself." In fatal cases prostration is soon manifested, with troubled respiration, indefinite pulsation, coldness, sinking and death.

In **Pneumonia**, or **Inflammation of the Lungs**, the ear placed at the side of the chest detects a crackling sound within, and tapping the ribs with the fingers elicits a dull heavy sound. The breathing is rapid and oppressed, the animal is unable to expand the lungs. A cough is present, not frequent but weak, and resembles a loud and forcible sigh; the expired air is also hotter than natural, and the pulse is rapid and oppressed; the ears and extremities are intensely cold, while the nose, instead of being hot and dry as in bronchitis, is very cold and moist or very wet. The temperature is increased in the early active stages, but the tendency to congestion within the lung tissue creates a somewhat early decline, which denotes sinking and death. Before the end the sufferer persists in sitting on his haunches with his fore legs apart, and later he stands on all four legs, which are separated, until he drops dead.

Pleurisy, Pleuritis, or **Inflammation of the Pleura,** *the lining membrane of the chest as well as covering of the lungs, &c.,* has also its special significations. The breathing consists of a prolonged inspiration which is somewhat slowly and carefully performed, and a sharp or somewhat halting or jerky expiration. The ear at the side detects in the first stages a sound of friction as the pleuræ of the lungs and ribs rub over each other in breathing. Later, this sound is gradually lost, disappearing from the bottom upwards as the accumulation of serum proceeds. The effusion of lymph also, which takes place during the active stages, serves to deaden the sound by uniting the lungs to the side and limiting their movement. A cough is present from the first, but it is short, paroxysmal, and evidently arrested by the extremely painful condition of the parts involved. Pressure on the sides or between the ribs inflicts severe pain, and the muscles of the sides may be observed to twitch or contract quickly. The state of the circulation causes the pulse to be small, hard and frequent. Animal temperature is also high. Expectoration is absent. A characteristic sign of pleurisy also in the later stages is the disposition to sit on the haunches as in pneumonia, and finally to stand until he drops dead.

In each of the foregoing diseases the animal indicates much suffering on account of the difficulty in breathing; he actually struggles for air as he sits or stands; the breath is offensive and the tongue hangs from the mouth apparently useless and is livid and extremely foul. As the chest fills with water, usually on one side only, the patient would lie, but the inconvenience he suffers causes him to rise almost at once. Dropsical swellings now appear, the respiration is laboured and painful, and the muscular spaces between the ribs are pressed outwards by the fluid within the chest. If the hand be carefully laid on these the heart-beats will be felt as a thrill as the fluid is moved by the pulsations. The tendency of the disease to attack one side only often renders the progress slow and protracted, the immediate cause of death being a form of internal drowning.

The *Treatment* is based on similar principles in each instance. Pure air is not only essential but curative, and is therefore indispensable in the routine. The best of nursing is required in order that comfort, warmth, and quietude may be ensured, and this, in conjunction with all known means of supporting the system by nutritious and digestible food, will fortify the system against the many depressing phases of disease, as well as aid the physiological action of remedies in the way of cure. With regard to medicines, the choice will lay with those of a stimulating, expectorant, and febrifuge character in order to support the system, control the circulation and promote free expectoration as a relief to the usually overcharged lungs in pneumonia and bronchitis. Bloodletting, emetics, and purgatives are so much poison and must be scrupulously avoided. To relieve the oppression of the chest the spongio-piline, as described under poultices, is an invaluable remedy; a good substitute is opodeldoc to which a small proportion of strong ammonia or turpentine is added, say one fluid drachm to one ounce of the former. This should be well rubbed into the sides. In the later stages vegetable tonics with the iodide of iron, one to three grains, will promote absorption of the chest effusion, or tapping must be resorted to, the trocar being passed through the space between seventh and eighth ribs, immediately above the sternum. In pneumonia and bronchitis nothing answers so well as the castor oil mixture, or mild salines for producing a lax state of the bowels, actual purgation being highly prejudicial.

In the *Distemper forms* of the two first-named diseases, which are characterised by great debility, the list of Expectorants will furnish appropriate formulæ for bolus or draught.

Verminous Bronchitis.—This form of disease, due to the presence of small worms in the air passages near the lungs, has been seen chiefly in young dogs. The parasite is located in numerous small elevations on the mucous membrane, giving rise to considerable irritation. The *symptoms* are those of bronchitis, the cough being short and husky, death following convulsions in most cases.

Treatment.—Stimulants and tonics should be given internally, and the patient caused to inhale dilute chlorine gas. The best method is the intra-tracheal method, or injection of the remedy direct into the windpipe by means of a suitable syringe. The most effectual remedies are "Sanitas" Oil or the "Sanitas" Fluid, turpentine, or solution of carbolic acid, three to ten drops of one of these being mixed with twenty or thirty of glycerine, to which three to ten drops of chloric ether is added, and the whole well shaken.

In the dog the worm proves to be one of the species known as *Strongylus*, a small white, slender, thread-like parasite, the male being about one-fourth of an inch in length, and the female not more than one-sixth or one-eighth of an inch. The mature female brings forth her young alive. The parasite has been named *Strongylus canis bronchialis*, and may possibly prove to be a stagal development of the *Strongylus filaria* of the sheep, &c.

Chronic Cough, by which is denoted a constant effort to discharge from the lungs, attended by a dry, harsh sound, usually commencing on the least exertion, short, and somewhat feeble, is common to animals taking little exercise, highly fed, and accustomed to warm rooms and soft comfortable beds. Violent paroxysms ensue on the infliction of unusual exercise, and the animal appears to be choking, the respiration being disturbed, and froth is ejected from the mouth. There are probably signs of indigestion with irregular bowels, &c., by which reflex nervous action upon the breathing apparatus is induced, leading to limited secretion and undue relaxation from want of nervous energy.

Cure depends upon removal of the causes, which should be carefully ascertained, the chief of which is doubtless chronic forms of indigestion inducing disturbance of the functional powers of the liver, spleen, pancreas, &c. Treatment of the cough alone is useless.

Asthma.—This painfully distressing disease finds its origin in a chronic form of bronchitis associated with thickening of the mucous membrane of the tubes, with more or less structural changes in the lung tissue as the result of high feeding and idleness. As dogs thus privileged grow old, the changes are completed: a fully distended stomach with increasing fat, exercising pressure, limits the respiratory act, and fully accomplishes that which is necessary to unfit the tissues for healthy function.

The *Symptoms* at the outset are those of indigestion, a depraved appetite, offensive mouth and breath, frequent vomition, flatulence, constipation, enlarged or hard abdomen. Piles are also common, or, if not developed, they are indicated by the animal drawing the anus over the ground, the hind paws being elevated on each side of his face. The animal is soon tired, hesitates to follow his owner, suffers from palpitation, has a capricious appetite, but is voracious after flesh. He is teased by a constant cough, which assumes such paroxysmal severity as to prostrate the sufferer, and he lies as if he were choking, but, after throwing out frothy matter, gains relief. Usually the dog appears to be dull, heavy, out of condition, and his coat is rough, and the skin sometimes has an unpleasant odour.

Treatment.—Aged animals should be destroyed by inhaling an overdose of chloroform, the most humane method of depriving them of life. In recent cases, when the animal is especially valuable, slight inhalations of chloroform, or the administration of chloric ether in doses of five to fifteen drops in a teaspoonful of water, may afford the needed relief. In less urgent cases one or other of the Expectorant formulæ will be useful as daily medicine. A hot bath, or stimulating liniment to the sides is also useful in cases of more or less urgency. In those of less severity, the patient being young, daily exercise is of great importance, the diet of flesh must be reduced, and vegetables substituted for the deficiency, or *Spratt's Fibrine* and *Beetroot cakes* may form the entire diet for some time. The action of the skin should be induced by regular cleansing and the use of the brush and comb. Aperients are called for to promote regular action of the bowels. Avoid such causes as cold and damp, especially while the health is precarious.

CHAPTER XII.

DISEASES OF THE CIRCULATORY SYSTEM.

Fatty Degeneration of the Heart—Rupture of the Heart—Valvular Disease—Pericarditis—Invasion by Parasites.

THE organs engaged in the circulation of the blood in canine animals are not subject to an extended list of maladies, as in the horse, for instance. The circumstances of food especially bring the dog within the limits of a special susceptibility to disease of the digestive track, but changes in the system of breeding, especially with reference to efficiency in various forms of sport, may remove the animal into the sphere of a new danger. Be this as it may, at present our list of diseases in connection with this particular class of organs is surprisingly limited.

Fatty Degeneration of the Heart is the common associate with asthma in pampered pets and constitutes a serious condition, the muscular tissue being replaced by adipose or fatty substance. The obvious result is a want of tone and energy in the beats or pulsations, and inability to propel the nutrient fluid along the channels of circulation. The various tissues therefore lack nourishment, become pallid and weak, which unfits the animal for any exertion, and a serious condition of the brain and nervous system is induced, not only in the want of nourishment, but in the defective supply of blood, syncope or fainting being a common symptom, sooner or later resulting in death. The disease is incurable, but may be prevented by permitting the animal to take regular exercise and other means of stimulating the natural functions.

Rupture of the Heart is not of common occurrence, but it is known in connection with improper feeding and want of judicious exercise. Dogs subjected to "a feast and a fast," and other treatment calculated to militate against health and condition, are likely to induce some form of degeneration of the organ, and in a moment of excitement, whether of play or work, rupture takes place at the weakest part, and death is certain.

Valvular Disease is not uncommon as the result of chronic rheumatism. It appears in the form of a deposit of fibrine from the blood, which may exist only as a roughness on the surface or be so large as to form a clot, and thus block up the opening to the vessels. Such conditions in their mildest form seriously interfere with the proper action of the valves, greatly diminishing the needful flow of blood; and when clots have formed the results are intensified, causing the patient to fall in repeated fits of fainting, or by completely plugging the vessels, sudden death is induced. *Treatment* is only palliative in the mildest forms of the disorder, the most useful agents being mild doses of calomel given alternately with iodide of potassium, the animal needing perfect quiet.

The Pericardium or Heart-Bag surrounds the heart and provides the fluid which moistens the surface during action. It usually suffers from disease in company with the pleura, or lining membrane of the chest, from which it derives a layer, internally and externally. An abnormal accumulation of thin reddish-looking fluid (serum) is the common result, producing inconvenience in proportion to the quantity, such as interference by pressure with the functions of the heart, as indicated by feeble pulse, obscuration of the heart sounds, tendency to fainting, anæmia, local dropsies, and eventually death. The disease is, however, rare in the dog, but as a result of injury is most common, bruising, puncture, or rupture from violent causes being the common forms.

Invasion by Parasites.—*Canine Hæmatozoa* is not an unfrequent event in dogs of the British Islands. The records of other countries where malarious influences abound furnish more frequent evidences. Two worms have been recognised: *Filaria immitis* or *Canis cordis*, and *Filaria sanguinolenta*, the former being generally understood to be the embryonic form of the latter.

Filaria immitis is said to be probably present in at least two-thirds of the dogs in the Chinese Empire, as estimated by microscopical examination of the blood. Singularly enough the embryos, though so numerous, do not occasion any appreciable inconvenience to the host, but move about briskly in a serpentine form within the blood-vessels. When fully developed as parent worms they take up their position within the heart, in some instances bundles or clusters of them being found, and individuals varying from one or two inches to six or seven in length. The general results of the presence of these worms is their interference with the valves, between which they may be forced by such bodily efforts as induce an inordinate flow of blood. The effects are seen somewhat later, as at the end of one or two days the animal exhibits a difficulty in respiration, dulness, and oppressed circulation, with great irregularity of the pulse, epileptic fits, &c., while fever is entirely absent.

Filaria sanguinolenta has a decided preference for various tissues of the body as well as the large aortic vessels, chiefly embedded in a mass of tumefaction, the result of their movements. In this they remain some time and bring forth their ova, which are subsequently hatched, and escape in all possibility as the mature worm, capable of propagating its species.

The tendency of the parasite to bore into the sentient structures gives rise to local irritation and the formation of small tumours. These are sometimes present on the surface or otherwise embedded within the deeper seated layers. Aggregations of such tumours occurring in various parts give rise to serious functional disturbance, consonant with the nature and position of the organ thus invaded.. *Pleurisy* also appears to have had its origin in some cases by the escape of the worms from the tumours in the substance of the gullet direct into the cavity of the chest, where they have been found crawling in the midst of recent tumefactions or adhesions created by their presence. *Paralysis of the hind limbs* is also seen, and is supposed to be the result of plugging of the small blood-vessels of the spinal cord by ova escaping by the aorta or chief artery. It is singular that the brain does not appear to suffer, the tumours, it is said, being seldom seen among the tissues in front of the heart. Doubtless, however, as may be hereafter demonstrated, other affections in various organs or viscera, as the kidneys, intestines, &c., may be due to similar causes.

CHAPTER XIII.

DISEASES OF THE DIGESTIVE SYSTEM.

The Teeth: Caries—Abscess of the Jaw—Diseases of the Tongue: Glossitis, Wounds, Paralysis—Ptyalism—The Lips—Pharyngitis—Choking—Structure of the Gullet—Indigestion—Vomition—Gastric Catarrh—Gastritis—Foreign Bodies in the Stomach—Ulceration—Worms in the Stomach—Colic—Diarrhœa—Dysentery—Constipation—Impaction—Enteritis—Prolapsus—Piles—Atony—Thickening—Hernia—Worms in the Bowels—Peritonitis—Ascites or Dropsy—Hepatitis, Acute and Chronic—Fatty Degeneration—Parasites in the Liver—Diseases of the Spleen and Pancreas—Goitre.

The Teeth are subject to disorder and discoloration from accumulations of so-called tartar at the neck, producing also irritation of the gums and the tooth cavity, usually ending in caries or displacement of the teeth and ulceration of the gums. The subjects are the well fed and pampered pets, especially old dogs, which contract a chronic form of dyspepsia, accompanied by offensive breath, flow of saliva from the lips, pain and inconvenience, until the animal becomes "broken mouthed"—that is, having scarcely a sound tooth.

To prevent these conditions the dog should be allowed to use and clean his teeth in the natural manner, namely, the picking of bones and other food sufficiently solid to require breaking down. For this purpose the Fibrine Cakes of Spratt's Patent are highly useful.

Broken Teeth are the result of carrying hard or heavy articles. **Displacement** is the result of irregular growth or accumulation of tartar, absorption of the alveolar margins, and ulceration of the gums. Extraction, with the after observance of hygienic rules, are the means of remedy.

Caries of the Teeth is the result of indigestion and improper feeding, probably derived from hereditary predisposition or taint. Breeders should especially note this fact. Excessive fœtor, unusual salivation, dulness, evidence of pain and fever, looseness of the teeth, which are encircled by deposits of tartar, evidence of pain on pressure, refusal of food, &c. The tooth is somewhat raised, and the gum inflamed, as the result of disease in the fang. *Treatment* consists of extraction, cleansing the mouth by antiseptic fluids as "Sanitas," &c. &c., and paying attention to the diet, exercise, and general welfare of the patient. When profuse bleeding follows extraction, a suitable plug of cotton wool steeped in a solution of alum or sulphate of iron will be usually sufficient.

Abscess of the Jaw, vulgarly known as *Canker of the Mouth*, results from neglect of the conditions essential to health, which leads to extensive caries and abscess of the fang of the tooth. Removal of the tooth is usually sufficient to liberate the pus; but in protracted cases the bone of the jaw swells, and the gums assume a spongy condition, with a liability to bleed profusely, causing high fever, salivation and inability to take food. These states may result in the discharge of matter by a fistulous opening.

Treatment.—Evacuate unopened abscesses; remove diseased teeth, and dress the parts regularly with astringent lotions, or simply "Sanitas" Fluid. Wash out the mouth also with the latter to remove the fœtor and sweeten the breath; and use a plug saturated in "Sanitas" for the cavity from which the tooth has been removed. Good food with stimulants and tonics will be required to restore the health and spirits of the patient.

Glossitis, or *Inflammation of the Tongue*, arises from punctures, bruises, scalding with hot food, the action of caustics, &c. Swelling and protruding of the organ from the mouth, profuse salivation, and probable soreness of the throat, with high fever, are the general signs.

Treatment.—Perfect quietness is essential. Syringe the mouth frequently with a solution of alum, or use an electuary as directed.

Wounds of the Tongue, *incised* or *punctured*, may be treated with astringent lotions thrown into the mouth by a syringe. During this treatment the animal must be fed on fluid rations, as Fibrine biscuits bruised and soaked in hot water or milk, and given when cool.

Paralysis of the Tongue is not common, but it occurs now and again in bulldogs and spaniels, hanging loosely and useless from one side of the mouth in a dry and often discoloured condition. In most cases the ascertained cause is nervous disorder. It is congenital in some animals, and therefore incurable.

Treatment comprises the use of nerve tonics, as strychnine. Purchasers of valuable dogs should be on the alert for this deformity, as unscrupulous dealers practise the surgical art of amputating the portion visible on the outer side of the teeth.

Ptyalism, or *Excessive flow of Saliva*, arises in the dog from the incautious use of mercurial ointment as a remedy for the mange, also when the mineral has been too frequently or too largely administered internally, when such *Symptoms* as the following are present: Discoloration or perhaps looseness of the teeth, sore and swollen gums, and in long-standing cases disease of the bones. Saliva drivels from the mouth, and when the jaws are separated the flow is largely increased. The animal is dull, highly sensitive to cold, and the body generally is cold, especially the ears and legs. A close examination is essential in order to decide accurately, as ptyalism arises from other causes, as defective teeth and disease of the mouth, &c. (*See* Mercurial Poisoning.)

The Lips are liable to invasion by warty growths, which sometimes affect the outer cheek, as well as internally, together with the tongue and palate. Increase in size, and their possible recurrence, may prove highly inconvenient and troublesome, besides being a serious disfigurement. The most effective treatment is that of constant excision by suitable sharp scissors or the knife, the parts being afterwards touched with lunar caustic.

Inflammation of the Pharynx or **Pharyngitis** always accompanies Laryngitis (which see), one of the common results being permanent thickening or ulceration of the lining membrane, the disease having assumed a chronic character. Free dressings with nitrate of silver are recommended, the mouth being kept open by means of the gag.

Choking.—Notwithstanding ample provision in the dog for bolting the food, this accident sometimes takes place, the usual seat of obstruction being the entrance to the pharynx. The *Symptoms* are frequent attempts to regurgitate or force out the obstruction; fluids passed into the mouth return immediately. There is also frequent cough, profuse salivation, great discomfort, an anxious look in the eyes, and sometimes the obstruction may be seen and felt on the outside.

Treatment.—Previous to actual surgical interference the nature of the obstruction should be ascertained, as sharp or angular substances are sometimes serious offenders, and should not be pushed downwards. A whalebone probe or a flexible tube specially made for the purpose will answer for pressing down a piece of meat, pudding, &c., but when bones or other hard and dangerous things are lodged in the passage, the throat forceps alone are useful, by which the body is seized and drawn through the mouth. During the operation the dog must be fixed securely, and the mouth held open by the gag. These methods may fail in consequence of the offending substance moving downwards and again retained within the gullet. In this case, seeing no direct possibility of moving the obstruction any further, the surgeon will not hesitate to open the gullet by incision from the outside, as experience shows the surprising aptitude for healing in the portions subjected to the operation. A fluid diet and attention to the wound comprise the after-essentials for a week or more.

Stricture of the Gullet is the probable result of repeated choking, considerable injury to the mucous membrane and even the muscular layer, arising from the swallowing of hard, and probably sharp, angular substances, as bones, &c. Similar states are also due to the presence and burrowing of a small round worm known as *Filaria sanguinolenta.*

The *Symptoms* are frequent and usually slight attacks of choking, which subside without treatment, or otherwise, after a dose of chloric ether in cold water. Its existence in sporting and other dogs which require heavy food is a serious drawback, the use of light and highly digestible food only being tolerated.

Inappetance, or *absence of desire for food*, is often a sign of being overfed and the beginning of serious states, and may arise from decayed teeth, sore tongue, mouth, or gums, choking, or muscular inability from paralysis of the jaws. The *treatment* must be based on the discovery and removal of the cause.

Indigestion is a disease of common occurrence in canine animals. The wandering mongrel alternately suffers from absolute want and over-repletion with unsuitable and highly indigestible food, and the highly favoured pets are the victims of a depraved appetite brought about by want of exercise, over-repletion, and often most unsuitable aliment. Allied causes are disease of the mouth or irregularities of the teeth, a torpid liver, worms or foreign substances in the stomach.

Symptoms.—A depraved appetite associated with frequent vomition, the ejected material passing down the nostrils. The bowels are constipated and distended by air, the result of fermentation, giving rise to colicky pains, dulness, and often excessive peevishness or unusual anger. The patient is often sensitive to cold, and seeks absolute quiet and warmth; the coat is rough, harsh and staring, and the temperature of the body irregular and unequal. In old-standing cases the sufferer lays on much fat, the hair falls off, and the state becomes one of general debility or anæmia.

Treatment.—Change of food and regular meals, substituting more digestible or less stimulating varieties as may be needed. Fresh air, regular exercise on foot. Purgatives are required for constipation and colic, assisted by occasional enemas; carbonate of soda or potash in water to relieve acidity and irritability of the stomach, and vermifuges to expel worms when they are known to be present.

Emesis or **Vomition** in the dog depending upon special nervous endowment, under ordinary conditions is a salutary process, intended as Nature's safeguard in the many dangers to which, as the scavenger of the earth, he is necessarily exposed. Thus irritant food is speedily ejected; and the organ also becomes specially excited under the stimulus of numerous ailments, when enforced discharge of the contents has the effect of a powerful sedative on the system. This special sensitiveness has led to egregious abuse in the employment of emetics for almost every disease, irrespective of the torture to which the creature is subjected. Their adoption should be regulated by great care and judgment, as they are likely to produce serious gastric disorder with *Continuous Vomition*, a condition usually indicative of acute irritation when it arises independently of medicinal agents.

Gastritic Catarrh, or *Catarrh of the Stomach*, vulgarly called "husk," consists of a congested and irritative, and more or less inflamed condition of the extensive mucous lining, arising from injudicious as well as erroneous feeding, the presence of parasites or indigestible foreign bodies.

The *Symptoms* comprise some amount of fever, irritability of the stomach, with frequent vomition, the fluid being of an acid character, and contains no food. Pressure over the region of the stomach causes severe pain in most cases. The animal is dull, dispirited, and tormented by a constant cough. By extension of the disease to the bowels, a fatal diarrhœa sets in, and the termination is usually fatal.

Treatment.—This is not always successful, the retention of food or medicine by the stomach being a matter of extreme difficulty. Small quantities only of anything should be given, and at frequent intervals. The best remedies appear to be prussic acid, chlorodyne, or opium, alternated with the carbonates of potash or soda. The injection of remedies beneath the skin offers a suitable method of treatment, thus avoiding the dilution as well as waste by the constant vomition. Some practitioners find great benefit from the administration of a pill containing one to three grains of opium, and sulphate of iron five to ten grains given morning and evening. If the vomition can be arrested, the use of vegetable tonics, as gentian or quinine, will be called for, and, in chronic cases, nux vomica in small and repeated doses.

Gastritis, or *Inflammation of the Stomach* of a true character, is seen only in connection with poisoning by irritants.

The *Symptoms* greatly resemble those of indigestion, developing slowly, and consist of thirst, fever, a habit of licking cool objects, depraved appetite, and subsequently frequent vomition. Pain is evinced by frequent whining, restlessness, moving from one place or position to another, and by stretching at full length, to present the abdomen to the ground. Pressure over the stomach causes pain; the pulse is accelerated and small, and animal temperature is increased. The mouth and tongue are dry, dirty and foul, breath offensive, mucous membranes injected, and vomition proceeds first by the ejection of simple fluid, which occasionally contains blood.

Treatment.—Precise measures consist of the administration of an agent which by chemical union with the poison renders it inert, details of which will be given under Poisons. Frequent draughts of soothing mucilaginous and alkaline solutions are advisable, and the application of counter-irritants, as mustard, in the form of plasters, is indispensable. With full abatement of all the symptoms, the animal enters upon the stage of convalescence, when vegetable tonics and alkalies will serve to promote sound recovery, during which the greatest care must be exercised in feeding.

Ulceration of the Stomach is occasionally seen as the result of malnutrition dependent upon wasting diseases, as distemper, or bad and insufficient food, with confinement in unsanitary places. The condition of defective health thus induced also secures the existence of other local evidences, the cornea being the common seat of the disease.

Foreign Bodies in the Stomach of the dog are common. Their name also is legion and we cannot enumerate them. The more common are stones, &c., which the animals are taught to seize or carry, which may be swallowed. Others have sharp prominences, and may seriously wound some of the structures, producing a train of morbid signs not always of simple interpretation, death only revealing the true nature of the case as well as its cause.

Worms in the Stomach.—These consist of several varieties of round as well as tape-worm, the chief of the former being the *Ascaris marginata*, or marginated round worm, and the *Spiroptera sanguinolenta*, and of the latter *Tænia cucumerina*, and more rarely *Tænia cænurus*, or gid tape-worm of the sheep.

Symptoms.—Nausea, retching, and vomiting proceed first in order, accompanied with fœtid breath, and a dry, troublesome, husky cough. Subsequently the bowels are irregular and colic ensues, with increase of the foregoing symptoms, especially gastric disturbance, often terminating with convulsions and death. Some dogs exhibit a voracious appetite in the early stages; notwithstanding the animal becomes poor and even emaciated, and towards the close there are signs of brain disturbance.

Treatment.—An effective remedy consists of oil of turpentine, one or more teaspoonfuls, proportionate to the size and build of the dog, in combination with one to three ounces of pure glycerine, followed in two or three hours by a dose of olive oil, or the Castor Oil Mixture. (*See* Aperients.) If needful these medicines may be repeated in three days.

Colic or Spasms, vulgarly known as *Gripes*, is a sign of bowel derangement, spasmodic in nature, and unassociated with tendency to inflammation. The *Causes* are irritants within the bowels, or the spasms may be due to reflex act on arising from morbid derangement in other organs, mostly the former, the irritants being foreign bodies, impacted food, disease of stomach, bowels, liver, or other contiguous organs. Colic is often present in diseases induced by mineral poisons, as in *lead colic*, and also those dependent upon animal poisons developed during certain diseases, as Distemper; it is also a common sign of worms. Puppies suffer frequently from changes in the quality of the mother's milk, and it also appears in pregnant bitches as a result of pressure on the neck of the bladder.

The *Symptoms* usually arise suddenly, the animal exhibiting signs of discomfort by moaning. The sleep is disturbed and he cries, rises, turns round, draws himself together, again lies down, but soon rises and repeats the various acts. Increase of pain is betokened by sharp and frequent cries; he is more restless and assumes every variety of position; the back is arched upwards, and the abdomen is distended when the colic is due to flatulence, or small, hard, and contracted in obstinate constipation. Fever is not present in true or simple colic.

Treatment.—Some practitioners resort to an emetic in the first instance. Others prefer to put the animal at once into a warm bath (90° to 104° F.), which frequently reduces the spasm, and promotes free action of the bowels, especially when conjoined with smart friction over the surface. If the pain is severe, anti-spasmodic draught No. 2 may be given at intervals of two or three hours; and mustard plasters may be applied to the surface of the abdomen, or a stimulating liniment should be rubbed in. When, however, some known irritant is present, an oleaginous aperient should be given in the first instance, as removal of the cause is specially curative.

Diarrhœa consists of a frequent passing of liquid fæces, attended with pain, spasm, or colic, and more or less straining. Acute cases have their origin in the presence of some irritant, which induces a catarrhal state of the mucous membrane, and inordinate secretion from the numerous intestinal glands as well as the membrane itself. Such irritants are food, intestinal worms, &c. Diarrhœa is also the result of blood disorder, terminating in wasting disease, or "breaking up of the system." It also depends upon an excessive secretion of bile, and may be caused by repeated overdoses of purgative medicines, inducing super-purgation. Chronic cases are denoted by intractable indigestion, and great debility in addition to the above, with more or less ulceration of the bowels, as seen near the anus, the opening of which is relaxed and dilated.

Treatment.—The patient demands the most careful nursing and *strict cleanliness*, with freedom from exposure to cold, otherwise acute cases have the tendency to assume the chronic form. A suitable dose of the castor-oil mixture (*see* Aperients) should be given in the first instance, which by removal of the original cause determines the recovery of the patient. If, however, the case assumes the chronic stage, one of the anodyne formulæ must be adopted, with astringent diet, as the symptoms indicate. Simple glycerine, vaseline, or "Sanitas" jelly, especially the latter, are eminently useful in soothing the anus and bowel, when smeared over it. When liver disorder is evident, calomel or podophyllin will be of service. Young puppies often suffer from a form of diarrhœa while deriving their sustenance from the mother. In that case the latter should receive a mild purgative; afterwards lime-water to drink, or a solution of carbonate of soda (5 to 10 grains to each ounce of water) mixed with the food. The disease is also a common associate with the early stages of distemper, the probable cause being the ingestion of unsuitable food and filth, or inhalation of the odours arising from drains, accumulations of manure, &c. Worms are a common cause. The usual remedy is half a dose of castor oil, with one to three drops of laudanum. Chronic forms degenerate into dysentery.

Dysentery consists of inflammation of the mucous membrane of the large bowels as a rule, followed by ulceration and discharge of blood. The evacuations contain no fæces, except at intervals, when solitary, dark, small, and offensive lumps are voided. The causes are those common to diarrhœa largely aggravated.

Symptoms.—In addition to the above, the animal suffers from abdominal pain, with rapidly forming debility and emaciation, also emanations of sickly odours from the skin and mouth. Shreds of the intestinal mucous membrane pass with blood among the offensive evacuations; the pulse and respiration are quick, nose dry and hot, mucous membranes injected, great thirst, but no appetite, gradual sinking, and death.

Treatment must be careful and persistent.

Constipation or **Costiveness** is the result of torpidity or comparative inaction of the bowels, the animal passing no fæces, or, otherwise, they are voided with much effort and pain, and are dry, small, and hard. The disorder is common to animals under confinement, especially when fed solely on animal food. Constipation, associated with fever, is one of the marked symptoms of liver disorder, but constipation pure and simple is not necessarily attended by fever, neither is it of long duration, and is amenable to ordinary remedies.

Treatment.—Change of diet is almost always essential. The flesh food should be reduced and the deficiency made up by vegetables, and a weekly feed of boiled liver will be helpful, conjoined with *regular feeding* times and *proper exercise.* In some cases the accumulation of fæces in the rectum is large, producing colic, and they may be felt on manipulating the abdomen by the hand as well as being evident in the bulging of the anus. Accumulations of this extreme nature sometimes prove fatal within a few hours in house and pet dogs. Removal of the accumulation of ingesta must be effected by means of the oiled finger, or when necessary broken down by he handle of a spoon, assisted by injections of warm water. A dose of the castor-oil mixture (*see* Aperients) should follow, and subsequently an occasional dose should be given if the disorder does not abate.

Impaction of the Bowels by means of various substances, as a bone of considerable size, or several pieces, a stone, accumulations of hardened fæces, or fibrous vegetable matter, which have been swallowed, constitutes an aggravated form of constipation. The formation of a calculus is of rare occurrence, but one such proves to be the cause now and again. Colic, constipation, and sometimes vomiting are present, especially after oleaginous purgatives have been administered. Enemas, assisted by external manipulation of the abdomen, often facilitates passage of the mass to the rectum and removed. A few days may be required for this purpose, during which the animal should receive only fluid laxative aliment, with opiates or other antispasmodics.

Enteritis, or *Inflammation of the Intestines.*—The muscular coat of the tube is the seat of the malady, the causes being impaction by indigestible substances, the passage of one portion passing within another, or some other form of strangulation; exposure to excessive cold and wet after removal of the coat; exhibition of poisonous doses of medicine or deliberate poisoning. It is also apt to arise from the absorption of local remedies used in excess for the eradication of mange.

Symptoms.—Continued pain and distress is evinced by cries and the appearance also of the eyes, with severe abdominal pain, high fever, and increase of temperature. Pressure on the abdomen increases the suffering; yet the animal finds some comfort in stretching himself on the ground, courting the coolness of the stones or earth to counteract the heat of the abdominal muscles. As a rule he seeks the quiet of a secluded corner, where he may be found, lying in perfect agony on his side and uttering piercing cries. The bowels are confined and the urine, voided only in very small quantities, is highly coloured and has a strong odour. The pulse is small, hard, and rapid; the nose is hot, thirst is considerable and the tail is firmly contracted over the anus and forward upon the abdomen. When the disease is due to poisons, vomiting is constant, the ejected fluids being mixed with blood. The mouth, ears, and legs become cold, the body smells disagreeably, the abdomen enlarges, the pulse and heart-beats becomes faint and at length imperceptible, and convulsions terminate in death. A chronic form of the disease may occur, which is indicated by intermittent colic, alternate constipation and diarrhœa, with tense abdomen, flatulence, &c., and more or less continuous vomiting, terminating in weakness, collapse, and death.

Treatment.—First learn the cause. If the disease arises from impaction, foreign objects, worms, &c., administer a *mild* dose of salad oil. Enemas of warm water will be useful, if assisted by breaking up of the fæces by the finger inserted within the rectum. Crude opium (one to three grains), chlorodyne, Indian hemp, &c., given in one or two teaspoonfuls of barley water, may be given to counteract pain and spasm, and may be repeated hourly as needed. Enemas containing one of these remedies are also of great value. A warm bath often proves highly beneficial if due care in drying, &c., is observed. In recovery the greatest care in feeding, &c., must be observed, or the animal when approaching convalescence will suddenly change, droop, and die from a recurrence of the malady. Poisoning must be met by appropriate remedies or antidotes. (*See* Poisons.)

Beef-tea, broth, milk, or cod-liver oil should be given with the medicines by the mouth, and by the rectum with astringents. Violent pain must be met by opium (one to three grains) hourly, or at longer intervals as needful to subdue the pain. Some practitioners add sulphate of copper with manifest benefit. A hot linseed poultice, or the spongio-piline (*see* Poultices) applied to the abdomen is often highly beneficial, and suppositories, or injections of an astringent nature should be employed in conjunction; iced water is sometimes added. Cleanliness, with fresh air, are all important in the means of cure.

Prolapsus Ani, or *Dropping of the Bowel*, appears in the form of an unsightly tumour beneath the tail, which often suffers considerable enlargement with the discharge of fæces, while some pain and difficulty attend the act. The usual *causes* are debility, the result of age, neglected constipation of a general character, as well as impaction of the rectum itself. It is also common in over-fed and idle dogs. It may be partial, consisting of the mucous membrane only, or the entire rectum may be everted, in which case swelling ensues with more or less strangulation, inducing changes which greatly militate against a speedy and successful return as well as retention of the organ.

Treatment consists of returning the bowels within the abdomen by means of careful side-pressure and manipulation with the fingers (the animal being held with the hind quarters raised considerably above the body), and afterwards dressed with cold astringent dressings. Injections or suppositories of the same nature should also be continued for several days, and the food should be fluid and laxative until the evidences of cure are established. In chronic cases the organ may become so mutilated and enlarged as to call for excision. *To prevent the disease*, avoid constipation of the bowels by a periodical feed of uncooked liver, boiled greens, or purgation.

Hæmorrhoids or **Piles** constitute a frequent disease in aged dogs, and those subject to constipation and a general state of relaxed fibre. Primarily they appear as simple bulbs or tumours located on the outer-side of the anal opening, or upon the lining mucous membrane within. They are, therefore, known as external or internal Piles, and consist of the enlarged veins of the locality, their condition being due to the pressure arising from straining to void fæces during constipation. Such pressure being long continued induces a tendency to ulcerate or slough, by which a number of sores are formed attended with more or less hæmorrhage constituting "bleeding piles." Further aggravation leads to the formation of *fistula*, which is an opening in a mass of condensed or diseased tissue, leading to a cavity, the situation of a former abscess. The lodgment of sharp, angular bones, or impaction by hard fæces lacerating the rectum, are also common causes. The liver is under disorder in most cases.

Treatment.—An oleaginous aperient is best for simple cases; but when the liver is at fault, an aloetic pill with calomel or the aperient blue pill should be given. Indigestion must receive appropriate treatment as detailed under that head, cod-liver oil forming a daily portion. *Local treatment* should consist of the application of cold water or ice for both forms, the latter being put inside and allowed to remain. Lotions of alum or the sulphates of zinc, copper, or iron, are also highly beneficial, but no permanent good can result unless the feeding is improved, and sufficient exercise is given to promote healthy function of the digestive organs in particular, and the system generally.

Atony of the Rectum is common to old dogs unable to take exercise. The gut is enlarged from constant impaction, and the glands of the vicinity discharge a foul-smelling fluid; the anus is also enlarged and ulcerated, from which a swelling arises and is continued downwards between the thighs along the course of the abdomen. It is common also to other diseases as a complication, viz., chronic diarrhœa and dysentery.

Treatment consists of supporting and improving the system by internal tonics and laxatives; the regular removal of fæcal accumulations, and constant administration of tonic astringent enemas, as solutions of tannic acid, sulphate of iron, &c.

Thickening of the Bowel, *leading to Stricture,* sometimes attended by dilation, is somewhat common to the duodenum. Such cases are always clearly manifested during life, and are usually traced to the action of some chemical or other irritant on the tissues of the bowels.

Hernia, or the passage of some portion of the intestines and their appendages, is not of common occurrence. In puppies hernia of the navel is now and again seen. It consists of the omentum or caul, which may be returned within the abdomen, and maintained by a bandage or truss, or excision of the whole protrusion by means of the ligature may be tried. Other forms need not be discussed here, as they are only of interest to the scientific operator in surgery.

Worms in the Intestines.—Several species of worms find their abode within the intestines of the dog, being chiefly of the classes commonly known as round and tapeworms. Their presence is in obedience to certain laws which regulate and ensure their being called into existence, as well as subsequent changes and developments.

The *Symptoms* generally denoting the presence of worms in the bowels are as follows: irritation, more or less persistent, inducing disorder, as variable and depraved appetite, loss of hair, and a rough unhealthy state of the skin; irregularity of the bowels, producing a discharge of fæces and fluid, which is slimy, exceedingly offensive, and contains the parasites; irritation of the anus, as shown by the creature licking it, or endeavouring to remove the annoyance by dragging himself in a sitting posture over the ground. As these signs continue, a state of general anæmia sets in, from which the animal dies or otherwise recovers and goes through similar suffering. Occasionally during life the worms migrate from the intestines to the stomach, from which they may be expelled in the resulting vomition; instances are also on record in which they have been known to pass to the windpipe or lungs and produce fatal consequences. The remedies for worms are numerous, formulæ for which will be found in Chapter VIII., one of the most efficacious being No. 3. p. 137.

Peritonitis, inflammation of the peritoneum or membrane which lines the cavity of the abdomen and invests the bowels, is frequently confounded with enteritis. It may be only partial; it is more frequently complete. The causes are external violence as severe blows, punctured wounds, &c.; it may also result from hernia, constipation, or exposure to damp and cold, and in females is apt to follow parturition.

Symptoms.—High fever with rapid, small, hard, and sharp pulse. Pressure on the abdomen induces severe pain, and to avoid being handled the sufferer seeks a quiet spot where he lies on his side, breathing with difficulty and constant pain, as evinced by frequent sharp cries. Constipation is present from the first. As the disease advances these signs are aggravated, the tongue is furred, dry, and offensive, thirst is great, and the urine is scanty and highly coloured. The abdomen enlarges from the accumulation of fluid, the legs and ears are cold, and death follows coma or delirium.

Treatment.—Continued fomentations, poultices (which see) or a mild stimulating liniment may be applied to the abdomen under gentle care; leeches often prove immediately beneficial. The only safe remedies are sedatives (*see* Febrifuges), especially aconite, digitalis, opium, or belladonna, given every four hours as required.

Ascites, or *Drops of the Abdomen*, is the frequent result of peritonitis, but it may arise from conditions totally apart from it, as anæmia following continued asthma or skin diseases, derangement of the liver, &c. Cold and damp are common causes in young dogs.

Symptoms.—Unusual enlargement of the abdomen, pale mucous membranes, general coldness and wasting of the body, rough staring coat, and falling of the hair, nausea, frequent vomition, and indigestion generally, husky cough, hurried respiration, subacute fever, intolerable thirst, dropsical states of the body generally, oppressed breathing, sinking, and death.

Treatment.—Tonics, with vegetable bitters and mild diuretics are useful. Absorption of the fluid may be promoted by regular, but small, doses of digitalis and iodide of iron. Cod-liver oil is highly nutritive and sufficiently laxative to promote free action of the bowels. The whole of the fluid may be drawn away by what is known as "tapping the belly," after which support must be afforded by a bandage placed round the body, and the operation may be required on future occasions to relieve the oppressed breathing from repeated accumulation of the fluid.

Hepatitis, or *Inflammation of the Liver*, is common to overfed and pampered animals, especially house pets taking little or no exercise. The disease in the acute form is said to be more common in tropical countries, and even the South of France, than in Great Britain, where it more frequently assumes the congestive form.

Symptoms.—The early manifestations are a dry or husky cough, accelerated pulse and respiration, rigors, or more commonly shivering fits, and pain on the right side which is aggravated by pressure; nausea and vomiting are present. In later stages the mucous membranes and the skin exhibit a tinge of yellow, which becomes more intense with the progress of the malady. The bowels are alternately relaxed or confined, and the evacuations are pale, the urine is deficient, having an orange colour; the pain of the right side is increased, and enlargement over the region of the liver is evident; bile mingles with the fluids ejected from the stomach. The animal is dull, the mouth and tongue are furred and with the breath are offensive, the abdomen enlarges and is pendulous, the bowels contain much flatus; there is intense thirst, absence of appetite, and the loss of flesh is very rapid.

Treatment.—Blood-letting to a moderate extent by means of the lancet, or abstraction by leeches after the hair has been removed is useful, especially if the hot (spongio-pilinē) poultice is immediately applied. Mustard plasters promptly are beneficial, or the hot bath may be tried, if the animal can be well protected afterwards. As medicines the salines, or febrifuge No. 3, may be given once daily for three or four days; or the febrifuge No. 6, three times daily, in simple water, thickened with treacle, until the acute symptoms are overcome, when vegetable tonics may be resorted to.

Chronic Hepatitis, like the acute form, in its true nature is congestive, due to similar causes, except in India and other hot countries, where continued high temperature and malaria are superadded.

The *Symptoms* are, in the main, those of acute hepatitis modified or less severe, making little progress one way or the other for some time. Jaundice and a peculiar haggard or dejected appearance, with loss of power, are prominent signs. The liver is generally increased, hard, and may be insensible to pressure. The belly, particularly on the right side, is swollen, and the animal is tormented by thirst, indigestion, flatulence, vomition, and irregularity of the bowels. The skin is dry, often scurfy, and discoloured by bile, and the hair is erect. Piles are common as a result of pressure obstructing blood circulation; and asthma, disease of the spleen, &c., are frequent accompaniments.

Treatment.—Promote regular action of the bowels by the use of saline aperient and febrifuge No. 3, or small doses of calomel, and podophyllin, rhubarb, or aloes on alternate days, with intermediate doses (two to four drops) of nitric or hydrochloric acid twice daily, or the iodide of potassium (five to ten grains) may be substituted for a time. Great benefit may arise from an application of strong iodine liniment, or ointment of biniodide of mercury—half strength, and repeated as needful—to the side after removal of the hair. The diet must be carefully regulated as well as digestible, and the action of the bowels should be largely maintained by enemas when the salines are not employed. Pet dogs recovering from the disease may prove useful as previously, but animals from which constant or phenomenal work is required are rarely capable, and for breeding purposes they should not be selected.

Fatty Degeneration of the Liver is an occasional result of hepatitis. In some instances it is enormously enlarged, and capable of being manipulated by the hand, causing a largely distended abdomen, irregular bowels, and anæmia, the patient finally becoming excessively lean and weak, with all the indications of chronic hepatitis.

Treatment.—Withdraw food containing fat, and substitute fibrine biscuits in moderate quantities, with enforced excercise daily. As a treat, give a meal of fresh liver, cut up and mixed with the usual food, and as a medicine give ten grains of chlorate of potash twice daily for some time.

Old and worn-out dogs frequently exhibit peculiar forms of malignant disease of the liver, spleen, mesentery, omentum, &c., which present some of the strangest combinations of incurable states. In all such instances common humanity suggests their destruction by a painless death, as prussic acid or an overdose of chloroform.

Parasitic Disease of the Liver is due to the presence of the fluke *Distoma conjunctum* in the bile ducts, inducing inflammation and numerous small abscesses. Various cystic or bladder forms of parasitism are also common; and round worms (*Filaria hepatica*) occupy the substance as well as the ducts of the liver, leading to the formation of cysts in the walls of the intestines.

Obstruction to the functions of the liver occasionally arises from the formation of biliary calculi, or *gall-stones*. Jaundice is a common sign, with more or less indigestion, and acute pain, evidenced by violence during their passage along the gall-ducts to the intestines, is not uncommon.

Treatment.—The pain is to be soothed by warm baths and the internal administration of opium, chloric ether, &c., measures which are also beneficial in the removal of the obstruction as well as the resulting jaundice. The presence of one stone suggests the presence and constant formation of many others, therefore, some alteration in the diet should be made, more frequent exercise being enforced, while one of the liver pills (*see* Aperients), or podophyllin and calomel are regularly given.

Disease of the Spleen and Pancreas is rarely recognised except in conjunction with morbid conditions of the liver, and chiefly after death. We have, therefore, but little information in reference to morbid signs during life, the principal being enlargement of the spleen, which may be felt on the left side of the front of the belly. The organ is then sensible to pressure, and the animal emits cries of pain when he is moved. A husky cough is present; the coat is rough and dirty; the bowels are relaxed, and the evacuations are yellow and mixed with froth, a state which alternates with constipation. The mucous membranes are pale, and fever is more or less present. Emaciation proceeds with the continuance of these signs, and the disease is practically incurable, depending on conjoint disease of the liver and other organs.

Goitre, or Bronchocele, is not unfrequent in newly born pups, associated with rickets, the probable result of parental mal-nutrition. Among older animals pugs are singularly liable, the swellings being known as "Kernels." The disease consists of enlargement of the thyroid glands, situate on each side of the throat, which has been known to cause obstruction to the flow of blood in the jugular veins, with resulting dulness, and even death. Pressure on the windpipe has also been known to produce suffocation. The diseased enlargement sometimes disperses spontaneously; otherwise painting with iodine, after removal of the hair, with internal administration of the drug, will accomplish its disappearance.

CHAPTER XIV.

DISEASES OF THE URINARY SYSTEM.

<small>Nephritis, or Inflammation of the Kidneys—Albuminous Nephritis—Calculi, or Stones in the Kidney—Hæmaturia, or Red Water—Atrophy and Hypertrophy—Worm in the Kidney—Impaction of the Ureters—Cystitis, or Inflammation of the Bladder—Stone in the Bladder—Rupture of the Bladder—Diabetes—Paralysis of the Bladder—Disease of the Prostate—Stone in the Urethra—Urethritis—Balanitis and Posthitis—Worm in the Urethra.</small>

THE urinary apparatus of the dog is probably subject to a greater number of disorders, occurring with greater frequency than is generally supposed among animals under confinement, especially when they are pampered and fed on all kinds of unsuitable aliment. Disorder of the digestive process is likely to derange the action of the kidneys, and from thence the various organs of the system are more or less influenced.

Nephritis, or *Inflammation of the Kidney*, arises from numerous causes, as blows, or strain on the loins; the action of cold after bathing or exposure to rain; irritation of the organ by calculi or stones, abscess, &c., and direct or indirect action of special remedies, as cantharides or turpentine, of which the dog is peculiarly susceptible, whether given by the mouth, absorbed by the skin, or carried to the stomach by the tongue, as the animal licks off external applications.

The *Symptoms* are a peculiar gait indicating stiffness in the loins, with probable pain under manipulation or pressure. Febrile symptoms are present, the pulse being rapid, wiry, and hard, nose and mouth hot and dry, mucous membranes reddened, and the bowels are acutely constipated. In females the act of urination is often attempted, and the quantity voided is small, highly coloured, and sometimes mixed with blood.

Treatment.—Leeches to the loins, or bleeding from the jugular vein. Castor-oil mixture as a laxative. Linseed mucilage or barley water should be used as a vehicle for medicines, as tartar emetic in doses of a quarter or half a grain twice or three times daily; or belladonna, opium, and camphor as anodynes; enemas containing one of the three latter drugs; hot spongio-piline poultices to the loins, frequently renewed. Bicarbonate of soda or potash are also useful in rendering the urine less acid and aseptic. Perfect quiet is essential, and, excepting very moderate exercise when the patient can bear it, all severe movement must be carefully avoided. A form of **Albuminous Nephritis** has also been noticed, constituting true *Bright's Disease*.

Calculi, or *Stones in the Kidney*, are by no means infrequent. One or both organs may be affected. They give rise to inflammation of the kidney, for which the appropriate treatment is required.

Hæmaturia, or *Red Water*, derives its name from the presence of blood in the urine.

The *Causes* are those which induce inflammation; more commonly calculi are present, the angular projections of which may seriously wound the organ or cause impediments to the flow of blood, set up inflammation, and even rupture of the vessels.

Symptoms.—Urination is attended with pain; heat, with tenderness of the loins; blood is discharged in three forms: during the act of urination, subsequent to it, or altogether independent of it. When it comes from the kidneys, it is diffused throughout the urine, which also contains threads of fibrine, not unlike small worms, either of a pale pink colour or white. Bleeding from the bladder is known by the first discharge of urine being free, but towards the end the blood comes floating in the urine. Bleeding from the urethra is unattended by signs of disease in the kidney or bladder. The blood is discharged pure and alone.

Treatment.—Avoid blood-letting. Mucilaginous fluids, as linseed tea, barley water, solution of gum, beef tea, &c., should be given freely, in which iron and opiates (*see* Styptics) should be given. Apply hot fomentations to the loins, the spongio-piline poultice, mustard, or ammoniacal embrocation. Enemas containing belladonna or opium to relieve pain and spasms. Tincture of cantharides, in doses of two or three drops in a wine-glassful of water, is often very useful.

Atrophy and **Hypertrophy**, terms which signify *Wasting* and *Enlargement*, are seen in the kidney. Few indications occur during life.

Worm in the Kidney is an occasional occurrence. The parasite is known as *Eustrongylus gigas*, a round worm, the female of which sometimes attains the length of three feet, and as large as the little finger. Enormous enlargement of the organ is one of the common results. The presence is not always denoted by definite signs during life.

Impaction of the Ureters may arise from the accumulation of small portions of calculi or sandy matter on their way from the kidneys, giving rise to acutely painful spasms, which yield to the action of opiates, or passage of the obstruction to the bladder.

Cystitis, or *Inflammation of the Bladder*, may arise from the absorption or imprudent use of turpentine, cantharides, &c., internally. Enlargement of the prostate gland by disease is the more frequent cause, as it obstructs the flow of urine from the bladder. Stricture of the urethra, calculi, and parasites act similarly.

Symptoms.—Extreme uneasiness, colic, frequent change of place and position, and putting the nose to the flanks, tenderness of the abdomen under pressure; fever is also present, with intense thirst; the hind limbs tremble, urine is voided in small quantities and under great pain, the bowels are costive, and vomition usually follows. Chronic forms greatly resemble the state of nephritis.

Treatment.—Hot baths, or the spongio-piline poultice round the abdomen and loins, with opiates, belladonna, &c., internally (*see* Anodynes), to overcome spasm of the urethra, and permit the flow of urine. Warm enemas are useful. Mucilage containing the carbonate of potash for drink. Pass the catheter, and remove urine. Explore for calculus, and regulate the bowels by means of a laxative dose of castor-oil mixture.

Calculus in the Bladder occurs in both males and females. More than one are usually present, the smallest being passed with sandy matter, forming one of the best diagnostic signs.

Symptoms.—Cystitis of an active kind is present in the stages of early formation, but as the calculi increase in size and number, the disease assumes the chronic form. The urine at first varies in colour: when blood is present it is red, otherwise it may be yellow, from the accumulation of crystals deposited from the urine. Later the flow of urine becomes more or less constant, but of uncertain quantity, sometimes suddenly suppressed, and giving rise to severe pain internally, while externally the skin is excoriated and tender over which the fluid passes.

Removal of the Stone by Operation is only possible in very large animals, and in them it is attended with risk, from the tendency to peritonitis, which is somewhat easily produced in the dog.

Rupture of the Bladder follows the obstruction of the urethra by pressure from diseased prostate gland, or small calculi becoming wedged within the urethra.

Symptoms.—The urine for some time passes only in drops; the animal moves very little, and always carefully; shortly the signs of acute inflammation of the bladder set in, and the sufferer soon sinks, and dies without excitement or struggle. After death the cavity of the abdomen contains blood and fluid, the peritoneum is congested, and the mucous coat of the bladder is acutely inflamed, the walls being torn in various directions. When calculi have had some share in the production of these states, one or more may be found in the abdominal cavity.

Diabetes, or *profuse urination*, is rarely seen in the dog, except as the result of the injudicious use of large doses of diuretic medicines. The habit of the animal to void urine repeatedly on being liberated for a run is due to the excitement of pleasure, and perfectly natural. It must not, therefore, be associated with probable disease.

Paralysis of the Bladder is the common result of continued retention of, and inordinate distension by, urine, in which cases, by removal of the direct cause, and absolute rest, the organ resumes its natural contractile powers. When it depends upon nervous diseases, injury to the spinal cord, apoplexy, &c., the inability to discharge the contents remains, when nerve stimulants, as strychnine, or probably the iodide of iron may be useful. *Removal of the urine* may also be required at stated intervals, which the canine practitioner will accomplish by means of a suitable catheter. Animals suffering from any urinary complaint should be removed to the surgeon's premises, where special attention can be bestowed.

Disease of the Prostate is common in the dog. It is generally a disease of senility, and as such proves incurable. The age of the patient renders treatment undesirable and a study of the causes will confirm the decision.

Calculus, or Stone in the Urethra, as a rule, originates in the bladder, but is retained in its passage from that organ, and becomes the source of irritation and stoppage of urine. In some instances it is situate in that portion of the canal lying within the pelvis, when removal can only be effected by an operation, for which the canine surgeon alone is competent.

Urethritis, or Inflammation of the Urethra, in its extended form, arises from participation in disease of the bladder, prostate gland, &c., and the presence of calculus. **Balanitis** consists of a similar state, but confined to the lining membrane of the prepuce or hood-shaped covering at the free extremity of the penis; and **Posthitis,** or Inflammation of the Mucous Membrane, investing the glans penis, are two local forms of urethritis dependent upon causes acting locally, as dirt, debility, want of exercise, overfeeding, &c., and is common to pet and watchdogs, and others affected with mange. These forms are common to dogs which are constantly at large, roaming our streets, and often as worthless mongrels, are the progenitors of the mongrel race. The disgusting scenes which ensue are a disgrace to our local forms of government, and their continuance is mainly responsible for the perpetuation of rabies. In the urethral form the glans penis is swollen, extruded, and mostly erect, a small quantity of pustular fluid oozing from the opening. Pain is evident in urination, and the animal constantly licks the exposed member. In other forms of the disease the prepuce is swollen and covers the glans penis, retaining the discharge to the further detriment of the organ, but allowing a portion to escape and accumulate in drying on the hairs around the orifice. By external pressure, which the animal stoutly resists, a large quantity of discharge may be obtained, sometimes having a disagreeable odour; and not uncommonly the diseased parts are invaded by abscesses and sinuses to a serious extent.

Treatment.—After a thorough cleansing, the long hairs should be removed to avoid the accumulation of discharge and dirt, the dog should be immersed in a warm bath, or fomentations may be locally applied. In either case care must be exercised in order to dry the patient and prevent his taking cold. Astringent lotions are then needed, or the "Sanitas" mixtures (*see* Antiseptics) will be highly beneficial. The bowels should be moved by the castor-oil mixture, and tonics, combined with mucilaginous fluids, are essential.

Parasitic Invasion of the Urethra is on record. In an instance falling beneath the notice of M. Séon, the worm was believed to be the male *Eustrongylus gigas*, upwards of four inches long, and was detected during an attack of urethral irritation and paroxysmal retention of urine, occupying the entire length of the urethra. Removal of the parasite afforded instant relief.

CHAPTER XV.

DISEASES OF THE GENERATIVE SYSTEM.

MALE ORGANS: Gonorrhœa—Imperforate Prepuce—The Penis—Amputation—Scrotal Inflammation—Orchitis—Abscess of the Testicles—Scirrhus.—FEMALE ORGANS: Metritis, or Inflammation of the Womb—Dropsy—Inversion, or Prolapsus—Hæmorrhage, or Flooding—Amputation—Tumours in the Vagina—Inversion, or Prolapsus—Amputation—Use of the Catheter.—DISEASES OF THE ORGANS OF LACTATION: Retention of Milk—Mammitis, or Inflammation of the Milk Gland—Malignant Tumours—Warts—Œstrum or Heat—Parturition.

Male Organs.—**Gonorrhœa**, improperly so-called in the dog, has been already described in the chapter on Diseases of the Urinary Organs, under the term Posthitis. The affection does not seem to arise from the transmission of contagious principles in canine animals, as in the human subject, therefore, the latter term is preferable.

Imperforate Prepuce occurs as a congenital malformation. The patient is unable to void urine in consequence of the penis being entirely invested by the prepuce, which has no opening. Retention of urine gives rise to considerable distress, with probable swelling of the prepuce and contiguous parts from infiltration, &c., of fluid. Such cases should receive prompt attention from the canine surgeon, who will secure relief by an operation.

The penis of the dog is subject to various forms of non-malignant growths, largely composed of the hypertrophied cells common to the epidermis, &c., sometimes also spreading over the glands, and inner as well as the outer surfaces of the prepuce. Such **Warts**, as they are commonly designated, may be small, single, hanging by a neck or cord, or otherwise flattened and diffused, forming large masses of a spongy and irritable nature, liable to bleed or discharge a thin, watery fluid. The necessary *treatment* consists of removal by amputation with knife or scissors when suitable, those of diffused character being freely as well as regularly dressed with caustic potash, nitrate of silver, or the mineral acids. Acetic acid has, however, special preference. Subsequently great care is required in order to avoid the injury of adjacent structures, which the ignorant in these essentials are apt to ignore.

Amputation of the Penis may be required as a result of the consequences just referred to, or by reason of abscess from neglected warts, cancer, &c., an operation calling for care and skill, which the qualified canine surgeon only can be expected to possess.

Scrotal Inflammation.—The bag or covering of the testicles is liable to become inflamed, and under circumstances of neglect, undue plethora, or other adverse states of the system, the disease is aggravated, and the tissues assume a hard, leathery, or semi-cartilaginous nature, and if wounded or abraided, the process of ulceration is established, and a condition not unlike that of cancer is the inevitable result of all such neglected cases. One of the early causes is probably excessive copulation in animals of a senile condition, an abnormal congestion of the tissues being established. The scrotum is acutely reddened, swollen, and sensible, and in a few days the surface is covered with pimples. These subsequently burst and discharge a thin fluid, which accumulates, and drying, forms a thick encrustation, but ultimately falls off and exposes an acutely inflamed and sensitive surface beneath. Further neglect ensures rapid ulceration, continued enlargement with malformation, and finally drying, with change to a cartilaginous state of the whole of the scrotum; or the parts may remain in the ulcerative condition until death carries off the patient.

Treatment.—Brisk cathartics to open the bowels at once, with one to four or five leeches to the inflamed scrotum, and after the lapse of twenty-four hours diligent bathing with hot water will be beneficial. When the pimples have formed apply frequently glycerine, to which boracic acid is added in the proportion of ten to fifteen grains to the ounce. Internally, use the iodide of potassium three to ten grains twice daily. When ulceration has set in use lotions of alum, zinc, boracic acid, or "Sanitas" Oil in glycerine. Sometimes the knife may be required to remove diseased masses, or it may be advisable to amputate completely the scrotum and testicles with it, for which the canine operating surgeon is competent.

Orchitis, or *Inflamed Testicle*, usually arises from pressure, blows, and possibly from unusual secretion stimulated by access to many females, or repeated stimulation without actual connection.

Symptoms.—The scrotum is full, tense, hot and shining, beneath which the swollen and inflamed testicles are detected by the fingers, simple pressure causing acute pain. In walking the dog carries the hind legs widely apart.

Treatment.—Administer a brisk cathartic, and apply leeches as desirable. At a later period cold applications, followed by iodide of potassium internally.

Abscess of the Testicles may follow orchitis, for which castration may be necessary. In other instances one or both may become *scirrhous*, and therefore useless, finally wasting considerably, but not always calling for removal.

Female Organs.—**Metritis**, or *Inflammation of the Womb*, is not a common disease.

Symptoms.—Acute fever, accompanied by an inflamed condition of the external genitals, from which a purulent, as well as fetid, discharge escapes. Such are the signs consequent on the absurd system of injecting fluids within the uterus and vagina, the object being to bring on the condition termed "heat." The disease may follow parturition, when, in addition to the above signs, the animal becomes acutely sensitive to pressure over the abdomen. Internally the finger will detect intense heat in the vagina and os uteri. Vomition, with great prostration is common, but the creature persists in sitting on her haunches; later the discharge proceeds from the vagina, the lips of which are tumefied, projecting, and hot, states which are aggravated by frequent attempts to urinate. When the disease accompanies parturition, or sets in soon after, the secretion of milk is usually absent, and the disease is likely to be associated with peritonitis.

Treatment.—The comfort of the patient must be ensured on every hand. The hot spongio-piline poultice is indispensable as long as the acute symptoms remain. Opium (one to three grains) is required to subdue the pain, with which extract of gentian should be combined, or a few drops of the aromatic spirit of ammonia may be added when the animal is prostrate. The discharge from the womb, &c., may be promoted by warm enemas, containing ten to twenty grains of boracic acid, administered with great care, particularly if the swelling of the passage is great.

Dropsy of the Womb, technically known as *Hydrops Uteri*, and *Hydrometra*, is often associated with indigestion and a state of obesity, especially in old animals which have bred largely, and indicate suppression or irregularity of the œstrum.

Symptoms.—Gradual enlargement of the abdomen, which may be mistaken for pregnancy, but is distinguished by the elastic, yielding sensation instead of the hard masses which the fœtal bodies present to the hands. Somewhat later the abdomen, in addition to further enlargement, becomes pendulous and heavy; the animal is excessively thirsty, feverish, and the appetite is very poor or absent; weakness and emaciation proceed, and at length she dies from exhaustion, when the womb is discovered to be charged with fluid, sometimes mere serum, or at others white and thick, from the admixture of cells derived from the lining membrane of the organ.

Treatment should be instituted early. When it is decided the fluid is the cause of the distension, it should be drawn off by means of the catheter passed through the contracted mouth of the womb, followed by regular washings with a solution of chloride of zinc (three grains to the ounce of water), the strength being supported by the regular administration of tonics, as iron, with gentian.

Inversion, or Prolapsus of the Uterus, is not infrequent, in the partial form, but protrusion of the entire organ rarely occurs. It constitutes one of the serious accidents of parturition, being dependent on causes which lead to violent straining during the act, such as improper traction, irritation of the organ, as wounds, bruises, &c. It may be mistaken for polypus, and also inversion of the vagina only.

Hæmorrhage, or Flooding, after parturition is not common in female dogs. If it should arise the womb may be stimulated to contraction by an astringent injection of one or two pints of cold water containing two or four drachms of tincture of oak galls.

Amputation of the Womb may be called for by reason of injury, or threatened mortification, &c. It has been successfully performed by qualified canine surgeons, the animals making good recovery. It is, however, a formidable operation, should be undertaken only after grave consideration, and by skilful hands.

Tumours in the Vagina or *birth passage* are not uncommon, sometimes proving troublesome, and even serious. They occur in sizes varying from small warty excrescences to large developments capable of obstructing the passage entirely. *Polypus* is the most common, being a smooth, vascular body, covered by the mucous membrane, and attached by a constricted neck, or pedicle, to the wall of the vagina, or womb. Care is especially needed in order that the growth may not be mistaken for inverted womb or vagina. Removal may be effected in one of several ways, as the situation or other circumstances may direct—viz., ligature applied to the neck, wh ch, causing death of the tumour, leads to its final removal; twisting of the neck is another form of strangulation, and attended with removal by severing the attachment; the tumour may be torn away when the neck is small; or by means of a suitable instrument, named the écraseur, the neck is compressed and partially sawn through, a safe preventive of subsequent hæmorrhage. Tumours having a large base or diffused growth and attachment, will require the constant application of caustics, the patient being meanwhile supported by good food and tonic medicines.

Inversion or **Prolapsus of the Vagina** occurs in aged or debilitated animals during "heat," and after frequent pregnancy, especially in those of the "bull" breed. Protrusion appears in various stages as a smooth, soft tumour, between the lips of the vagina, when careful distinction must be made, the appearances being liable to be confounded with tumour, or inversion of the womb (which see).

Treatment consists of first clearing the organ from extraneous matters, and noting the existence of abrasions, &c., by the animal's movements, or sitting on it; after which it must be returned as described under Inversion of the Womb, its retention being also secured by the injection of astringents, as there detailed.

Amputation of the Vagina is resorted to in cases where the organ has received severe injuries, &c., for which the canine surgeon will be required.

The Use of the Catheter is often called for in the female during pregnancy, and prolapsus, polypus, &c., of the vagina, the act of urination being interfered with by pressure or change of position in the organs. The passage to the bladder is situated within the vagina, distant from half an inch to two inches, depending on the size of the animal, and is easily reached by first opening the lips by the finger of the left hand, and passing the tube carefully forwards along the floor. Entrance to the bladder is denoted by the stream of urine which flows through the tube.

Diseases of the Organs of Lactation.—Retention of Milk.—The process of milk secretion in its ordinary course, is somewhat in advance of the period of parturition. The mammary glands, of which there are eight or ten, become charged with blood, and are perceptibly enlarged, extending from the breast backwards to the space between the thighs. Subsequently, near the time of delivery, milk is actually secreted in readiness for the young family shortly requiring it. Possibly the secretion may be somewhat in advance of birth, over-abundant, or the pups being small in number, do not drain the whole of the teats; sometimes also several teats are rejected, although there are sufficient young to drain the whole. There are also additional causes, as cold, damp quarters and unsuitable food, which by setting up disorder of digestion, seriously alter the quality of the secretion, probably also its constitution, when its undue retention becomes an additional source of irritation and disorder, the end of which is inflammation. To prevent this early attention should be given to the animal, the overcharged glands being relieved by removal of the milk, as the teats are carefully drawn, pressure commencing from above and continued downwards to the apex.

Mammitis, or *Inflammation of the Milk Gland*, arises from injuries, retention of milk, and exposure to cold, damp, &c., during lactation. Whatever tends to arrest the process also disorders the secretion, which curdles, forming hard masses composed chiefly of caseine, of which the milk of canine animals contains a considerable quantity.

Symptoms.—Febrile disturbance is severe from the outset to the end of the disease; the affected glands being red, hot, hard, and excessively painful. The milk when pressed out contains clots, and later is mixed with blood, subsequently pus, when the milk disappears. An abscess forms in the part most actively inflamed, and in some cases involves every section of the gland, terminating in *lacteal fistulæ*, openings or sinuses which refuse to heal, constantly discharging a mixture of pus, blood, milk, &c. The terminations are induration and functional destruction of the gland, probably causing death of the sufferer.

Treatment.—Bleeding by leeches in the early stages, followed by a saline aperient and the hot spongio-piline poultice diligently applied for hours. Perfect quiet must be maintained, with fresh air and a comfortable bed. The pups should be encouraged to suck, or in case of their death, the gland must be drawn frequently in order to avoid abscess. Injection within the gland of a solution of carbonate of potash is highly useful, but is a somewhat difficult task for amateurs minus a proper syringe. Some good may be effected by administering the solution by the mouth. Open abscesses as soon as pointing is present, observe cleanliness, and use the "Sanitas" Antiseptic Mixture as a dressing.

The disease is apt to assume the chronic form when the ordinary substance of the gland becomes indurated, or hard, having a gristly constitution. Some cases also assume the cancerous state. Induration must be met by outward application of iodine ointment, or the gland may be painted by the tincture. Hand friction is also useful. When the enlargement is considerable the weighty parts may be suspended in a bandage passed round the back.

Malignant or **Lacteal Tumours** are the result of injury to the gland inflicted by the pups in suckling, or by human violence. They are characterised by enormous and rapid growth, and their disposition to ulceration from even slight bruises or other forms of simple injury. *Treatment* by excision under chloroform is the only effectual course, although specially severe, as the whole of the affected section of the gland must be removed.

Warts are also common to the milk-gland, being confined to the skin as a rule, and are neither malignant nor extensive. (*See* Skin Diseases.)

Parturition.—We have now to notice certain conditions relating especially to the female of the canine race, which are of essential importance with reference to breeding.

Œstrum or **Heat** is purely a physiological condition of the system, manifested by signs indicative of desire for connection with the male. Its occurrence and duration varies with climate and other conditions, as health, &c. Spring and autumn are the seasons in which it is seen in this country, the manifestations being excitability, unusual liveliness, desire for the company of males, with whom the bitch is playful. For this she will steal away, if unobserved, frequently preferring the attentions of a number of the ugliest curs, and if allowed full liberty, her progeny will, as a natural consequence, be a mixture of breeds. The greatest watchfulness is, therefore, needed at such times if purity is desired. From the same cause also *super-*

fœtation is common, the animal " throwing " or giving birth to pups at intervals of two, three, four, or even seven days, each bearing unmistakable evidences of separate parentage. *Epileptic fits* occur in some animals during the prevalence of œstrum, but subside with the attendant excitement and as impregnation proceeds. It is also remarkable in closely kept and unimpregnated animals, that after the subsidence of the venereal excitement, say from the fortieth to the sixtieth day, they behave as though they were pregnant and about to give birth; they make their bed, are uneasy, constantly moving about, &c., while the mammary glands appear swollen, the vulva is dilated, and the lining membrane is reddened, a discharge of viscid mucus escaping from the passage. Milk is also obtained from the teats, and such animals have been known to rear the puppies of other females as tenderly as those of her own body. *Pregnancy* is usually detectable at the end of the fourth week, by exploration of the abdomen. At this period the teats enlarge, the abdomen becomes round and drooping, and by successive stages the signs are more pronounced; when at the end of about the ninth week, or within a period of from fifty-five to seventy days, delivery is effected. Meanwhile the signs already alluded to are present as conducive to the process.

Parturition usually takes place as the creature lies upon her side, the process extending over variable time, and is attended by severe muscular throes which cause the sufferer to cry piteously. Owing to the cartilaginous condition of the bony framework, the pups are exceedingly elastic and yielding, a state often highly conducive to delivery in *malposition*, which however is somewhat rare in this animal. When such occurs it may be usually traced to the mother being served by animals of larger breed than herself, or when she exhibits the tendency of "throwing back," that is, giving birth to pups which resemble former sires. *Untimely and persistent interference* during parturition is often attended with fatal results. Canine patients possess an exceedingly nervous temperament, and more than actual assistance is baneful. Simple exploration with the forefinger well oiled, will usually suffice to indicate the state of affairs; more than this will often induce severe fever, and interruption to the natural process. Removal of fæces and urine by assisted means, or the use of a warm enema, may conduce to a more favourable state by affording room for the fœtus. As a rule, direct interference for the removal of the pups is not called for; when it otherwise happens, the services of an experienced canine surgeon should be secured, especially when the sufferer is valuable. *Abnormal positions*, as a rule, occur when the pup approaches the vaginal passage, where its progress is impeded by various causes, but finally yields to the application of various forms of traction. This should be always and only exerted during the natural throes, otherwise the strength of the patient may be exhausted. The presentation of one forefoot only, when the head is properly placed may not prevent delivery, providing good hold is obtained. Unusually large heads sometimes prove insurmountable, and such call for reduction before delivery can be effected. As traction agents, a piece of tape, or small cord, a loop of wire, &c., have frequently done good service in the absence of direct suitable instruments; but the canine surgeon has his *répertoire* from which he can make useful selection.

After-treatment of the Patient consists of careful feeding, avoidance of excess or deficiency, good beds, comfortable quarters, &c., above all taking care that the mother has no more pups than she can properly find milk for. Any excess of these should be suckled by a foster-mother. But this requires great care, otherwise the milk so conveyed may contain the seeds of some constitutional taint, by which the hopes of the owner may be grievously frustrated. Should any objection be made by the foster-mother towards the stranger, it is a common practice to remove her own pups temporarily, and present the stranger over which her milk has been sprinkled. It also happens occasionally that the natural mother will devour the fœtal membranes or "cleansing," so-called, and the morbid appetite may also extend to her pups. Such animals repeat the vice at each parturition, the cause being assigned to a disordered digestion. If this be correct, the exhibition of a cathartic will be of service, and she should be zealously watched, but kept as quiet as possible.

CHAPTER XVI.

DISEASES OF THE EYES AND EARS.

ORGANS OF VISION: Simple Ophthalmia, or Conjunctivitis—Cataract—Iritis—Amaurosis, or Gutta Serena—Staphyloma—Hydrophthalmia—Distension, and Dislocation of the Eyeball—Tumour of the Haw—Dermatoid Conjunctiva—Ulceration of the Eyelids—Ectropion—Entropion—Watery Eyes. ORGANS OF HEARING: Otitis — Internal Canker—External Canker—Abscess of the Ear-flap, or Blood Abscess—Polypi, or Tumours within the Ear—Squamula, or Scurfiness of the Ear-flap—Ticks—Mange of the Ear.

Organs of Vision.—Simple Ophthalmia, commonly known as *Conjunctivitis*, or inflammation of the investing membrane, the conjunctiva, arises from external injury, as blows, stings, insinuation of foreign bodies, cold winds, foul emanations in the kennel, and a chronic form is apt to arise from mal-nutrition dependent on disordered stomach and digestion; it is also an accompaniment of distemper.

Symptoms.—Intolerance of light, closed eyelids, from which flows an abundant watery secretion. On separation of the lids, which the sufferer strenuously opposes, the membranes are observed to be highly injected, and the organ is susceptible to pressure or light. Unless the disease is speedily arrested, permanent blindness by destruction of the organ is certain.

Treatment.—Carefully remove all foreign substances when present. Avoid the stimulus of light by placing the patient in a darkened room, allowing ample fresh air. Cover the affected member with the hot spongio-piline poultice, and administer a mild aperient. Ordinary cases readily yield to this treatment. Severe forms call for the application of leeches, the spongio-piline, first soaked in a hot infusion of poppy-heads, or it may be saturated with hot water, pressed out, and a few drops of laudanum poured on. The cathartic also must not be omitted. Chronic cases are denoted by watery eyes, opacity of the eyeball, and red membranes. Such call for the use of astringent lotions of zinc or nitrate of silver. Paint the eyelids outwardly with iodine, and intermediately use cold water applications. Some practitioners place a seton behind the poll. When ulceration of the cornea is present, blow upon the spot a little dry oxide of zinc, and repeat daily as required. Total loss of vision in these cases results from implication of the humours as well as the deeper-seated tissues of the eyeball.

Cataract.—Several forms of this affection are observed. It consists of the opaque deposit of inflammation more or less interfering with the transparency of the optical tissues, of the lens, and occurs in three forms, viz., lenticular, or opacity of the lens; capsular, opacity of the capsule of the lens, and capsulo-lenticular, signifying that both the lens and its capsule are involved. Cataract may be peripheral or central, limited or diffused, and on these peculiarities depend the interference or otherwise with the vision. Cataract is common to old dogs, but it may occur at any age. The first is due to want of vitality; the second arises from causes inducing inflammation.

Symptoms.—Defective vision, or absolute blindness in proportion to the position and extent of the cataract. On examination of the eye, an opaque speck, or body, of variable size is seen through the pupil by daylight, or better in a dark place by the aid of a lighted candle.

Treatment.—Recent cases in suitable subjects may be benefited by an operation for which special talent is required. Few dogs are worth the expense.

Iritis.—Inflammation of the iris, or circular membrane of the eye, is the result of injury, or the membrane is involved in the inflammation in common with other tissues of the organ.

Symptoms.—The colour of the iris is changed to a reddish brown, by the presence of blood and the bringing into view blood-vessels not discernible in the healthy state, and the colour spreads also beyond the circle of the cornea. The patient cannot bear the light, and to shut it out the pupil contracts, and is more or less immovable by reason of the inflamed condition of the structures. The unopposed progress of the disease leads to extravasation of blood, deposit of opaque lymph, possibly the formation of pus, and total destruction of the organ as far as vision is concerned.

Treatment.—Local bloodletting by lancet or leeches; hot fomentations; secure free action of the bowels, the patient being kept in a dark, but airy room. Considerable fever is usually present, which must be met by febrifuges; and when it has subsided daily doses of iodide of potassium with extract of gentian may be given to remove the deposit of inflammation. A seton behind the head is often beneficial.

Amaurosis, or *Gutta Serena*, also known as *Glass Eye*, is a serious impairment of vision, due to disordered, if not structural, changes in the condition of the optic nerve, retina, or brain, the result of violent shocks, as falls, blows, &c. The first effect is probably paralysis, or inflammation accompanied with extravasation of blood, lymph deposits, or formation of tumour, with ultimate suspension or total loss of nerve power. The disease may be associated with extreme debility, the result of anæmia, hæmorrhage, inordinate lactation, or other causes.

Symptoms.—Defective vision, in some instances developing slowly, and in others very suddenly. In the first instance the animal fails to see objects until he is close upon them, and in the latter he approaches with great caution and uncertainty, usually relying on his acute sense of smell as he moves about alone. Ultimately the power of vision is entirely absent. Any signs of unusual heat, pain, or redness of the eyes, or cloudiness of the pupil, which may have been observed in the early stages, have now passed away. The pupil is dilated, the eyelids are also widely apart, the strongest light may be thrown upon the organ, but it remains motionless, bright, clear, and reflecting from the posterior surface of the rays as they fall upon it. Only one eye may be affected at the outset, but as a rule both become diseased eventually. Generally both are implicated from the beginning.

Treatment is most unsatisfactory, except in very slight cases, and when the disease has been attacked in the earliest stages. The approved remedies are blisters or setons behind the head; the former may be rubbed in around the orbits, or strong ointment or liniment of iodine may be substituted. As the nervous system is greatly at fault, nux vomica or strychnine may prove useful, in conjunction with nutritious and easily digested food, fresh air, and other stimuli of healthy function.

Staphyloma, so-called from its resemblance to a grape, is the result of ulceration of the cornea, an accompaniment of simple ophthalmia associated with distemper. A circular depression on the outer surface is first formed, and shortly, as a result of pressure from within, the internal membrane is pushed forwards, assuming a conical form, opaque from infiltration, and often very irritable. When it is associated with escape of the aqueous humour and subsequent granulation and disease of the eyeball, the latter may call for extirpation. Simple staphyloma may, however, yield to the action of astringents, as nitrate of silver; sometimes opacity of a permanent character remains.

Hydrophthalmia, or *Dropsy of the Aqueous Chamber*, is usually confined to one organ, the cause being direct injury. When the disease is congenital, both eyes may be involved.

Symptoms.—The eyeball is prominent, enlarged, and protrudes from the orbit; it is also tense and unyielding beneath the fingers. The cornea is opaque, and presents a dull appearance from infiltration of fluid, the pupil is stationary and the vision impaired, if not lost. The disease may originate in the anterior chamber, but as a rule both eventually suffer.

Treatment consists of draining off the fluid by means of the trocar and cannula, at various intervals, followed by the application of cold water, or astringent and evaporating lotions.

Distension of the Eyeball from extravasation of blood and serous effusion as the result of direct injury, was successfully treated by Blaine, evacuation being secured by means of a couching needle. He proposed to consider such states as *traumatic dropsy*.

Dislocation of the Eyeball is common to small animals having large and prominent organs, being caused by injuries from other dogs in combat, or by the claws of a cat.

Treatment is by operation, which must be performed by the practised canine surgeon.

Tumour and Enlargement of the Haw, *or Cartilago Nictitans.*—The formation of tumour may find attachment to the substance of the cartilage, interfering greatly with vision, and producing a copious flow of tears known as *watery eye*. They are caused by various forms of irritation, and are also congenital. Removal by knife or scissors is the only effectual plan.

Enlargement is caused by cold, injuries, irritation, &c., or it may be congenital, inducing pain, becoming acutely inflamed, and producing abundant lachrymation. *Treatment* consists of scarifications to the membrane, followed by hot fomentations, or the spongio-piline poultice, aided by a laxative internally. Subsequently, astringent lotions to the affected parts. Complete amputation may be called for.

Dermatoid Conjunctiva.—This is usually a congenital defect. A portion of the conjunctival membrane covering the eyeball is thickened, and organised similar to the skin, bearing a tuft of strong hairs. Early attention is called to the defect by a profuse lachrymation and inconvenience, amounting to opacity of the eyeball with absolute loss of vision. The tuft, together with the thickened membrane, should be subjected to complete extirpation with the knife.

Ulceration of the Eyelids is a frequent accompaniment of mange, but more frequently arises from persistent scratching the parts with the feet, when the eyes are "watery." It is attended by swelling, with loss of hair and the formation of numerous small sinuses. The best application is the ointment of nitrate of mercury, the animal being secured against injuring the parts.

Ectropion, *or Eversion of the Eyelids*, consists of a turning outwards of the extreme edges, with exposition and bulging of the conjunctival membrane. It is rare in the dog.

Entropion *is the reverse of Ectropion.* The edges of the lids curl inwards, the eyelashes creating continued painful irritation of the eyeball.

Watery Eyes are the result of the latter malformation, which leads the dog to scratch with his hind feet, and commit serious injury to the parts.

Treatment consists of a surgical operation, by which an eliptical portion of the lid is removed from the skin, and the parts are drawn together and maintained by sutures. Healing of the wound causes shortening of the lid, and consequent removal of the lashes from contact with the eyeball.

In *ectropion* excision of the internal or lining membrane is effected, and this brings the eyelid into close apposition with the surface of the eyeball.

Organs of Hearing.—Otitis.—Inflammation of the internal structures of the ear, although in common with other affections of the organ, is not so frequent as formerly, yet it is by no means rare. It may be justly termed the precursor of *canker*, having its origin in the same conditions, being an irritable state of the local nerves, evinced by pain and high vascularity of the internal organs.

Symptoms.—The head is carried towards one side, and the feet are often used to scratch the ear on the affected side, or he rubs it on the ground, against the wall, and other stationary objects. He also suddenly shakes the head, and flaps the ears with violence, as the paroxysms of pain occur. The roots of the ears are hot and painful in the acute stages, and the patient is feverish; occasionally also some amount of brain disturbance is evident in the appearance of signs not unlike those of epilepsy in more advanced cases (*see* Mange of the Ear), having their origin in disease of the internal osseous structures. Simple cases have been known to be frequently rendered formidable by the use of improper remedies, especially caustics, one of the most common results being *deafness*, which is also a sequel of internal canker and absurd mutilation of the ears. The needful remedies for otitis will be detailed under.

Internal Canker, which may be defined as an acute inflammation of the skin which forms at the inner lining of the external ear. In long-standing cases, the disease is associated with *External Canker* (which see). The early forms of derangement consist of swelling of the skin, with blocking of the natural opening, by which the secretion of the ceruminous glands is retained, creating pain and irritation, especially from its liability to undergo decomposition, forming at first a red, but soon changing to a black, and offensive matter which oozes from the canal. The discharge also dries on the surface of the ears, induces ulceration, the formation of abscess and discharge of pus. Cases aggravated by neglect exhibit the formation of fungoid tumours, which block up the passage, and discharge matter which accumulates among the hair, and creating irritation, induces the formation of ulcers over the entire face. Canker is especially a disease common to dogs with long hair. The *Causes* are, accumulation of dirt and cerumen in the ear, or, in water dogs, the entrance of water, producing irritant and cooling effects, disturbing the circulation as well as the nervous power. Thus soapsuds carelessly allowed to enter during washing have a similar effect. Dogs suffering from mange are liable to canker from extension of the irritation to the organ. External canker is also a further complication.

Treatment comprises perfect quiet, keeping the animal

from entering the water, absolute cleanliness of the ears, with repeated application of suitable remedies, and, meanwhile, securing the ears from damage by flapping by means of a suitable cap or bandage. Diligent attention only will be rewarded by improvement and cure. The best applications are the ointments of carbonate or oxide of zinc, applied once or even twice a day, after the ears have been carefully syringed, or "mopped out" by means of a small piece of sponge on the end of a stick, "Sanitas" Fluid forming an admirable agent for purifying and stimulating the parts to healthy action. In simple *Otitis* a diligent use of the Fluid, with a dose of laxative medicine will be probably all that is required. The fever of Internal Canker is also beneficially treated by means of a laxative, as the castor-oil mixture, or, if unusually severe, a saline cathartic may be called for.

External Canker is the term used to denote the diseased changes which take place on the lower margins of the ear-flaps. As already pointed out, the affected animal shakes his head violently, by which the ends of the ears are caused to strike the sides of the face and top of the head, or the collar, if such is worn, with violence. They are bruised and inflamed; shortly swelling, thickening, and ulcerative changes follow, and the disease from the first assumes an obstinate or chronic character. As these conditions arise from the irritation due to the existence of Internal Canker, that disease must receive appropriate attention. The flaps of the ears in recent cases may be first cleansed from all accumulations of dried pus, dirt, &c., and afterwards covered with an application of "Sanitas" jelly, calamine, or oxide of zinc ointment. Older-standing cases may call for the application of the nitrate of silver to stimulate healthy healing power, the ears being secured from injury by means of a cap properly fitted and secured over the head.

Abscess of the **Ear-Flap**, or *Blood Abscess*, is large, painful swelling, of sudden appearance, due to bruising by violent shaking of the head. The tumour is tense, but is found to contain a yielding substance within, which proves to be a large clot of blood, with a thin red fluid, the result of rupture of the vessels and escape of the contents within the areolar tissue. *Treatment* consists of opening the abscess by free incision across its entire extent, and liberation of the contents, dressing the wound regularly several times daily with "Sanitas" Fluid, or compound tincture of aloes and myrrh, and putting on the cap.

Polypi, or *Tumours within the Ear*, consisting of fibrous or cartilaginous growths, are common results of internal canker, situate near the auditory canal. *Treatment* consists of removal by excision, ligature, or torsion, and the subsequent application of lunar caustic.

Squamula, or *Scurfiness of the Ear-flap*, may exist in conjunction with irritation and bruising as the result of internal canker in the early stages, also from dirt and the presence of parasites, one of which is the common tick, *Ixodes reticulatus*, usually found on the margin of the ear. The best remedy is the following mixture :— Olive oil and turpentine, equal parts, one or two drops being sufficient for each tick.

Mange of the Ear, or *Auricular Acariasis*, is a form of parasitic disease common to sporting dogs, inducing persistent irritation, recurring fits of extreme uneasiness, and sometimes epileptiform seizures, or violence which has been mistaken for rabies, the animals being dealt with accordingly. The best remedies are a five per cent. solution of sulphide of potassium, which should be frequently injected within the ear; and, as used by Nocard, olive oil, 100 parts, naphthol, 10 parts, sulphuric ether, 30 parts : mix, and keep in a well-stoppered bottle. A portion to be injected into the ear daily, after which the orifice is to be closed with cotton wool to prevent loss of effect by evaporation. Deafness is a common result.

CHAPTER XVII.

DISEASES OF THE NERVOUS SYSTEM.

Epilepsy—Vertigo—Neuralgia—Apoplexy—Tetanus, or Locked-jaw—Chorea—Cramp—Injuries to the Head: Concussion—Compression—Apoplexy—Encephalitis—Hydrocephalus—Paralysis—Parasitism.

THE brain of the dog species is generally well developed, and in some breeds it is of a remarkable character, being very much larger in many of the pet varieties, and in proportion to their bodies, than in the dogs of larger breeds and massive corporeal development. The natural intelligence is also acute, and many instances occur from time to time in the experience of the canine surgeon which are evidences of a high order of animal instinct. Some animals are very clever in simulating illness or lameness, and succeed in the clever deception as to excite human pity for their apparently urgent and serious malady. Numerous instances of this kind have come under our observation. Recognising such acuteness, and the evidences also of contemporary nervous sensibility in various forms, we shall be prepared to admit the necessity for careful regulations in the form and dose of all the remedies we are called upon to administer; and likewise, as strangers, our mode of approach or handling the patient. Neglect of these has often had the effect of raising a tumult of excitement, or developing a fit of convulsions.

Epilepsy, or **Fits**, is a state of nervous disorder characterised by a loss of consciousness, and accompanied by violent convulsions, dependent upon some peculiar form of irritation of the brain or other distant parts of the nervous system. The *Causes* may be due to the state of the blood in such diseases as anæmia, plethora, distemper, &c. It has also been traced to

Missing Page

collar, if worn, should be removed. In epilepsy the owner should first secure the sufferer to prevent his running away, and as soon as the fit is over cold water should be applied to the head, protection from the sun being meanwhile secured. A dose of purgative medicine should speedily follow, and perfect quietude must be enjoined. The dieting, &c., must be careful, regular meals and digestible food in moderate quantity being allowed; the nervous irritation and resulting fever may be controlled by regular doses of chloral hydrate, or belladonna. In *chronic cases* the blister or a seton may be advisable, applied to the head, or the continued internal administration of bromide of potassium, nitrate of silver, or sulphate of iron.

Neuralgia.—It is beyond all doubt that dogs under certain circumstances are occasionally liable to neuralgia. The victim of the malady is seized very suddenly, the violent pain being indicated by fits of howling or screaming, arising suddenly during states of apparent ease and composure. The head is drawn towards the side or upwards, the animal gradually rising upon the hind feet, finally falling over, and remaining on the ground, crying with intense pain.

Apoplexy.—This disease is common to the hot months of summer when dogs are put to severe exertion. It also follows sunstroke, especially in long and tedious cases. Tightly fitting collars, and heavy chains, especially when the dog pulls heavily, or when the neck is short, are common causes. Plethoric and idle dogs, especially when old, are predisposed to the disease. It occurs as an effect of severe straining in parturition; but it may depend also upon sudden suppression of milk immediately before, or at the time of giving birth, when the animal is too plethoric, or as a result of removing the young, and of constipation.

Symptoms.—In the early or partial stages of unconsciousness, the pulse is slow and full, the eyes are bloodshot and fixed, and the pupil dilated; breathing heavy and stertorous. The animal is sometimes delirious.

Treatment.—Blood should be abstracted from the

jugular vein by preference. Subsequently, if the animal lives so long, a blister should be applied to the same part and along the spine. The best internal remedy is ammonia. Cold water continuously applied to the head is also of great service. Ammonia should be held to the nostrils for inhalation, and the gums may be rubbed with spirit of wine. In the parturient form of this disease many complications arise, and the animal does not succumb so early. A brisk purgative should be promptly administered, the action of which may be stimulated and nervous power restored by small and frequent doses of the aromatic spirit of ammonia. The milk should also be continuously drawn from the gland.

Tetanus, or *Locked Jaw.*—Notwithstanding the high state of development in the nervous system, and his liability to nervous disorders, the dog is rarely affected with tetanus. The form with which we are most familiar is that induced by poisoning with strychnine, in which the jaws are fixed, tightly closed, and often including the tongue, which is seriously injured.

Treatment is unsatisfactory, perfect quietude being all-essential.

Chorea, commonly known as *St. Vitus's dance*, is a spasmodic form of nervous derangement, most probably due to a low state or debility of the system generally and the nervous centres in particular. It may assume the local or general form.

The *Symptoms* consist of a series of sudden spasms or contractions which are confined to a set of muscles, or sometimes to one muscle, or even the part only of one, followed immediately by relaxation. Thus, one limb or other part of the body may be seized, the alternate contractions and relaxations being continuous, induces a varied appearance, sometimes even grotesque, but always evidently attended with severe strain and discomfort. The most searching investigations hitherto carried out have failed to point out the exact condition of the nerve structures involved, or the means of absolute cure.

Treatment.—We have found strychnine a valuable remedy, and under its judicious use better results have been attained than with others. The dose is from one-fortieth to one-tenth of a grain, or of nux vomica one to two grains, twice daily in bolus, and *always after a meal*. Some practitioners prefer the *liquor strychnia*, one fluid drachm of which contains half a grain of the alkaloid, as being more effective as well as more readily administered. The seton is also employed, together with blisters, and sometimes mercurial ointment in chronic cases, the parts selected being the back of the head, along the spine, &c., as indicated by the symptoms. The hot bath often soothes and rests the patient. Fresh air and walking exercise must be given according only to ability, never to tire or distress; and when the strychnine can be safely dispensed with, a change to cod-liver oil and iron tonics will be advisable. Give plain nourishing diet, always ensuring an appetite for the following meal. Remove constipation by enemas only as a safe precaution against exhausting the little strength of the patient.

Cramp differs from chorea in the continuance of painful spasm in a portion only of a muscle, arising from some cause local or general in its nature. Thus it may be due to poisoning, rheumatism, or the effects of cold after being in the water. The hind limbs are most commonly seized.

Treatment consists of the hot bath, followed by swathing in heated rugs or flannel until the body is thoroughly dried, and afterwards removed singly. The best remedy is the anodyne mixture No. 6, followed by friction to the part. Subjects of the malady should have dry beds and quarters, with freedom from cold draughts.

Injuries to the Head usually result in signs which vary with the amount of actual damage inflicted, and the area over which the effects are distributed. The indications are those of *concussion* and *compression of the brain*, with more or less *damage to the coverings*, and *apoplexy*. Under these circumstances it is frequently a question of difficulty to estimate to what extent these conditions may exist.

In *Concussion of the Brain* the animal is said to be stunned, that is, motionless and insensible; respiration is slowly performed, pulse small, rapid, and feeble; eyelids separated, pupils contracted as a rule, but insensible to the stimulus of light. Sensation slowly returns, and the patient usually vomits; the movements in progression are deliberate and dreamy, the head is carried below the level of the spine, and the animal moves in an uncertain way reeling or falling against objects, having no power to avoid them.

Recent Compression is indicated by the existence of fracture of the bones of the skull, the plates of which are depressed upon the brain substance. Insensibility is partial or complete according to the extent of the injury; respiration slow, oppressed, and noisy; the pulse also slow, and probably intermittent; eyelids separated, pupils dilated and unaffected by light; the whole muscular system is relaxed; thus, the limbs are subject to no control, but lie as when the animal fell to the ground, and both urine and fæces are voided without effort.

Apoplexy from injury to the head is due to compression by the bones of the cranium, and, as in the ordinary form, spontaneous recovery of consciousness may result from the brain accommodating itself to the situation; but the recovery is attended with unequal power in progression, the animal always moving to the right or left as the position of the injured parts will indicate.

In these cases the animal gradually acquires consciousness, and with it the liability to *Encephalitis*, or an inflammatory condition of the coverings of the brain, otherwise known as *Meningitis*, which is indicated by unusual excitement and probably convulsions, terminating in insensibility, paralysis, and death, according to the extent to which the organs are involved. The animal should, therefore, be kept perfectly quiet throughout the apoplectic stages, frequent applications of cold water to the head being desirable. Blood-letting by leeches, or the usual method, may be adopted, and the dormant powers restored by small and frequent doses of *liquor ammonia*. The injured cranium must also receive attention by the attendant surgeon, appropriate after-treatment having the object of preventing the recurrence of inflammation.

When *Encephalitis* has set in, the applications of cold water to the head should be diligently pursued; the bowels should be moved by mild aperients and enemas, the violence of the attack being controlled by aconite, prussic acid, &c. Chronic states should be met by blisters or setons externally, and internally by the bromide of potassium.

Hydrocephalus, or *Dropsy of the Brain,* usually common in delicate, highly-bred toy dogs, as terriers and French poodles, is doubtless due to a senseless plan of mating without regard to stamina of constitution. The result is either a monstrosity or weakly and attenuated, never useful, but always worthless and positive pests in the household. Such creatures are fit subjects of dropsy of the brain, and after suffering from confirmed lethargy, somnolence, inability for any exertion, paralysis of a partial or complete nature sets in, and the owner discovers he is possessed of an object of real misery, which, however, soon terminates in death.

Paralysis in the dog more frequently arises as the result of other diseases or injuries than as a distinct affection, the usual course being through their serious effects upon the spinal cord.

Symptoms.—Weakness, unsteady gait, crouching and reeling of the hind quarters, accompanied with twitchings of the muscles locally or generally. The acute form progresses rapidly, all power being lost in a few hours or less, and the animal falls, and lies in a helpless condition. Palsy or paralysis signifies disablement by loss of power, of sensation, or of both. In chronic cases the weakness continues, other signs are delayed, and the animal loses flesh and becomes a spectacle of misery and suffering. Complete paralysis is common when the brain is the seat of the injury or disease as the exciting cause. Partial paralysis arises from disease of one side only, and it is in the reverse side of the body. In injuries or diseases of the spinal cord the paralysis is limited to the parts behind the seat of disease. Vomition is a conspicuous sign in acute paralysis, and is often associated with severe abdominal pain. Blindness may be also present. The disease supervenes upon all forms of debility and anæmia, being as common in the extreme condition of obesity as in other instances.

Treatment of the patient should be entrusted to the canine surgeon.

Parasitism of the nervous system of the dog is somewhat rare. The common form is the gid hydatid *Cænurus cerebralis*, derived from the sheep, which is located in the brain, and is indicated by dulness, gradual loss of sight, and an increasing tendency to move in a circle, which point to compression of the brain. It is questionable whether the animal lives long enough to enable the parasite to effect its liberation by the usual process of growth, invasion, and ulceration of the tissues; if so, the time of suffering may be shortened by an operation for liberating the offender. This is, however, somewhat doubtful.

CHAPTER XVIII.

DISEASES OF THE SKIN.

Alopecia, or Baldness—Anasarca, or Dropsy of the Cellular Tissue—Eczema, Surfeit, or "Red Mange"—Erythema—Warts.—PARASITIC DISEASES OF THE SKIN, ANIMAL PARASITES: Scabies, or Sarcoptic Mange—Follicular Mange—The Harvest Bug—Fleas—Lice—Ticks. VEGETABLE PARASITES: Tinea Tonsurans, or Ringworm—Tinea Favosa, or Honey-Comb Ringworm.

THE literature of skin disorders in canine animals has remained incomplete during long periods; but in recent years observant men have laid all lovers of the race under perpetual obligation by their diligent investigations, and the liberal publication of their views and discoveries. It was formerly thought that the dog could not perspire. This statement implied the total absence of sudorific glands, whose especial office is the production of the secretion commonly known as sweat. Physical conditions gave the denial to this theory, as it became evident under certain forms of disease in which the functions of the kidneys were suspended, that the skin vigorously eliminated in an aeriform state the effete products which imperilled the animal's existence. The progress of histology, or the study of the ultimate tissues of the animal body, has decided the existence of sudoriparous glands in the skin of canine animals, which assume an activity of secretion proportionate to muscular exertion. Nevertheless, the office mainly consists of sending forth the waste and useless products of decomposition in the form of exhalation or vapour, any appreciable moisture being probably the after-result of cooling and condensation. As we recognise the existence of these organs, we look in other directions for the causes which secure the genesis of maladies formerly attributed to their absence. The skin of the dog requires especial care. It is liable to various forms of disease which owe their origin entirely to the absence of proper regimen and sanitary excellence. Deficiency of air, exercise, or food, as well as excess of the latter, and especially when unsuitable, work out their results in disaster and peril to general health. *Mismanagement* of this kind is the sure road to the end alluded to, *general foulness of the skin* being a significant danger-signal. Immediately it is observed the proprietor should resort to a thorough cleansing by water and "Sanitas" Dog Soap, using warm water in winter, and on all occasions taking especial care to remove moisture from the skin as much as possible by friction with dry cloths, and with protection from cold draughts. Conjointly a vegetable diet should be substituted, along with regular exercise. Spratt's Beetroot cakes admirably come to the relief of the owner under these circumstances, often saving the lives of useful servants when they are being ignorantly killed with kindness.

Alopecia, *Baldness, or Loss of Hair*, may be partial or complete, sometimes being confined to a few or single patches on various parts of the head, body or legs, or it may extend to a large surface by the destruction of the hair follicles in various forms of skin disorder, which operate through the medium of blood supply. The state is that of local congestion, and death of the hair bulb in severe instances, which ensure permanent baldness. The disease is the common result of mismanagement, as improper food, want of exercise, fresh air and grooming. The most efficient *remedy* is one part of the ordinary ointment of cantharides reduced by mixing four, six, or eight of pure lard, which should be well rubbed in twice or three times weekly. Iron and vegetable tonics should be given internally.

Anasarca, or *Dropsy of the Cellular Tissue* beneath the skin, is generally seen below the jaws, on the breast, and along the abdomen. The *cause* is some form of local irritation, as colds from entering ice-cold water, the effects of irritating mud or limy soil. It is also due to debilitating influences, especially diseases of a prostrating character.

Treatment.—Remove the cause; followed by the administration of nitric ether, ten to thirty or sixty drops, with five to twenty grains of powdered gentian.. In other cases the treatment will be regulated by the disease with which it is associated.

An acute form of inflammation of the skin of the scrotum, probably of the nature of erysipelas, has been described in Chapter XV., on the Diseases of the Male Organs of Generation (which see). The disease has been considered as a form of *cutaneous tuberculosis* by Continental veterinarians.

Eczema, *Dermatitis,* or *Surfeit,* commonly known as "Red Mange," and technically *Eczema rubrum,* consists of a vesicular inflammation of the skin, sometimes acute, or otherwise chronic in its character. It is a common disease of canine animals, being a frequent attendant upon other affections, as indigestion, distemper, and in females after pupping. Sudden chills after being heated are common causes in sporting dogs. Two forms are observed, the local and general. The first usually affects the head, neck, and back; in the latter all parts of the body suffer, but especially the thin skin on the inner sides of the arms, thighs, and over the belly. The skin is very red, and covered with vesicles or small bladders, which are sometimes isolated, or otherwise running together form larger vesicles, which shortly burst, and drying on the surface, agglutinates the hairs into tufts or masses of various size. Somewhat later they decompose, emitting a putrid odour. Severe irritation follows, to allay which the dog bites, scratches, or tears himself severely, producing sores which, in many cases, yield to no treatment. This is especially the case with those which occur on the loose skin in the bend of joints, a chronic state being general throughout the disease. Ultimately the skin assumes one or other of the following forms, viz., a constant state of scurfiness with loss of hair, or the skin is immensely thickened, drawn into folds destitute of hair, and exhibiting ugly cracks, at the bottom of which ulceration, with more or less discharge, proceeds. At certain local points also, large and bare tumours of similar callous substance are found, as on the elbows and buttocks, states especially common to animals kept in confinement and subjected to neglect.

Treatment.—First open the bowels by a dose of the castor-oil mixture; or in the early stages of the acute form reduce the dose one-third, and subsequently give salines, as Epsom salts. Some prefer opium and calomel in one-grain doses of each daily, a remedy seldom used with safety in the hands of amateurs in medicine. Such remedies secure the reduction of fever, after which tonics, as iron and gentian, or the *liquor arsenicalis*, are indicated, especially if debility sets in early. Special forms of fever arising from the severity of the skin affection may call for very active measures, as opium and calomel internally, with repeated fomentations, or baths of hot water containing glycerine and boracic acid, or even opium. Chronic cases are not always manageable, yet good may be done by repeated dressings with lunar caustic, and the skin generally dressed with zinc ointment. The disease is apt to exhibit phases of severe excitement, the result of change in temperature and derangement of the digestive functions. The animal is maddened by severe itching of the skin, and can scarcely be restrained from injuring himself. For this fomentations with warm water containing opium may suffice; in some cases they afford no relief, and remedies of an entirely opposite nature are required—viz., lotions of nitrate of silver, ointment of nitrate of mercury, &c., applied as circumstances require. The diet must be carefully regulated, less animal food being allowed, the exercise regular and duly proportioned to the strength of the patient. Neglect of these precautions is sure to bring on a fresh attack of the complaint. A common practice exists in the use of mercurial or blue ointment for the cure of this malady. The owner who is wise will avoid the remedy entirely except under the care of the canine surgeon.

Erythema is a diffused form of irritation of the skin, usually considered to be of a congestive character, preceding true inflammation, and affecting such parts as receive a large quantity of blood for the supply of the sebaceous glands within the structure. It arises from disorder of the stomach or system generally, as indigestion, worms, teething, chills, &c. As the active symptoms decline, the skin throws off a considerable number of scales or scurf, and shortly the affected parts resume their natural appearance. This is the usual course under ordinary management, but persistence of the cause eventually develops true inflammation or eczema, already described.

Treatment consists of replacing animal food by a variety less stimulating and partially vegetable; giving regular exercise, especially in the open air, and away from home. Irritation of the skin may be allayed by water containing a few drops of laudanum, or a lotion containing five grains of the sulphate of zinc to the ounce may be used. Boracic acid, five to ten grains to the ounce of water, is also highly effectual.

Warts, technically termed *Verrucæ*, often prove troublesome to the dog. They consist of inordinate as well as deformed growths of the dermis, or deeper layer of the skin, and appear to be due to some special form of local irritation. They are to be seen on the free edges of the ears, lips, and especially the eyelids; and in some animals the mucous membrane of the mouth and prepuce is a common location. Other parts of the skin are also liable to invasion, but probably not so frequently as those already named. The enlargements partake of a variety of forms. They are sometimes diffuse, or spread over the surface of the skin, at others they rise erect, and subsequently assume a spherical or other form, being very mobile, and united to the tissues of the true skin by a narrow cord-like neck. Their presence gives rise to various forms of inconvenience, such as friction against other objects, laceration, &c., and considerable irritation in old-standing cases by the cracking of the scales, and subsequent ulceration between them.

Treatment.—In the diffused variety the regular application of caustic, as the nitrate of silver, or strong acetic acid, will be required. Those attached to the skin by a constriction or neck, are easily removed by ligature, torsion, or the écraseur. Early attention when the growths are small is likely to be of greatest service.

Parasitic Diseases of the Skin.—The affections of this class are numerous and important. They arise from the irritation produced as the result of the efforts of the *animal parasites* in obtaining a nidus or hatching-place for their eggs. Some of these occupy their position for such a length of time when undisturbed as to indicate the permanence of their home; others are ephemeral in their visits, being endowed with organs of free locomotion, as legs and wings of considerable power. In the first order we place the various forms of mange, or itch animalcules, and in the latter, fleas, ticks, lice, and other insects, amongst which the harvest bug is a common example. In addition to these, we have also to notice another variety—viz., *vegetable parasites*, which likewise prove exceedingly troublesome to canine animals, as well as disappointing to the hopes and aspirations of the owner.

Animal Parasites of the Skin.—These are included under the term *Dermatozoa*, which embraces a great variety in the forms of animal life. Their movements are directed in the search for suitable breeding-places, as well as for their natural sustenance, and thus a large amount of tissue is destroyed, accompanied by severe irritation, which induces a form of active inflammation, or true dermatitis. We call the disease *mange*, as especially the result of the presence of the acarus, or mange insect; it is, notwithstanding, true inflammation of the skin. Contagion plays the essential part, as true mange cannot exist without the parasite. It may attack the best of animals, but the common subjects are those debilitated by want of food and necessary care, whose hunger leads them to prowl, and ferret out from the dirtiest places the wherewith to appease their hunger, and there meet with the acari; or it may be in the company of infected dogs that the disease is contracted. The differences exhibited by various forms of parasitic disease in their potency of contagion, depends on the habits of the acarus. Infection, as we understand it, is not a term of suitability; the parasite does not become aeriform, nor is it, as far as can be ascertained, carried by the air.

Scabies, or *Mange of the Dog*, technically known as *Sarcoptic Scabies*, is the analogue of "itch" in mankind, and the "scab" of sheep. The producing parasite is the *Sarcoptes canis*, which usually first invades the parts least disturbed by the feet of the sufferer; thus we find the back of the neck is the spot where the earliest signs may be looked for. From thence it spreads rapidly, as the army of acari have multiplied by thousands or even millions. Their operations give the subject no rest. He loses his appetite, is depressed, puts on a haggard look, and is feverish. He is continually scratching, and the wildest paroxysms are usually evident after eating, drinking, or lying in the warmth of a fire. *He enjoys being scratched by the fingers*, and places himself suitably for its being continued over the entire body. From this point the disease becomes intensified, as every spot, bed, &c., frequented by the patient, and also the sufferer's claws, become infected, and shortly provide a fresh colony of acari ready for further attack when the dog again visits the spot. If the reader has attentively studied the paragraphs dealing with the symptoms of *erythema* and *eczema*, he will be able to realise by the changes produced by the parasite how rapidly the disorganisation proceeds, constituting true forms of those diseases. The parasite burrows beneath the cuticle, and may be found on raising the scabs which cover the wounded parts. This is the sure diagnostic sign of the disease, and the essential proof that it is not simple eczema or "red mange."

Treatment.—Successful issues attend only diligent and orderly application of the remedy. The hardened cuticle and protecting scabs are safe refuges to the acari, therefore, if we desire to destroy them, the above-named barriers must be removed. The affected animal should be placed in a warm bath, and washed thoroughly with "Sanitas" Dog Soap, taking care to remove or break up the encrustations or scabs, as they are swollen and raised by the water. An ounce of potash placed in the water will greatly promote the operation. Not a spot, however small, must be omitted. The ears and feet also must come in for their share of the general scrutiny and cleansing. The owner need not be in haste to remove the dog from his bath. The warmth will comfort him, and, with fresh additions of heated water after the first washing, it will be advisable to include one or two teaspoonfuls of "Sanitas" Oil mixed with an equal bulk of glycerine. Next comes the operation of dressing. The dog is removed from the bath, carefully drained under protection from the cold, and the dressing, whatever it may be, is patiently and carefully rubbed in. In order to realise how much of both is required, the operator must endeavour to think how he would like to have it done to himself under similar circumstances. The process will be needed at intervals of at least three or four days, long hair being carefully removed, or even entire shaving must be resorted to. A muzzle should be in readiness to prevent the animal using his teeth. We also recommend care in its selection, as some of these appliances are perfect tortures, fitting badly and inflicting pain on the suffering creature. For various forms of mange dressings *see* Chapter VIII. under Parasiticides.

Follicular Mange differs from *Sarcoptic Mange* both in respect of the parasite and its location. The former is the analogue if not the identical parasite *Demodex folliculorum* common to mankind; indeed, this form of human itch has been transferred to the dog, and back again to mankind. The location of the parasite is the bag or pouch-like sebaceous glands and hair follicles; it is microscopical, possesses a large abdomen, several pairs of short legs, elongated after the form of a shrimp, and is endowed with remarkable powers of multiplication. The disease produced is much less susceptible of medical treatment, and there is also at first much less irritation and resulting fever. It appears in patches, first about the head, face, lips, &c., and later it invades the legs, loins, belly, sides, and scrotum in the male. The discharge from the sebaceous glands partakes of pus as well as the excess of a morbid secretion, by reason of which the sufferer presents a loathsome appearance and highly offensive odour. The animal shakes himself instead of using his feet, and he refuses to be handled. When the hairs are plucked singly from the follicles, the parasite may be detected at the root by means of a microscope; the pus and also the secretion from the gland likewise furnish the same conclusive evidence. The first signs of the malady consist of small bare patches, on which appear red spots, which proved to be the enlarged ducts of the sebaceous glands, filled with serum, and later, with pus. These subsequently burst and form scales, and occasionally one or more pustules become confluent, or united, especially when the skin is acutely inflamed; the hair is also freely shed over the entire body, and the animal suffers much from cold, requiring ample clothing, especially in adverse seasons. Further aggravation arises from the formation of sores and cracks, the result of death of the tissues of the skin, blood and pus flowing freely from the discharging surfaces.

The principles of *Treatment* laid down for sarcoptic mange must be rigidly adopted in this disease. Frequent and thorough dressing must be persisted in, especial attention being directed to removal of the crusts in order that the dressings may reach the parasites within the hair follicles. Suitable formulæ will be found in Chapter VIII. under the head of Parasiticides. As in sarcoptic mange the removal of hair by close clipping, or even shaving, must be carried out efficiently and without hesitation when desirable. The advice concerning removal of the crusts given under sarcoptic mange is especially needed, frequent baths and subsequent dressings, probably continued for months, being needed before any improvement is evident. As we have already remarked, the parasites, by reason of their location, are extremely difficult to attack, and even, if we are successful, yet another problem awaits us, viz., the ova, which may be hiding away on such parts as have been restored by destruction of the parents. Care must be exercised also with regard to lodging and beds. Kennels require cleansing, and nothing answers so effectually as strong and boiling-hot solutions of caustic potash or soda, which should be used liberally by means of a large painter's brush. The best bed is pine shavings, frequently renewed; when they are not accessible, clean hay or straw may be used, which should be regularly dressed with water containing one-twentieth part of crude "Sanitas," and allowed to dry before being put into use. Beds of whatever kind, having served their purpose, should be summarily burned.

The Harvest Bug, or *Leptus autumnalis*, the larval hexapod of the *Tetranychus autumnalis*, proves a troublesome parasite to the human subject, giving rise to painful boils. It also attacks animals, especially dogs, during the hot months of July and August, afterwards passing through other developmental changes, and is lost sight of. When it reaches the skin it may be detected by its bright red colour, and if not speedily removed it shortly burrows in the skin, giving rise to irritation. When the parts are rubbed the parasite ejects an acrid secretion, which, with the burrowing operations, produces severe pain. In the dog it may be usually found on the head, neck and back, which are involved in severe eczema, and on the inflamed parts the offenders may be readily observed by means of an ordinary lens. The disease yields very tardily, perhaps owing to the difficulty of reaching the parasite. Paraffin has been found effectual; carbolic acid in glycerine is not certain, as, owing to the susceptibility of the dog to the action of the drug, only weak solutions could be used.

Fleas, *Fulex irritans*, are terrible pests to the dog. Their presence in pet dogs is a serious drawback, and their extermination becomes a disideratum. If not removed they cause severe and continued irritation, seriously affect the health, and reduce the animal to a state of anæmia and debility. Cleanliness in the kennel, as in all other respects, is absolutely essential to prevent the attack, regular washing of the animal with "Sanitas" Dog Soap being effectual. For especial remedies, *see* Parasiticides, in Chapter VIII.

Lice, *pediculi*, do not prove so troublesome or painful as fleas. They are, however, more loathsome, and we shudder to think of the possibility of their transmission to ourselves. Well-kept dogs receive them only by contact with others infected. Mongrels and wandering curs obtain them in the dirt and filth among which they seek their food, or by contact with their infected fellows. They always retire before the resolute acts of cleanliness. Simple cases are cured by ordinary washing with "Sanitas" Dog Soap. Confirmed cases require the application of a special Parasiticide.

Ticks are summer visitants, which not only produce severe irritation by boring into the skin, but debilitate the sufferer by sucking his blood, and by their effects on the nervous system have been known to induce paralysis. The species common to our dogs is the *Ixodes ricinus*, an innocent offender as compared with certain varieties common to South Africa, which are known to kill not only dogs, but also oxen. They are usually found in the ears, but may attach themselves to other parts where the hair is thin. The best remedy is to cut each tick in half by scissors, after which the embedded portion may be removed by forceps, or a drop of turpentine will answer the purpose.

Vegetable Parasites.—Of this class two are common to canine animals. They are true fungi in nature, attach themselves to the epithelium or scarf skin, as well as the hairs proceeding from it, and are readily detected under an ordinary microscope. They prevail in damp, dark, and ill-drained places, and young animals are especially susceptible of attack ; but in all cases want of condition and general cleanliness predisposes the animal to their effects. They are also communicable from other species of animals to the dog, and he may convey them to others besides his own, or even to mankind by contagion alone. This may be mediate or immediate, and from the nature of the spores, it is believed that the air may act as a suitable medium. After being deposited on the skin, the process of incubation commences, and occupies from eight or ten to fourteen days, when they produce a colony of spores, and from the circumstance of their common arrangement in the form of a circle, the disease they produce is familiarly known as Ringworm.

Tinea Tonsurans, or *Ringworm*, is occasionally seen in the dog. It occurs in circular patches, destitute of hair, except a few which by the action of the fungus, are broken and lifeless, standing among the enlarged cells, and projecting irregularly. Growth is on the external margin ; thus, the skin first affected is left smooth, and covered with glistening scales, or an aggregation forming a grey crust, each of which contain the spores of the fungus *Achorion lebertii,* or *Trichophyton tonsurans*. Constant cleansing with "Sanitas" Soap and warm water, and subsequent dressings with the tincture of cantharides, or iodine ; dilute mineral and acetic acids, mercurial, or nitrate of silver ointment, tincture of iron, &c. &c., usually effect a cure. The disease is liable to be mistaken for *Herpes circinatus*, or vesicular ringworm, a form of local eczema common in young dogs as a result of indigestion, teething, &c., on the cessation of which it disappears.

Tinea Favosa, or *Honeycomb Ringworm*, variously

known as *Achorion Schönleinii* or *Tricophyton favosa*, is a parasitic fungus of peculiar form and growth. It has a special preference for the hairs. Having entered the hair follicle it throws out a mass of fungoid cells around the base, and growing, encircles the hair in such a manner that the latter appears to be growing out of a cup. A number of these may unite, and thus a large and unsightly tumour is formed, with the loss of surrounding tissue by resulting absorption. It is supposed the dog catches the complaint from mice, in which it is quite common. The tumour is usually located about the head. It is also peculiar as emitting a smell not unlike the urine of the cat, probably derived from the course of destruction of animal tissue.

Treatment consists of entire removal of all the diseased hairs and fungus crusts by means of a paper knife or suitable instrument, and immediately burned. *The bare fingers must not come into contact with the diseased mass.* Appropriate dressings will be found in the list enumerated for *Tinea tonsurans*. The most effective are solution of corrosive sublimate (poison) and the nitrate of silver ointment.

CHAPTER XIX.

LOCAL INJURIES.

Anchylosis, or Stiff-joint—Sprain of Muscle and Sinew—Congenital Deformity—Dislocations—Fracture of Bone—False Joint—Lameness—Sprain of Muscle—Sprain of Tendon—Lameness of the Feet—Carpet Fever—Injuries by Thorns, Nails, &c.—Raw, Bruised and Bleeding Feet—Mange of the Foot—Overgrown Claws—Wounds—Hæmorrhage, or Bleeding.

Anchylosis, or *Stiff-joint*, is not uncommon in canine animals, being due to some injury and consequent inflammation, with the formation of *exostosis*, or bony deposit. The latter accumulates largely at the ends of the bones, eventually uniting them, causing the animal to carry the limb in a more or less flexed position, and is unable to put it to the ground, or bear any weight upon it. The parts commonly affected are the phalanges, or small bones of the feet, which suffer from being trodden, run over, or bruising from falling objects. The elbow also suffers as a result of dislocation which has not been reduced. Sprains of ligament also end in exostosis and anchylosis, and, on that account, all such injuries should receive prompt attention. Blisters frequently applied, and the actual cautery, are often attended with good results in the early stages.

Sprains of Muscle and Sinew are common to sporting dogs, especially greyhounds. They are met with in all forms, varying from slight extension, or laceration of fibre, to "breaking down," or rupture of the sinews. Cure is effected by complete rest, the administration of laxative medicine, and cold water externally.

Congenital Deformities of the extremities are not uncommon in puppies. They present such a variety of forms that intelligible description fails in the small space allotted. When the animal is of valuable or special strain, the best course is to submit the case to a well-known canine surgeon for opinion as to procedure.

Dislocations.—Displacement of bones in their union to form joints is common in dogs of all ages. They present various aspects as well as difficulties, and the patient should be placed in the hands of the skilled canine surgeon.

Besides reduction, the after-treatment of dislocation is often important. Bandages and splints, as for fractures, may be required, being retained by starch, melted pitch, &c., until the parts have assumed a healthy condition, the use of the limb being also suspended. Blisters, or even firing, may be called for at a later stage in order to hasten the cure.

Fracture of Bone is frequent in dogs. They originate from falls, blows, kicks from horses, or being run over by vehicles; and, as a rule, are readily distinguished by the crepitus, deformity, pain on movement of the injured member, inability to use it, with subsequent swelling and inflammation. The power of reparation is ample in the dog, he is also less liable to systemic disturbance, and on this account an attempt to restore by treatment is always advisable in ordinary cases.

The *treatment* of these cases should be entrusted to the canine surgeon.

False union may arise from bones improperly set, when the appliances are too slack, or the animal has used the limb too soon. In such cases the limb is bent, unsightly, and gives rise to lameness. The common plan is to destroy the recent callus by fracture, and reset the limb with care, when good results may be obtained. Such a severe operation should call for the use of an anæsthetic as chloroform.

Lameness arising from various causes is common in canine animals. The usual signs consist of inability to support the weight of the body without limping, or the limb may be carried, and during rest the affected part is indicated by the dog as he licks or even bites it.

Sprain of Muscle is usually denoted by heat, and swelling and great tenderness over the seat of injury, the limb being carried in a semi-flexed state, and the foot near the ground. The severe forms are attended with more or less fever and inaction of the bowels; the injured spot is often licked.

Treatment.—Sprain of muscle usually yields readily to absolute rest, and the hot spongio-piline poultice frequently renewed to maintain heat. Pain may be reduced by adding a drachm of the tincture of belladonna or opium to the material after being slightly wrung out. The bowels should be moved as directed, and when the state of the animal calls for it, give a febrifuge.

Sprain of tendon may be detected in a somewhat similar manner to the above, with the exception of the evidence of immediate swelling. Pressure will, as a rule, elicit the existence of pain, or, when a joint is sprained, flexion and extension will succeed.

Treatment.—Cold water applications continually are indicated; or evaporating lotion may be used to saturate a *thin* bandage surrounding the injured part. The bowels will also need attention as already referred to in preceding paragraphs.

Subsequent treatment for Sprains is carried out as follows: When the heat, pain, and inflammation are subdued the parts may be smartly rubbed two or three times daily by the hand, using soap liniment seven parts, and laudanum one part. Five or six minutes may suffice for the operation, the last portions being rubbed to dryness of the hair, &c. When swelling or thickening remains, and is cool, the following liniment should be employed: Soap liniment four ounces, tincture of iodine one ounce. Apply morning and evening with friction as already directed.

Lameness of the Feet arises from several causes. *Foot-founder* consists of inflammation of the skin between the balls or pads, arising from the irritation of dust, sand, or wet, during long and tedious journeys, especially in dogs which have been at rest some time. It is also a common result of "frost-bite." In such instance the resulting pain and fever are sufficient to throw the dog off work entirely for some time.

House and Pet Dogs likewise suffer from a similar but slightly chronic form by long confinement indoors, in which indigestion and the irritation from the heat and dust of carpets equally contribute. The disease has been facetiously termed "carpet fever," as indicating the systemic character, the accompaniments being redness, soreness, and pain of the skin in the spaces between the pads. *A cure* is effected in these foot diseases by first opening the bowels, and applying several times daily a lotion of zinc or alum in slight cases. The "Sanitas" Jelly also answers well for the purpose. When the pain is severe, and fever runs high, the hot spongio-piline poultice is the best application frequently renewed, after a patient fomentation with hot water, or a hot bath in which the animal may be placed if able to stand. As soon as he is able to walk, he should wear boots or some other protection until the feet assume their former coolness and hardness. The disease is apt to recur on application of the causes.

Injuries by Thorns, Nails, &c., are best treated by removal of the offending substance, dirt, &c., and the application of "Sanitas" Jelly or the "Sanitas" Veterinary Ointment, with the exhibition of a laxative, &c., as already pointed out.

Raw, Bruised and Bleeding Feet are the result of long journeys and the irritating dust, &c., of the roads, and usually yield to continued rest, laxatives, and the applications already advocated.

Mange of the Foot is the common result of using the member to allay the irritation of the body, and presents the usual local indications, with ulceration of the toes and loosening of the claws. The latter should be removed, and the usual dressings for mange applied, or the foot may be enveloped in tow saturated with "Sanitas" Fluid, or well smeared with the "Sanitas" Veterinary Ointment.

Overgrown Claws are the usual result of a luxurious life, especially on carpets. In the absence of wear they grow rapidly, and curling beneath eventually wound the pads or the interspaces. They should be severed a little in advance of the pad, by means of stout wire cutters, and regular outdoor exercise enjoined.

Wounds of various kinds are inflicted on the skin of dogs, and include all the varieties known in animal surgery—viz., *incised, lacerated, contused,* and *punctured*.

Incised Wounds are produced by some cutting instrument, the skin being evenly divided without loss of substance. They may prove serious by contemporaneous wounding of blood vessels.

Lacerated Wounds are caused by hooks, nails, &c., which tear the skin unevenly, and sometimes seriously interfere with the vitality of the parts, and subsequent healing. Sloughing is, therefore, not an uncommon result.

Contused Wounds are the effects of blows, falls, &c., in which the tissues are more or less disorganised and the vitality destroyed. Sloughing is a frequent after-occurrence.

Punctured Wounds are caused by the entrance of sharp

bodies, as nails, thorns, or splinters of wood, &c. They are dangerous according to the depth, especially as some of the internal organs and cavities may be injured.

Treatment consists of closing incised wounds by means of sutures, always first ensuring the absence of foreign bodies. Some lacerated wounds will also admit of this treatment, but, as a rule, sutures do not answer effectually. Bandages, or other forms of support may be needed according to the peculiarities of the case. These, as well as contused wounds, are often benefited by stimulating applications to the surrounding parts, as soap liniment, containing a few drops of ammonia, alternated with fomentations, or the spongio-piline poultice. Punctured wounds call for the prompt removal of the offending instrument, for which incision may be required. Inject healing fluids by means of a syringe.

Wounds of Arteries and Veins.—These are distinguished by the colour of the blood, that from an artery being scarlet, and venous blood is a modena red. Remedies known as styptics are used to stop the flow of blood by forming a plug over the situation of the wounds. Such are astringents which act by coagulating the fibrine, of which the blood is largely composed. Examples are, cotton wool, German tinder, as mechanical agents; tannic acid, lunar caustic, and perchloride of iron, are chemical styptics; and the hot iron a corrosive agent. A simple method of arresting blood in a limb consists of passing a cord or handkerchief round and above the wound, and tying to form a loose loop. A stick is then passed through half way, forming two convenient handles for twisting the ligature, the result being pressure, and arrest of the flow of blood. This being accomplished, the local wound can be treated more efficiently, the animal being saved from severe loss of blood.

CHAPTER XX.

POISONS.

Empirical Poisoning—Accidental Poisoning—Wilful and Malicious Poisoning—Symptoms of Poisoning—Treatment—Mineral Poisons—Vegetable Poisoning—Animal Poisons—Snake, or Viper Bite—Wasps, Hornets, and Bees—Destruction of Dogs.

THE death of animals by poisoning arises in three ways :

In *Empirical Practice* many persons make use of remedies the nature and action of which they know little or nothing ; they also continue the use of a remedy without being able to perceive that it is unsuitable, or probably dangerous. In this way an ordinary medicine acts with the virulence of a poison.

Accidental Poisoning takes place in a variety of ways, chiefly through the absolute carelessness on the part of those who have the custody of remedies. They are sometimes carelessly left within reach of the animal, or become mixed with the food; and preparations for external use may be given internally. Vermin poisons reach the meal-tub or the feeding-trough ; large doses of medicines are also given too frequently; thus, the remedy which might have effected a cure proves a deadly poison.

Wilful and Malicious Poisoning, happily, is not frequent. Yet one hears now and again of a favourite pet, or the first animal of a special strain, having won high honours, is found dead or dying at the time, or before, he reaches his home. Such acts characterise fiends and fools who fail to see that others read them accurately by their daily lives, which have a full renown for many similar accomplishments.

The *Symptoms of Poisoning*, as a rule, are quickly

developed, generally after a meal, or they may be associated with some special act or circumstance, as the giving of a tit-bit by an admiring stranger, or immediately after the external use or internal administration of a remedy. Such facts being kept in mind, precise attention may be directed to the probable cause with the result of showing whether the signs are due to malicious intent, poisonous agents, or mistakes in medicines. Concise information on these points, as far as they are elucidated, should always be sent in writing to the canine surgeon when summoned.

The precise *Treatment of Poisoning* must always be left with the canine surgeon. He alone can provide the acknowledged antidote. The owner may alleviate to an extent the pangs and sufferings of the patient, for instance in diarrhœa or dysentery, by the giving of milk with egg beaten up, thick flour or starch with water will be useful; and when abdominal pain is acute a dose of laudanum, twenty-five or thirty drops, or three to five grains of the gum. Syrup of white poppies, one to three or four drachms, also proves a useful agent. If vermin powder has been taken, give broth or thick soup; and when hellebore or colchicum is the cause, add to the milk and eggs nitrous ether, ammonia, or spirits, as gin, whisky or brandy, to obviate the extreme depression which ensues.

Mineral Poisons.—These comprise a variety of substances used in medicine or otherwise, the most active of which are preparations of arsenic, lead, mercury and zinc, and copper.

The *General Symptoms of Poisoning by Minerals* are as follow: irritation and violent pain in the stomach and bowels, with vomiting, diarrhœa, painful straining, the evacuations being mixed with blood, cramps of the limbs and collapse. The membrane of the bowels is sometimes also removed, and may be found in the evacuations, as in the case of *arsenic*, the *compounds of mercury*, and even *mercurial ointment* when largely used to the skin. To the latter metal also is ascribed the *mercurial eczema* which arises from long continuance of its use externally as well as internally. Salivation is also present, and the breath as well as the secretions of the skin are highly offensive. Poisoning by *lead*, or *plumbism*, is denoted by general failure of function in the digestive apparatus, a blue line forming along the gums, vomition, colic, vertigo, with gradual paralysis and death. *Acute poisoning by copper* resembles that of violent irritants generally, as already detailed; the *Chronic form* greatly resembles that of slow arsenical poisoning, as impaired appetite, constipation, imperfect nutrition, weakness, and occasionally bloody urine. In this class of poisons *carbolic acid* must be included. Few remedies in medicines have had a greater responsibility as a toxic agent than this, especially in dogs and cats. Whether used externally, internally, or licked by the animal, it produces severe and immediate depression, weakness of the heart, with ultimate paralysis of the organ, convulsions and speedy death. In our experience dogs have simply laid down, become quite listless, breathing slowly, with evident oppression, and died in unconsciousness, when the medicine has been largely applied to wounded surfaces. Whatever may be its vaunted virtues as a sanative dressing in other animals, the serious drawback to employment in the same direction among canine and feline animals is that its general effects are those of a powerful poison.

In case of absorption of the remedy sufficient to produce poisoning, Broad, of Bath, recommends the continued application of cold water as a spray, or by means of the rose on a watering-pot, until convulsions cease. The animal should also be thoroughly cleansed by means of cold water and hard soap, or the whole of the skin may be well rubbed with oil. The animal should receive stimulants internally.

In *Vegetable Poisoning* the symptoms are mainly different to those induced by the metallic salts. *Strychnine*, is perhaps the most common of dangerous drugs, and being recognised as one of the most fatal, is ignorantly selected by the wilful poisoner. Death sometimes arises from overdoses or long continuance of the drug. Dogs are specially susceptible of its effects, the symptoms being severe tetanic convulsions, rigidity, and straightening of the spine, with elevation of the head and tail, rigidity of the legs, retraction of the muscles of the face and mouth, inducing a remarkable grin of the features. All the symptoms are sudden and simultaneous. Many antidotes have been tried, the most effectual being the monobromide of camphor in doses of one to one-and-a-half drachms, given by the stomach. Recovery has also been effected by the continued use of chloroform, and subsequently belladonna and opium; also hydrocyanic acid somewhat later.

Tobacco, and also *Hellebore Infusions*, sometimes used as Parasiticides in Mange, &c., prove dangerous as violent poisons, being absorbed through the skin, especially where it is rendered sore by the parasites. The signs are great depression, with vomition, failure of the heart's action, and death. To counteract these states the animal should be immediately washed in clean cold water.

Snake and *Viper Bites* are forms of *Animal Poisoning*. The first is common abroad, and exceedingly fatal; the latter is seen in England, and is likewise dangerous in the dog. The affected animal suffers from extreme distress, depression and difficult respiration, with rapid decomposition of the blood, local swelling, paralysis, terminating in violent convulsions. If the part bitten is a limb, a ligature should be applied *above* the wound, sufficiently tight to prevent absorption. Strong solution of ammonia, largely diluted, should be administered internally at frequent intervals, and the wound promptly cauterised, or dressed freely with the undiluted ammonia. Artificial respiration must be persistently carried on from the first, and conjointly with cold affusions, with the object of producing stimulus to the nervous system. The *Bite of the Dog* should also receive the same treatment, especially if he be suspected of rabies. In mankind the ligature, with prompt suction of the wound as an encouragement to bleeding, is essential.

It now appears to be fairly demonstrated that great similarity of action in the poison of snake-bite also exists in the *Indian arrow-head poison*, or, technically, *curare* and *wourali*, death arising from paralysis of the muscles of respiration, in addition to the action upon the heart. In order to avert death, the utmost endeavours must be made to promote artificial respiration, contemporaneous with other means described, by which life is preserved long enough for the other remedies to act in the neutralisation of the toxic agent.

Wasps, hornets, bees, &c., in this country, are troublesome pests to the dog. Those animals used for hunting purposes, and others which act as marauders, disturb the insects by accidentally upsetting the nests. The hornet's sting is often rapidly fatal, giving no opportunity for treatment. To escape an attack from the infuriated insects it is common to raise a dense smoke, or take refuge behind thick bushes, and, best of all, to rush into water when at hand. The best local as well as internal remedy is ammonia; the common washing-blue is also effective externally; and a third popular agent is carron-oil, a compound of linseed oil and lime-water in equal parts. Such, however, is the severity of the poison, especially that of the hornet, that the dog frequently dies before anything can be done in the way of treatment.

The Destruction of Dogs.—An effective and speedy method of putting useless and other animals out of existence is a subject of importance. When they have served us faithfully, having also grown old, decrepit, and often offensive, a burden to themselves also, we grieve to witness their condition, and desire to see their misery terminated. *Euthanasia*, an easy or calm death, is what we prefer; many methods are speedy, but the results are agonising. Thus, *prussic acid* is probably the most speedy and powerful poison, but the convulsions are horrifying. An *electric shock*, sufficiently powerful, is surprisingly effective, but is cumbrous in its application. *Pithing* and *drowning* are objectionable on grounds so obvious that their discussion is unnecessary. The *hypodermic method*, or simply injecting the lethal dose beneath the skin, is, perhaps, the most speedy; but we object to the evidences, although it is probably certain the animal is totally unconscious of all suffering. For large numbers of animals nothing supersedes the *lethal chamber*, in which death comes on as quietly as ordinary slumber; yet we hesitate to send our favourite to die in such motley company. Dr. Gordon Stables recommends first a dose of chloral in the form of syrup to induce sound sleep, during which the animal is caused to inhale an over-dose of chloroform. In our practice we omit the chloral as an unnecessary delay, and simply place the animal recumbent, cover him with a woollen rug, doubled, then introduce beneath it a sponge fully saturated with chloroform, which is held close to the nostrils. He thus breathes only the vapour of chloroform. Death is speedy and minu- all suffering, occupying less time than is required for writing the few and imperfect lines discussing this special method.

INDEX.

ABDOMEN, dropsy of the, 200
Abscess, 112
,, of the ear-flap, 227
Abuse of medicines, 115
Achorion lebertii, 247
,, Schönleinii, 248
Active aperient, 162
Alopecia, 237
Alteratives, 119
Amaurosis, 222
Anæmia, 140
Anasarca, 238
Anchylosis, 209
Anodynes, 120
Anthrax, 147
Antispasmodics, 121
Antiseptics, 121
,, importance of, 115
Antiputrescents, 121
Aperients, 122
Aphonia, 174
Apnœa, 146
Apoplexy, 231
Appetite, 109
Arrow-head poison, 257
Arteries, wounds of, 253
Ascaris marginata, 191
Ascites, 200
Asthma, 179
Astringents, 122
Atony of the rectum, 198
Auricular acariasis, 228

BAKEWELL'S MOTTO FOR BREEDING, 31
Baldness, 237
Bandy-legs, 144
"Barry," story of, 59
Beagle, 34
Bedlington Terrier, 75
"Belton Greys," 10
"Bernard de Meuthon," 58
Black Poodle, 99
,, Pug, 95

Black and Tan Terrier, 69
Bladder, paralysis of, 207
,, rupture of, 207
,, stone in, 207
Bleeding from the nostrils, 173
,, piles, 197
Blenheim Spaniel, 88
Blister fluid, 123
,, ointment, 123
,, sweating, 124
Blisters, 123
Blood abscess, 227
,, diseases, 138
Bloodhound, 28
,, breeding of the, 31
,, origin of, 29
Blood poisoning, 167
"Bloom of Health," 108
"Blue Peter," 93
Blue pill, 122
Bob-tailed Sheepdog, 81
Bolus, the, 117
,, for diabetes, 122
,, ,, hæmorrhage, 122
,, stomachic, 137
Bone, disease of, 249
Borzoi, 50
Bowel, stricture of the, 199
,, atony of the, 198
,, dropping of the, 196
,, thickening of, 198
Bowels, inflammation of the, 194
Brain, injuries of the, 233
,, compression of the, 234
,, dropsy of the, 235
Breaking-down, 249
,, the Fox Terrier, 41
Breeders of the Blenheim Spaniel, 89
,, ,, Bloodhound, 31
,, ,, Dandie Dinmont, 69
,, ,, Old English Mastiff, 52
Breeders of Pugs, 90, 95

262 Index.

Breeding, Bakewell's plan, 31
Bright's Disease, 205
Broken-haired Terrier, 70
Bronchitis, 175
   ,, verminous, 178
Bronchocele, 203
"Bull-cross" in Fox Terrier, 41
Bull-dog, 63
  ,, Terrier, 65
Bruises, or cuts, lotion for, 134

CANINE HÆMATOZOA, 182
Canis cordis, 183
Canker, external, 226
  ,, internal, 227
  ,, of the mouth, 185
Carpet fever, 251
Castor-oil mixture, 122
Catarrh, 170
Cartilago nictitans, 224
Cataract, 221
Catarrh of the stomach, 189
Catheter, use of, 215
Caustic lotions, 125
  ,, potash, 124
Caustics, 124
"Cecil" on the Foxhound, 32
Celebrated breeders of Bloodhounds, 31
Charbon, 147
Characteristics of the Irish Setter, 12
Chloroform, inhalation of, 133
Choking, 187
Cholera, 148
Chorea, 232
Chronic cough, 179
  ,, ,, mixture for, 131
  ,, hepatitis, 201
Circassian Wolfhound, 51
Circulatory system, diseases of, 180
Classification of disease, 116
Claws, overgrown, 252
Cleanliness, importance of, 114
Cleanly poultice, 136
Clever Spaniel, 19
Close-breeding, 31
Clumber Spaniel, 15
Clysters, 125
Cocker Spaniel, 17
Cockermouth Beagles, 34
Cænurus cerebralis, 236
Colic, 191

Collie, the, 83
Colour of the Greyhound, 88
  ,, Setters, 9
Common tick, 246
Constipation, 194
Contagious diseases, 146
Continuous vomition, 189
Contused wounds, 252
Cooling lotion, 134
Cordial drench, 127
Cordial pill, 127
Cordials, 127
Coryza, 170
Costiveness, 194
Cough, chronic, 179
  ,, mixture, 131
Cow Dog, 82
Cramp, 233
Crooked legs, 144
Cultivation of the truffle, 43
Curare poisoning, 257
Cystitis, 206

DANDIE DINMONT, 73
Dane, the Great, 54
Dachshund, 36
Deerhound, 50
Degeneration of the heart, 182
Demulcents, 129
Dermatitis, 238
Dermatoid conjunctiva, 224
Dermatozoa, 242
Destruction of dogs, 258
Diabetes, 207
  ,, bolus for, 122
Diaphoretics, 128
Diarrhœa, 192
  ,, mixture for, 120
Digestive system, diseases of, 184
Digestives, 128
Diphtheria, 148
Disease, classification of, 116
  ,, prevention of, 114
  ,, treatment of, 109
Diseases of the blood, 138
Dispensing of medicines, 117
Disposal of rabid dogs, 162
Distemper, 150
Distoma conjunctum, 204
Diuretics, 128
Dog, origin of, 1
  ,, general management of, 100

Dog, habits of the, 1
Dogs, destruction of, 258
Draught, the, 118
  ,, how to administer the, 118
Dressing, 102
  ,, for fleas, &c., 135
Dropsy of the abdomen, 200
  ,, ,, cellular tissue, 238
  ,, ,, eye, 323
  ,, ,, womb, 213
Dislocation of the eyeball, 224
Dislocations, 249
Drugging, indiscriminate, 115
Dysentery, 193

EAR, TUMOURS IN THE, 228
Ears, diseases of the, 225
Eczema, 238
  ,, of distemper, 154
  ,, *Epizootica*, 156
  ,, *rubrum*, 238
Effective poultice, 136
Electuary, the, 118
Embrocation, sedative, 129
  ,, stimulating, 129
Emesis, 188
Emetics, 130
Encephalitis, 234
Enema, the, 125
  ,, funnel, 126
  ,, gaseous, 126
  ,, syringe, 126
English Setter, 8
Enlargement of the kidney, 206
Enlargements, dispersion of, 129
Enteric distemper, 153
Enteritis, 195
Ephemeral fever, 110
Epilepsy, 229
Epistaxis, 173
Erythema, 240
Essentials of the Greyhound, 24
Eustrongylus gigas, 206, 209
Exercise, importance of, 115
Expectorants, 130
Eyeball, dislocation of the, 223
  ,, distension of the, 224
Eyelids, affections of, 225
Eyes, diseases of the, 220
  ,, lotion for the, 134
  ,, wash for the, 123
  ,, watery, 225

FALSE UNION OF BONE, 250
Filaria hepatica, 202
  ,, *immitis*, 182
Family of Terriers, 66
Fatty degeneration of the heart, 181
Featherstone Castle Setter, 7
Febrifuges, 131
Feeding, systematic, 114
Feet, wounds of the, 252
Fever, 110
  ,, bolus, 131
  ,, ephemeral, 110
  ,, mixture, 132
  ,, specific, 111
  ,, symptomatic, 110
Field Spaniels, 13
Filaria sanguinolenta, 182, 187
Fistula, 197
Fits, 229
Fleas, 246
  ,, dressing for, 135
Fluid blister, 123
  ,, healing, 134
Fomentations, 132
Foreign bodies in the stomach, 190
Foxhound, the, 32
  ,, "Cecil" on the, 32
Fox Terrier, 39
  ,, ,, controversy on the Bull cross, 41
Fracture of bone, 249
Fresh air, importance of, 114
Funnel, the enema, 126

GALL STONES, 202
Gaseous enema, 126
Gastric catarrh, 189
Gastritis, 190
General management of the Dog, 100
German Badger Terrier, 36
Gervase Markham on the Bloodhound, 28
Glanders, 156
Glass-eye, 222
Glossitis, 185
Goitre, 203
Gonorrhœa, 210
Gordon Setter, 10
Great Dane, the, 54
Greyhound, the 20
Gullet, structure of the, 187
Gutta serena, 222

HABITS OF THE DOG, 1
Hæmaturia, 205
Hæmorrhoids, 197
Hair, loss of, 236
Harrier, the, 34
Harvest Bug, 243
Haw, diseases of the, 224
Healing lotion, 134
Health, signs of, 108
Heart, diseases of, 182
Heart-bag, 182
Hepatic distemper, 153
Hepatitis, 200
 ,, chronic, 201
Herpes circinatus, 247
Hernia, 198
Highland Sheep-dog, 83
Honeycomb ringworm, 247
Hot poultice, 136
Hounds, 28
Husk, 189
Hydrocephalus, 235
Hypodermic injections, 132

ICTERUS, 145
Importance of antiseptics, 115
 ,, ,, exercise, 115
Inappetence, 188
Incised wounds, 252
Indigestion, 188
Inflammation, 111
 ,, of the bladder, 206
 ,, ,, bowels, 195
 ,, ,, brain, 194
 ,, ,, bronchial tubes, 175
 ,, ,, ear, 225
 ,, ,, eyes, 220
 ,, ,, liver, 200
 ,, ,, lungs, 176
 ,, ,, milk gland, 216
 ,, ,, peritoneum, 199
 ,, ,, scrotum, 211
 ,, ,, spleen, 203
 ,, ,, stomach, 190
 ,, ,, testicle, 212
 ,, ,, tongue, 185
 ,, ,, urethra, 208
 ,, ,, womb, 212
Inhalation of chloroform, 133
 ,, ,, "Sanitas," 133
Injections, 125

Injuries, local, 245
Inter-breeding, 144
Internal astringents, 122
 ,, canker, lotion for, 134
 ,, styptics, 137
Intestinal distemper, 153
Irish Setter, 12
 ,, Terrier, 77
Iritis, 221
Italian Greyhound, 91
Itch, 242
Ixodes ricinus, 246
 ,, *reticulatus*, 228

JAUNDICE, 145
Jaw, abscess of, 185
Joint, stiff, 209

KENNELS, 102
Kibblehound, 36
Kidney, diseases of, 206
 ,, stone in the, 205
 ,, wasting of the, 206
King Charles Spaniel, 87
Knox, Mr., on points of the Setter, 12
Knuckling, 37

LACERATED WOUNDS, 252
Lacteal tumours, 217
Ladies' toy dogs, 86
Lameness, 251
"Landseer Dog," 57
Laryngitis, 173
Leptus autumnalis, 245
Leuchæmia, 145
Leucocythæmia, 145
Llewellyn Setter, 7
Lice, 246
 ,, dressing for, 135
Liniments, 129
Linseed mucilage, 127
Liver, diseases of the, 200
 ,, pills, 122
Local injuries, 248
Locked jaw, 232
Lord Lovat Setter, 7
Loss of hair, 236
 ,, voice, 174
Lotion for canker, 134
 ,, sprains, 134
Lotions, 133

Lotions, caustic, 125
,, cooling, 134
,, eye, 134
,, healing, 134
Lunar caustic, 124

MAD DOG, SEIZURE OF THE, 163
Maltese Dog, 97
Malicious poisoning, 254
Malignant distemper, 156
Mammitis, 216
Management of the dog, 103
,, ,, pet dogs, 103
,, ,, whelps, 102
Mange, 242
,, dressings for, 135
,, in the ear, 228
,, ointment, 134
Marlborough Spaniel, 89
Mastiff, 52
,, distinguished breeders of the, 52
Measles, 157
Medicines, abuse of, 115
,, dispensing, 117
,, relative doses of, 118
Medicated poultice, 136
Meningitis, 234
Metritis, 212
Mild oleaginous purge, 122
Milk, retention of, 215
Mineral poisoning, 255
Mixtures for diarrhœa, 120
,, stomachic, 136
Modern Foxhound, 32
,, Retriever, 48
Mucilage of linseed, 127
Mustard embrocation, 129

NEPHRITIS, 214
Neuralgia, 231
Newark Castle Setter, 7
Newfoundland, 55
Norfolk Retriever, 48
,, Spaniel, 17
Nostrils bleeding from, 173
,, tumours in, 173
Noted St. Bernards, 62
Nursing, 119

OBESITY, 140
Œstrum, or heat, 217

Ointments, 134
,, blistering, 123
,, for mange, 134
Old English Mastiff, 52
Orchitis, 212
Origin of the Bloodhound, 29
,, ,, Clumber Spaniel, 89
,, ,, Dog, 1
,, ,, Gordon Setter, 10
,, ,, Otterhound, 38
Orloff Wolfhound, 51
Otterhound, 37
Otter Terrier, 39
Overgrown claws, 252
Ozæna, 171

PANCREAS, DISEASES OF, 203
Paralysis, 235
,, of the bladder, 207
,, ,, tongue, 116
Parasitic ozæna, 171
Parasiticides, 135
Parasites in the heart, 182
,, ,, liver, 202
Parturition, 218
Pasteurian system, 166
Pathology, 109
Pediculi, 246
Peking Pugs, 95
Penis, amputation of, 211
,, wash for, 123
Pentastoma denticulatum, 172
Pericardium, diseases of, 182
Peritonitis, 199
Pet dogs, management of, 103
Pharyngitis, 186
Piles, 197
Pill, the, 117
,, to administer a, 117
,, for diabetes, 122
Plethora, 130
Pleurisy, 176
Pneumonia, 176
Poisoning, 254
,, treatment of, 255
Poisons, 254
Polypus, 173
,, in the nostril, 173
,, ,, vagina, 214
Pomeranian, 86
Pointer, 4
Poodle, 99, 100
Poultice, 136
Prepuce, imperforate, 210

Prevention of disease, 114
" rabies, 164
Price of the Fox Terrier, 42
"Prince Leopold," 98
Profuse urination, 207
Prolapsus ani, 195
Prostate, disease of, 208
Ptyalism, 186
Pug Dog, 94
Pulex irritans, 246
Pulmonary distemper, 153
Purgatives, 136
Putrilage, 149
Pyrenean Wolfhound, 51

RABIES, 157
Rabid dogs, disposal of, 162
Rabbit Beagle, 36
Rachitis, 143
Recent cough, mixture for, 131
Rectum, atony of, 198
Red Poodle, 100
" mange, 238, 243
" water, 205
Relative doses of medicines, 119
Regularity of feeding, 114
Remedies for worms, 137
Respiratory system, diseases of, 170
Retriever, 48
Rheumatism, 141
Rickets, 143
Ringworm, 247
Rough Terrier, 70
Round worms, remedies for, 138
Rupture of the heart, 181
Russian Setter, 6
" Wolfhound, 50

ST. BERNARD DOG, 58
St. Vitus's Dance, 232
Saliva, flow of, 186
"Sanitas," inhalation of, 133
" preparations, 116
Sarcoptes canis, 242
Sarcoptic scabies, 242
" mange, 242
Scab, 242
Scabies, 242
Scotch Collie, 85
" Greyhound, 20
" Setter, 10
Scurfy ears, 228

Sedative embrocations, 129
Seizure of mad dogs, 163
Septicæmia, 167
Serous cyst, 113
Setters, 6
Sheepdog, 81
Siberian Wolfhound, 50
Simple fever, 110
Skin, diseases of, 236
" parasites of, 241
Skye Terrier, 71
Small-pox, 169
Smooth Collie, 85
" English Terrier, 67
Snake bites, 257
Snoring, 174
Sore throat, 173
Soothing embrocation, 129
Spaniel, 13, 18
Spasms, 191
Specific diseases, 146
" fever, 111
Spiroptera sanguinolenta, 191
Spitz Dog, 86
Spleen, diseases of, 203
Spongio piline, use of, 136
Sprains, 250
" lotions for, 134
Stagbound, 32
Staphyloma, 223
Stiff joint, 248
Stimulants, 136
Stimulating embrocation, 129
Stings of wasps, 258
Stomach catarrh, 189
" foreign bodies in, 190
" worms in, 191
Stomachic bolus, 137
Stomachics, 137
Stone in the bladder, 207
" " kidney, 205
" " urethra, 208
Stricture of the bowel, 199
Strongylus filaria, 178
Styptics, 137
Subcutaneous injections, 132
Surfeit, 238
Sussex Spaniel, 14
Sweating blister, 124
" embrocation, 129
Symptomatic fever, 110
Symptoms of poisoning, 254
Syringe, clyster, 126
Systematic feeding, 115

"TAIL OR NO TAIL," 82
Tænia cucumerina, 191
" *cænurus*, 191
Tapeworm, remedy for, 138
Teeth, diseases of, 184
"Tell," measurements of, 61
Terriers, family of, 66
Tetanus, 232
Tetranychus autumnalis, 245
Ticks, 246
Tinea favosa, 247
" *tonsurans*, 248
Tongue, diseases of, 185
Tonics, 137
Toy dogs, 86
" Terrier, 98
Treatment of abscess, 113
" disease, 109
" fever, 111
" inflammation, 112
" poisoning, 255
" rabies, 167
" serous cyst, 113
Trycophyton favosa, 249
" *tonsurans*, 247
Truffle, the, 43
" dog, 44
" " training the, 45
Tuberculosis, 168
Tweedside Spaniel, 18

URÆMIA, 145
Ureters, impaction of, 206
Urethra, stone in, 208
Urethritis, 208

VAGINA, amputation of, 215
" inversion of, 215
" tumour in, 214
Value of Spaniels, 90
Valvular diseases of the heart, 181

Variola, 169
Vegetable parasites, 247
" poisoning, 256
Veins, wounds of, 253
Verminous bronchitis, 178
Verrucæ, 240
Vertigo, 230
Voice, loss of, 174
Vomition, 188
" continuous, 189

WARTS ON THE SKIN, 240
Wash for the eyes, 123
" " penis, 123
Wasp stings, 258
Wasting of the kidney, 206
Water Spaniel, 18
Weight of Italian Greyhound, 92
Welsh Cocker, 17
" Terrier, 79
Whelps, 102
Whippet, 80
Wilful poisoning, 254
Wolfhound, 51
Womb, amputation of, 214
" prolapsus of, 214
Worm medicines, 137
" in the kidney, 216
" " urethra, 209
Worms in the intestines, 198
" " stomach, 191
Wounds, 252
" lotion for, 134
" of arteries and veins, 253
" of the feet, 252
" " tongue, 185
Wourali poisoning, 258

YORKSHIRE DOG, 70
Youatt on the Setter, 7

Printed by BALLANTYNE, HANSON & CO.
London and Edinburgh.

www.ingramcontent.com/pod-product-compliance
Lightring Source LLC
Chambersburg PA
CBHW022106230426
43672CB00008B/1297